GUITAR
FOR
DUMMIES®

GUITAR FOR DUMMIES®

by Mark Phillips and Jon Chappell

IDG Books Worldwide, Inc.
An International Data Group Company

Foster City, CA ♦ Chicago, IL ♦ Indianapolis, IN ♦ New York, NY

Guitar For Dummies®

Published by
IDG Books Worldwide, Inc.
An International Data Group Company
919 E. Hillsdale Blvd.
Suite 400
Foster City, CA 94404
www.idgbooks.com (IDG Books Worldwide Web site)
www.dummies.com (Dummies Press Web site)

Library of Congress Catalog Card No.: 98-87102

ISBN: 0-7645-5106-X

Printed in the United States of America

10 9 8 7 6 5 4

1E/SQ/RQ/ZY/IN

Distributed in the United States by IDG Books Worldwide, Inc.

Distributed by Macmillan Canada for Canada; by Transworld Publishers Limited in the United Kingdom; by IDG Norge Books for Norway; by IDG Sweden Books for Sweden; by Woodslane Pty. Ltd. for Australia; by Woodslane (NZ) Ltd. for New Zealand; by Addison Wesley Longman Singapore Pte Ltd. for Singapore, Malaysia, Thailand, Indonesia and Korea; by Norma Comunicaciones S.A. for Colombia; by Intersoft for South Africa; by International Thomson Publishing for Germany, Austria and Switzerland; by Toppan Company Ltd. for Japan; by Distribuidora Cuspide for Argentina; by Livraria Cultura for Brazil; by Ediciencia S.A. for Ecuador; by Ediciones ZETA S.C.R. Ltda. for Peru; by WS Computer Publishing Corporation, Inc., for the Philippines; by Unalis Corporation for Taiwan; by Contemporanea de Ediciones for Venezuela; by Computer Book & Magazine Store for Puerto Rico; by Express Computer Distributors for the Caribbean and West Indies. Authorized Sales Agent: Anthony Rudkin Associates for the Middle East and North Africa.

For general information on IDG Books Worldwide's books in the U.S., please call our Consumer Customer Service department at 800-762-2974. For reseller information, including discounts and premium sales, please call our Reseller Customer Service department at 800-434-3422.

For information on where to purchase IDG Books Worldwide's books outside the U.S., please contact our International Sales department at 650-655-3200 or fax 650-655-3297.

For information on foreign language translations, please contact our Foreign & Subsidiary Rights department at 650-655-3021 or fax 650-655-3281.

For sales inquiries and special prices for bulk quantities, please contact our Sales department at 650-655-3200 or write to the address above.

For information on using IDG Books Worldwide's books in the classroom or for ordering examination copies, please contact our Educational Sales department at 800-434-2086 or fax 317-596-5499.

For press review copies, author interviews, or other publicity information, please contact our Public Relations department at 650-655-3000 or fax 650-655-3299.

For authorization to photocopy items for corporate, personal, or educational use, please contact Copyright Clearance Center, 222 Rosewood Drive, Danvers, MA 01923, or fax 978-750-4470.

is a trademark under exclusive license to IDG Books Worldwide, Inc., from International Data Group, Inc.

About the Authors

Mark Phillips is the Music Editor for both *Guitar* magazine and *GuitarOne* magazine and the Director of Music for Cherry Lane Music. He earned his bachelor's degree in music theory from Case Western Reserve University where he received the Carolyn Neff award for scholastic excellence, and his master's degree in music theory from Northwestern University, where he was elected to Pi Kappa Lambda, the most prestigious U.S. honor society for college and university music students. While working toward a doctorate in music theory at Northwestern, Phillips taught theory, ear-training, sight-singing, counterpoint, and guitar.

Formerly, Phillips was the Director of Popular Music at Warner Bros. Publications where he wrote *Understanding Rhythm* and arranged *The Young Guitarist's Library* and edited or arranged the music of Neil Young, James Taylor, Joni Mitchell, The Eagles, Rush, and Led Zeppelin. At Cherry Lane Music, he wrote *Metallica Riff by Riff* and edited or arranged the music of John Denver, Bonnie Raitt, Van Halen, Guns 'N' Roses, and Metallica.

Jon Chappell is a multistyle guitarist, transcriber, and arranger. He attended Carnegie-Mellon University, where he studied with Carlos Barbosa-Lima, and he then went on to earn his master's degree in composition from DePaul University, where he also taught theory and ear training. He is currently Editor-in-Chief of *Guitar* magazine in New York, Technical Editor of *Guitar Shop Magazine,* and Musicologist for *Guitarra,* a classical magazine. He has played and recorded with Pat Benatar, Judy Collins, Graham Nash, and Gunther Schuller, and he has contributed numerous musical pieces to film and TV. Some of these include *Northern Exposure, Walker, Texas Ranger, Guiding Light,* and the feature film *Bleeding Hearts* directed by actor-dancer Gregory Hines. In 1990, he became Associate Music Director of Cherry Lane Music where he has transcribed, edited, and arranged the music of Joe Satriani, Steve Vai, Steve Morse, Mike Stern, and Eddie Van Halen, among others. He has 11 method books (selling in excess of 100,000 copies) to his name, and Chappell is the author of the textbook *The Recording Guitarist — A Guide for Home and Studio,* published by the Hal Leonard Corporation.

ABOUT IDG BOOKS WORLDWIDE

Welcome to the world of IDG Books Worldwide.

IDG Books Worldwide, Inc., is a subsidiary of International Data Group, the world's largest publisher of computer-related information and the leading global provider of information services on information technology. IDG was founded more than 25 years ago and now employs more than 8,500 people worldwide. IDG publishes more than 275 computer publications in over 75 countries (see listing below). More than 90 million people read one or more IDG publications each month.

Launched in 1990, IDG Books Worldwide is today the #1 publisher of best-selling computer books in the United States. We are proud to have received eight awards from the Computer Press Association in recognition of editorial excellence and three from *Computer Currents'* First Annual Readers' Choice Awards. Our best-selling *...For Dummies*® series has more than 50 million copies in print with translations in 38 languages. IDG Books Worldwide, through a joint venture with IDG's Hi-Tech Beijing, became the first U.S. publisher to publish a computer book in the People's Republic of China. In record time, IDG Books Worldwide has become the first choice for millions of readers around the world who want to learn how to better manage their businesses.

Our mission is simple: Every one of our books is designed to bring extra value and skill-building instructions to the reader. Our books are written by experts who understand and care about our readers. The knowledge base of our editorial staff comes from years of experience in publishing, education, and journalism — experience we use to produce books for the '90s. In short, we care about books, so we attract the best people. We devote special attention to details such as audience, interior design, use of icons, and illustrations. And because we use an efficient process of authoring, editing, and desktop publishing our books electronically, we can spend more time ensuring superior content and spend less time on the technicalities of making books.

You can count on our commitment to deliver high-quality books at competitive prices on topics you want to read about. At IDG Books Worldwide, we continue in the IDG tradition of delivering quality for more than 25 years. You'll find no better book on a subject than one from IDG Books Worldwide.

IDG BOOKS WORLDWIDE

John Kilcullen
CEO
IDG Books Worldwide, Inc.

Steven Berkowitz
President and Publisher
IDG Books Worldwide, Inc.

VIII WINNER
Eighth Annual Computer Press Awards ≥1992

IX WINNER
Ninth Annual Computer Press Awards ≥1993

X WINNER
Tenth Annual Computer Press Awards ≥1994

XI WINNER
Eleventh Annual Computer Press Awards ≥1995

IDG Books Worldwide, Inc., is a subsidiary of International Data Group, the world's largest publisher of computer-related information and the leading global provider of information services on information technology. International Data Group publishes over 275 computer publications in over 75 countries. More than 90 million people read one or more International Data Group publications each month. International Data Group's publications include: **ARGENTINA:** Buyer's Guide, Computerworld Argentina, PC World Argentina; **AUSTRALIA:** Australian Macworld, Australian PC World, Australian Reseller News, Computerworld, IT Casebook, Network World, Publish, Webmaster; **AUSTRIA:** Computerwelt Osterreich, Networks Austria, PC Tip Austria; **BANGLADESH:** PC World Bangladesh; **BELARUS:** PC World Belarus; **BELGIUM:** Data News; **BRAZIL:** Annuário de Informática, Computerworld, Connections, Macworld, PC Player, PC World, Publish, Reseller News, Supergamepower; **BULGARIA:** Computerworld Bulgaria, Network World Bulgaria, PC & MacWorld Bulgaria; **CANADA:** CIO Canada, Client/Server World, ComputerWorld Canada, InfoWorld Canada, NetworkWorld Canada, WebWorld; **CHILE:** Computerworld Chile, PC World Chile; **COLOMBIA:** Computerworld Colombia, PC World Colombia; **COSTA RICA:** PC World Centro America; **THE CZECH AND SLOVAK REPUBLICS:** Computerworld Czechoslovakia, Macworld Czech Republic, PC World Czechoslovakia; **DENMARK:** Communications World Danmark, Computerworld Danmark, Macworld Danmark, PC World Danmark, Techworld Danmark; **DOMINICAN REPUBLIC:** PC World Republica Dominicana; **ECUADOR:** PC World Ecuador; **EGYPT:** Computerworld Middle East, PC World Middle East; **EL SALVADOR:** PC World Centro America; **FINLAND:** MikroPC, Tietoverkko, Tietoviikko; **FRANCE:** Distributique, Hebdo, Info PC, Le Monde Informatique, Macworld, Reseaux & Telecoms, WebMaster France; **GERMANY:** Computer Partner, Computerwoche, Computerwoche Extra, Computerwoche FOCUS, Global Online, Macwelt, PC Welt; **GREECE:** Amiga Computing, GamePro Greece, Multimedia World; **GUATEMALA:** PC World Centro America; **HONDURAS:** PC World Centro America; **HONG KONG:** Computerworld Hong Kong, PC World Hong Kong, Publish in Asia; **HUNGARY:** ABCD CD-ROM, Computerworld Szamitastechnika, Internetto online Magazine, PC World Hungary, PC-X Magazin Hungary; **ICELAND:** Tolvuheimur PC World Island; **INDIA:** Information Communications World, Information Systems Computerworld, PC World India, Publish in Asia; **INDONESIA:** InfoKomputer PC World, Komputek Computerworld, Publish in Asia; **IRELAND:** ComputerScope, PC Live!; **ISRAEL:** Macworld Israel, People & Computers/Computerworld; **ITALY:** Computerworld Italia, Macworld Italia, Networking Italia, PC World Italia; **JAPAN:** DTP World, Macworld Japan, Nikkei Personal Computing, OS/2 World Japan, SunWorld Japan, Windows NT World, Windows World Japan; **KENYA:** PC World East African; **KOREA:** Hi-Tech Information, Macworld Korea, PC World Korea; **MACEDONIA:** PC World Macedonia; **MALAYSIA:** Computerworld Malaysia, PC World Malaysia, Publish in Asia; **MALTA:** PC World Malta; **MEXICO:** Computerworld Mexico, PC World Mexico; **MYANMAR:** PC World Myanmar; **NETHERLANDS:** Computer! Totaal, LAN Internetworking Magazine, LAN World Buyers Guide, Macworld Netherlands, Net, WebWereld; **NEW ZEALAND:** Absolute Beginners Guide and Plain & Simple Series, Computer Buyer, Computer Industry Directory, Computerworld New Zealand, MTB, Network World, PC World New Zealand; **NICARAGUA:** PC World Centro America; **NORWAY:** Computerworld Norge, CW Rapport, Datamagasinet, Financial Rapport, Kursguide Norge, Macworld Norge, Multimediaworld Norge, PC World Ekspress Norge, PC World Nettverk, PC World Norge, PC World ProduktGuide Norge; **PAKISTAN:** Computerworld Pakistan; **PANAMA:** PC World Panama; **PEOPLE'S REPUBLIC OF CHINA:** China Computer Users, China Computerworld, China InfoWorld, China Telecom World Weekly, Computer & Communication, Electronic Design China, Electronics Today, Electronics Weekly, Game Software, PC World China, Popular Computer Week, Software Weekly, Software World, Telecom World; **PERU:** Computerworld Peru, PC World Profesional Peru, PC World SoHo Peru; **PHILIPPINES:** Click!, Computerworld Philippines, PC World Philippines, Publish in Asia; **POLAND:** Computerworld Poland, Computerworld Special Report Poland, Cyber, Macworld Poland, Networld Poland, PC World Komputer; **PORTUGAL:** Cerebro/PC World, Computerworld/Correio Informático, Dealer World Portugal, Mac*In/PC*In Portugal, Multimedia World; **PUERTO RICO:** PC World Puerto Rico; **ROMANIA:** Computerworld Romania, PC World Romania, Telecom Romania; **RUSSIA:** Computerworld Russia, Mir PK, Publish, Seti; **SINGAPORE:** Computerworld Singapore, PC World Singapore, Publish in Asia; **SLOVENIA:** Monitor; **SOUTH AFRICA:** Computing SA, Network World SA, Software World SA; **SPAIN:** Communicaciones World España, Computerworld España, Dealer World España, Macworld España, PC World España, PC World Electronic; **SRI LANKA:** Infolink PC World; **SWEDEN:** CAP&Design, Computer Sweden, Corporate Computing Sweden, Internetworld Sweden, it.branschen, Macworld Sweden, MaxiData Sweden, MikroDatorn, Nätverk & Kommunikation, PC World Sweden, PCaktiv, Windows World Sweden; **SWITZERLAND:** Computerworld Schweiz, Macworld Schweiz, PCtip; **TAIWAN:** Computerworld Taiwan, Macworld Taiwan, NEW ViSiON/Publish, PC World Taiwan, Windows World Taiwan; **THAILAND:** Publish in Asia, Thai Computerworld; **TURKEY:** Computerworld Turkiye, Macworld Turkiye, Network World Turkiye, PC World Turkiye; **UKRAINE:** Computerworld Kiev, Multimedia World Ukraine, PC World Ukraine; **UNITED KINGDOM:** Acorn User UK, Amiga Action UK, Amiga Computing UK, Apple Talk UK, Computing, Macworld, Parents and Computers UK, PC Advisor, PC Home, PSX Pro, The WEB; **UNITED STATES:** Cable in the Classroom, CIO Magazine, Computerworld, DOS World, Federal Computer Week, GamePro Magazine, InfoWorld, I-Way, Macworld, Network World, PC Games, PC World, Publish, Video Event, THE WEB Magazine, and WebMaster; online webzines: JavaWorld, NetscapeWorld, and SunWorld Online; **URUGUAY:** InfoWorld Uruguay; **VENEZUELA:** Computerworld Venezuela, PC World Venezuela; and **VIETNAM:** PC World Vietnam.   5/7/98

Dedication

From Mark:

For my wife, Debbie; my children, Tara, Jake, and Rachel; and my parents, Aaron and Dorothy.

From Jon:

For my wife, Mary, and my children, Jennifer, Katie, Lauren, and Ryan.

Authors' Acknowledgments

The authors gratefully acknowledge the folks at IDG: John Kilcullen and Kathy Welton (the folks who make the decisions at the highest levels), our acquisitions editor, Mark Butler (for believing in us), our project editor, Kyle Looper (our savior, our hero!), copy editor Bill Barton (don't miss much, do ya, Bill?), technical editor Lisa Sullivan (for keeping our feet on the ground); Keith Mardak of Hal Leonard; Peter Primont, Ted Piechocinski, Sharon Seidl (for all the great photos), as well as Arthur Rotfeld, Sean McDevitt, and Fred Hand of Cherry Lane Music. Special thanks to Woytek and Krystyna Rynczak of WR Music Service for their speedy and accurate music typesetting.

Special thanks from Mark to his guitar teachers, Joe Monk and Kent Sidon.

Special thanks from Jon to TJ Baden of Taylor Guitars; Lloyd Schwartz and Dale Krevens of Tech 21; Douglas Chin; Gary Cook, Paul Youngblood, Kellie Wilkie, and Leanna Harshaw of the Roland Corporation for supplying the technology that helped create the CD.

Publisher's Acknowledgments

We're proud of this book; please register your comments through our IDG Books Worldwide Online Registration Form located at http://my2cents.dummies.com.

Some of the people who helped bring this book to market include the following:

Acquisitions, Editorial, and Media Development

Project Editor: Kyle Looper

Acquisitions Editor: Mark Butler

Copy Editor: William A. Barton

Technical Editor: Lisa M. Sullivan

Editorial Manager: Leah P. Cameron

Media Development Manager: Heather Heath Dismore

Editorial Assistants: Paul Kuzmic, Donna Love

Production

Project Coordinator: Valery Bourke

Layout and Graphics: Lou Boudreau, Linda M. Boyer, J. Tyler Connor, Angela F. Hunckler, Heather N. Pearson, Anna Rohrer, Brent Savage, Janet Seib, Deirdre Smith

Proofreaders: Christine Berman, Kelli Botta, Laura Bowman, Michelle Croninger, Rachel Garvey, Nancy Price, Rebecca Senninger, Janet M. Withers

Indexer: Liz Cunningham

Special Help

Barry Childs-Helton, Senior Copy Editor
Steve Hayes, Associate Acquisitions Editor
Allison Solomon, Administrative Assistant

General and Administrative

IDG Books Worldwide, Inc.: John Kilcullen, CEO; Steven Berkowitz, President and Publisher

IDG Books Technology Publishing: Brenda McLaughlin, Senior Vice President and Group Publisher

Dummies Technology Press and Dummies Editorial: Diane Graves Steele, Vice President and Associate Publisher; Mary Bednarek, Director of Acquisitions and Product Development; Kristin A. Cocks, Editorial Director

Dummies Trade Press: Kathleen A. Welton, Vice President and Publisher; Kevin Thornton, Acquisitions Manager

IDG Books Production for Dummies Press: Michael R. Britton, Vice President of Production and Creative Services; Cindy L. Phipps, Manager of Project Coordination, Production Proofreading, and Indexing; Kathie S. Schutte, Supervisor of Page Layout; Shelley Lea, Supervisor of Graphics and Design; Debbie J. Gates, Production Systems Specialist; Robert Springer, Supervisor of Proofreading; Debbie Stailey, Special Projects Coordinator; Tony Augsburger, Supervisor of Reprints and Bluelines

Dummies Packaging and Book Design: Robin Seaman, Creative Director; Kavish + Kavish, Cover Design

◆

The publisher would like to give special thanks to Patrick J. McGovern, without whom this book would not have been possible.

◆

Contents at a Glance

Cartoons at a Glance

By Rich Tennant

page 9

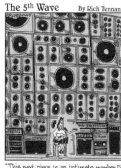

page 39

page 87

page 285

page 313

page 155

page 251

Fax: 978-546-7747 • E-mail: the5wave@tiac.net

Table of Contents

Introduction

So you wanna play guitar, huh? And why wouldn't you?

Because you may as well face it: In the music world, guitars set the standard for *cool* (and we're not *just* being biased here). Since the '50s, many of the greatest showmen in rock 'n' roll, blues, and country have played the guitar. Think of Chuck Berry doing his one-legged hop across the stage (the "duck walk") while belting out "Johnny B. Goode," Jimi Hendrix wailing on his upside-down, right-handed (and sometimes flaming) Stratocaster, Bonnie Raitt playing slide guitar, Garth Brooks with his acoustic guitar and flannel shirts, B.B. King's authoritative bending and expressive vibrato on his guitar "Lucille," or George Benson's mellow jazz guitar stylings. (Even Elvis Presley, whose guitar prowess may not have exceeded five chords, still used the guitar effectively on stage as a prop.) The list goes on.

Playing electric guitar can put you out in front of a band, where you're free to roam, sing, and make eye contact with your adoring fans. Playing acoustic guitar can make you the star of the vacation campfire sing-along. And playing any kind of guitar can bring out the music in your soul and become a valued lifetime hobby.

About This Book

Guitar For Dummies has been carefully crafted so that you can find what you want or need to know about the guitar and no more. Because each chapter is as self-contained as possible, you can skip information that you've already mastered and not feel lost. Yet, at the same time, you can also follow along from front to back and practice the guitar in a way that builds step-by-step on your previous knowledge.

To find the information you need, you can simply look through the Table of Contents to find the area that you're interested in, or you can look for particular information in the Index at the back of the book.

Guitar For Dummies delivers everything the beginning to intermediate guitarist needs: From buying a guitar to tuning the guitar, to playing the guitar, to caring for the guitar, this book has it all!

Finding a guitar

Believe it or not, many would-be guitarists never really get into playing because they have the wrong guitar. Maybe the strings are too difficult to push down (causing a great deal of pain). *Guitar For Dummies*, unlike *some* other books we could mention, doesn't assume that you already have the right guitar — or even any guitar at all, for that matter. In this book, you find everything you need to know (from a buyer's guide to buying strategies, to guitars and accessories for particular styles) to match yourself with the guitar equipment that fits your needs and budget.

Playing the guitar

Most guitar books want you to practice the guitar in the same way that you practice the piano. First, you learn where the notes fall on the staff; then you study about the length that you're supposed to hold the notes; then you move on to practicing scales; and the big payoff is to practice song after unrecognizable song that you probably don't care about playing anyway. If you're looking for this kind of ho-hum guitar book, you've definitely come to the wrong place. But don't worry, you can find no shortage of that kind of book.

The truth is that many great guitarists don't know how to read music, and many who can read music learned *after* they learned to play the guitar. Repeat after us: *You don't need to read music to play the guitar*. Chant this mantra until you believe it, because this principle is central to the design of *Guitar For Dummies*.

One of the coolest things about the guitar is that, even though you can devote your lifetime to perfecting your skills, you can start faking it rather quickly. We assume that, instead of concentrating on what the 3/4 time signature means, you want to play music — real music (or at least recognizable music). We want you to play music, too, because that's what keeps you motivated and practicing.

So how does *Guitar For Dummies* deliver? Glad you asked. The following list tells you how this book starts you playing and developing real guitar skills quickly:

- ♪ **Look at the photos:** Fingerings that you need to know appear in photos in the book. Just form your hands the way we show you in the photos. Simple.

- ♪ **Read guitar tablature:** Guitar tablature is a guitar-specific shorthand for reading music that actually shows you what strings to strike and what frets to hold down on the guitar for creating the sound that's called for. Tab (as it's known to its friends and admirers) goes a long way toward enabling you to *play* music without *reading* music. Don't try this stuff on the piano!

♪ **Listen to the CD:** You can listen to all the songs and exercises on the CD in the back of the book. Doing so is important for a couple of reasons: You can figure out the rhythm of the song as well as how long to hold notes by listening instead of reading. We could tell you all sorts of really cool things about the CD, such as how it has the featured guitar on one channel and the accompaniment on the other (so that you can switch back and forth by using the balance control on your stereo) or how the book and CD are tightly integrated so that you can always find the track you're looking for easily, but, aw shucks, we don't want to brag on ourselves too much.

♪ **Look at the music staff as you improve:** To those who would charge that *Guitar For Dummies* doesn't give you diddley in terms of reading music, we respond: "Not so, Fret Breath!" The music for all the exercises and songs appears above the shortcut methods. So you get the best of both worlds: You can associate the music notation with the sound you're making after you already know how to make the sound. Pretty cool, huh?

Caring for your guitar

A serious guitar is a serious investment, and, as with any other serious investment, you need to maintain it. *Guitar For Dummies* provides the information you need to correctly store, maintain, and care for your six-string, including how to change strings and what little extras to keep stashed away in your guitar case.

Not-So-Foolish Assumptions

We really don't make many assumptions about you. We don't assume that you already own a guitar. We don't assume that you have a particular preference for acoustic or electric guitars nor that you favor a particular style. Gee, this is a pretty equal-opportunity book!

Okay, we do assume some things. We assume that you want to play a *guitar,* not a banjo, Dobro, or mandolin, and we concentrate on the six-string variety. We also assume that you want to start playing the guitar quickly, without a lot of messing around with reading notes, clefs, and time signatures. You can find all that music-reading stuff in the book, but that's not our main focus. Our main focus is helping you make cool, sweet music on your six-string.

What You're Not to Read

We started out with a book full of only cool, exciting, and useful stuff, but our editor told us that we needed to throw in some boring, technical stuff for balance (just kidding!).

Actually, knowing the theory behind the music can sometimes help you take the next step after mastering the basics of a technique. But those theoretical and technical explanations aren't really necessary for you to play basic music. For this reason, we use two icons, Theory and Technical Stuff, to mark those explanations that you may want to skip at first and then come back to later, after you're getting more advanced and developing an intuitive feel for the instrument.

Conventions We Use in This Book

This book has a number of conventions that we use to make things consistent and easy to understand. Here is a list of conventions:

♪ **Right hand and left hand:** Instead of saying "strumming hand" and "fretting hand" (which sounds really forced to us), we say "right hand" for the hand that picks or strums the strings and "left hand" for the hand that frets the strings. We apologize to those left-handed readers who are using this book, and we ask that you folks read right hand to mean left hand and vice versa.

♪ **Dual music notation:** The songs and exercises in this book are arranged with the standard music staff on top (occupying the exalted, loftier position that it deserves) and the tablature staff below for the rest of us to use. The point is that you can use either of these methods, but you don't need to look at both at the same time as you must while playing the piano.

♪ **Up and down, higher and lower (and so on):** If we tell you to move a note or chord up the guitar neck or to play it higher on the neck, we mean higher in pitch, or toward the body of the guitar. If we say to go down or lower on the neck, we mean toward the headstock, or lower in pitch. If we ever mean anything else by these terms, we tell you. (Those of you who hold your guitar with the headstock tilted upward may need to do a bit of mental adjustment whenever you see these terms. Just remember that we're talking pitch, not position, and you should do just fine.)

How This Book Is Organized

We separate the book into two distinct kinds of chapters: information chapters and playing chapters. Information chapters tell you stuff about the nuts and bolts of the guitar, such as tuning the guitar, selecting the right guitar, and caring for the guitar. The playing chapters provide you with the information you need to (you guessed it) play the guitar.

Each playing chapter contains exercises that enable you to practice the skill we discuss in that particular section. And at or near the end of each playing chapter, you find a section of songs that you can play that use the techniques in that chapter. At the beginning of each "Playing Songs" section is a section called "About the Songs," where you can find a list of skills you need and special information about each song.

We divide the chapters in *Guitar For Dummies* into eight logical parts for easier access. The parts are organized as follows:

Part I: So You Wanna Play Guitar

Part I provides three information chapters on some guitar basics that you need to know before you can start playing. Chapter 1 helps you understand what to call the various parts of the guitar, and what they do. Chapter 2 tells you how to tune the guitar, both in reference to itself and to a fixed source — such as a tuning fork, piano, or electrical tuner — so that you can be in tune with other instruments. Chapter 3 covers the basic skills you need to know to be successful in this book, such as how to read guitar tablature, how to pick and strum, and how to produce a clean, clear, buzz-free tone.

Part II: So Start Playing: The Basics

In Part II, you begin to actually play the guitar. All the chapters in this part deal with playing the guitar, so "strap" yourself in (and get used to bad puns). Chapter 4, the first playing chapter, provides the easiest way to start playing real music, with major and minor chords. Chapter 5 goes over how to play simple melodies by using single notes, and Chapter 6 adds a little bit of *oomph* with some basic 7th chords. Remember the old joke about the tourist who asked the New York beatnik, "How do you get to Carnegie Hall?" Answer: "Practice, man, practice." Well, you may not be headed for Carnegie Hall (but then, who are we to say?), but practicing the basics is still going to be important if you want to become a good guitar player.

Part III: Beyond the Basics: Starting to Sound Cool

Part III moves beyond the simple stuff into some intermediate material. Chapter 7 provides you with the techniques that you use in playing in position, which not only makes you sound cool, but makes you look cool, too. Chapter 8 tells you about playing barre chords, which refers to using one finger to lay across all the strings and then making chords in front of that finger. Chapter 9 goes into some special techniques for creating particular guitar effects, all with pretty cool-sounding names such as hammer-ons, bends, and slides.

Part IV: A Cornucopia of Styles

Part IV, the final part of playing chapters, gives you the methods that you use in particular music styles. Chapter 10, about the rock style, tells you about playing lead by using the pentatonic minor scale, playing solos in a box, and other rock stylings. (The chapter also gives you some information on country-style pickin' with the pentatonic major scale.) Chapter 11, on blues, provides more lead boxes and special blues articulations and tells you how to get your mojo working. Chapter 12, on folk music, provides you with the specific picking patterns that give folk music its distinctive sound (and throws in some country finger-pickin' techniques as well). Chapter 13, on classical guitar, introduces you to techniques necessary to play Bach and Beethoven.

Part V: Gearing Up: A Buyer's Guide

Part V contains two chapters designed to help you find the equipment that's right for you. Chapter 14 covers finding not only your first practice guitar, but also finding the second and third guitars (often more difficult decisions than your first). Chapter 15, on guitar accessories, gives you a primer on guitar amps, as well as the little extras you need for a well-rounded assortment of equipment.

Part VI: Care and Feeding

Part VI contains two chapters on how to care for your guitar. Chapter 16 covers the process of changing strings, something you gotta know if you're going to play the guitar for more than a month. Chapter 17 covers the basic maintenance and repairs that can save you money at the guitar store and keep you playing well into the night.

Part VII: The Part of Tens

The Part of Tens is a ...*For Dummies* trademark that provides fun and interesting information in a top-ten-style format. Chapter 18 should inspire you with ten great guitarists. And, Chapter 19, on ten classic guitars, may lure you to your local guitar store to acquire one of these babies for yourself.

Appendixes

The appendixes in this book cover two important issues. Appendix A succinctly explains what all those strange symbols on the staff mean and tells you just enough about reading music to get you by. Appendix B tells you about the CD that accompanies this book.

Icons Used in This Book

In the margins of this book, you find several helpful little icons that can make your journey a little easier:

Skip to a real song for some instant guitar gratification.

Something to write down on a cocktail napkin and store in your guitar case.

Detailed explanations of the trivial and obscure you can skip if you want.

The whys and wherefores behind what you play.

Expert advice that can hasten your journey to guitar excellence.

Watch out, or you could cause damage to your guitar or someone's ears.

Where to Go from Here

If you're a beginner and are ready to start playing right away, you can skip Chapter 1 and go straight to Chapter 2, where you get your guitar in tune. Then browse through Chapter 3 on developing the skills that you need to play and dive straight in to Chapter 4. Although you can skip around somewhat in the playing chapters, if you're a beginner, we urge you to take the chapters in order, one at a time. Moreover, you should stick to Chapter 4 until you start to form calluses on your fingers, which really help you to make the chords sound right without buzzing.

If you don't yet have a guitar, you should start in Part V, the buyer's guide, and look for what you need in a basic practice guitar. You're better off not splurging on an expensive guitar until you're sure that this instrument is for you. After you buy your ax, you can get on with playing, which is the real fun after all, right?

Part I
So You Wanna Play Guitar

The 5th Wave   By Rich Tennant

"Why can't you play guitar like everyone else?"

In this part . . .

Good morning, ladies and gentlemen, and welcome to *Guitar For Dummies*. Prior to takeoff, please ensure that you review Chapter 1, which outlines the various parts and names of both the electric and acoustic guitars, and don't forget to check your guitar's tuning, as outlined in Chapter 2. Finally, consult Chapter 3 (or the card located in the seat pocket in front of you) to review important operator information prior to actually engaging the instrument. Sit back. Your flight time with the guitar may last the rest of your life, but you're sure to enjoy the ride!

Chapter 1

Guitar 101

● ●

● ●

All guitars — whether painted purple with airbrushed skulls and lightning bolts or finished in a natural-wood pattern with a fine French lacquer — share certain physical characteristics that make them behave as guitars and not violins or tubas. If you're confused about the difference between a headstock and a pickup and you're wondering which end of the guitar to hold under your chin, this chapter is for you. The following sections describe the differences among the various parts of the guitar and tell you what those parts do. You also find out in this chapter how to hold the instrument and why the guitar sounds the way it does.

And, in case you took us seriously, you *don't* hold the guitar under your chin — unless, of course, you're Jimi Hendrix.

Anatomy of a Guitar

Guitars come in two basic flavors: *acoustic* and *electric*. From a hardware standpoint, electric guitars have more components and doohickeys than do acoustic guitars. Guitar makers generally agree, however, that making an acoustic guitar is harder than making an electric guitar. That's why, pound for pound, acoustic guitars cost just as much or more than their electric counterparts. But both types follow the same basic approach to such principles as neck construction and string tension. That's why both acoustic and electric guitars have very similar constructions, despite a sometimes radical difference in tone production (unless, of course, you think that Segovia and Metallica are indistinguishable). Figures 1-1 and 1-2 show the various parts of an electric guitar and an acoustic guitar.

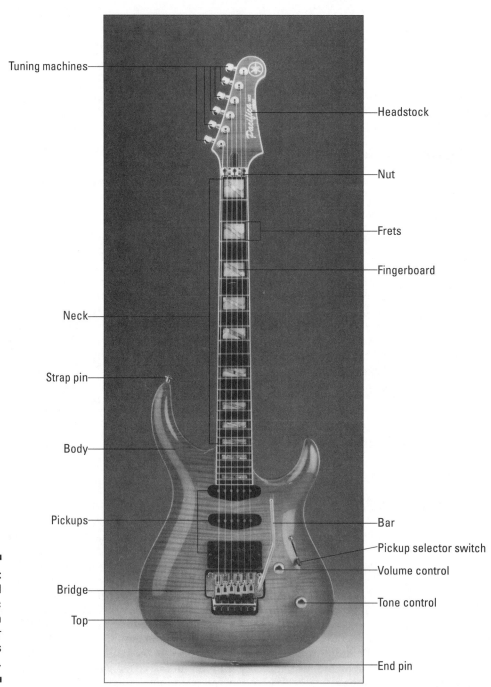

Tuning machines

Headstock

Nut

Frets

Fingerboard

Neck

Strap pin

Body

Pickups

Bar

Pickup selector switch

Volume control

Tone control

Figure 1-1:
A typical
electric
guitar with
its major
parts
labeled.

Bridge

Top

End pin

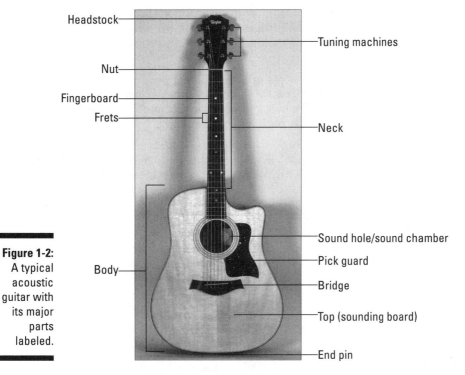

Headstock

Tuning machines

Nut

Fingerboard

Frets

Neck

Figure 1-2:
A typical
acoustic
guitar with
its major
parts
labeled.

Body

Sound hole/sound chamber

Pick guard

Bridge

Top (sounding board)

End pin

The following list tells you the functions of the various parts of a guitar:

♪ **Back (acoustic only).** The part of the body that holds the sides in place; made of two or three pieces of wood.

♪ **Bar (electric only).** A metal rod attached to the bridge that varies the string tension by tilting the bridge back and forth. Also called the tremolo bar, whammy bar, vibrato bar, and wang bar.

♪ **Body.** The box that provides an anchor for the neck and bridge and creates the playing surface for the right hand. On an acoustic, the body includes the amplifying sound chamber that produces the guitar's tone. On an electric, it consists of the housing for the bridge assembly and electronics (pickups as well as tone and volume controls).

♪ **Bridge.** The metal (electric) or wooden (acoustic) plate that anchors the strings to the body.

♪ **End pin.** A metal post where the rear end of the strap connects. On electro-acoustics, the pin often doubles as a *jack* so that you can plug in a cord to access the guitar's internal pickup.

♪ **Fingerboard.** A flat, planklike piece of wood that sits atop the neck, where you place your left-hand fingers to produce notes and chords. The fingerboard is also known as the *fretboard*, because the frets are embedded in it.

♪ **Frets.** 1) Thin metal wires or bars running perpendicular to the strings that shorten the effective vibrating length of a string, enabling it to produce different pitches. 2) A verb describing worry, as in "He frets about how many little parts are on his guitar."

♪ **Headstock.** The section that holds the tuning machines (hardware assembly) and provides a place for the manufacturer to display its logo. Not to be confused with "Woodstock," the section of New York that provided a place for the '60s generation to display its music.

♪ **Neck.** The long, clublike wooden piece that connects the headstock to the body.

♪ **Nut.** A grooved sliver of stiff nylon or other synthetic substance that stops the strings from vibrating beyond the neck. The strings pass through the grooves on their way to the tuners in the headstock. The nut is one of the two points at which the vibrating area of the string ends. (The other is the bridge.)

♪ **Output jack (electric only).** The insertion point for the cord that connects the guitar to an amplifier or other electronic device.

♪ **Pickup selector (electric only).** A switch that determines which pickups are currently active.

♪ **Pickups (electric only).** Barlike magnets that create the electrical current, which the amplifier converts into musical sound.

♪ **Sides (acoustic only).** Separate curved wooden pieces on the body that join the top to the back.

♪ **Strap pin.** Metal post where the front, or top, end of the strap connects. (Not all acoustics have a strap pin. If the guitar is missing one, tie the top of the strap around the headstock.)

♪ **Strings.** The six metal (for electric and steel-string acoustic guitars) or nylon (for classical guitars) wires that, drawn taut, produce the notes of the guitar. Although not strictly part of the actual guitar (you attach and remove them at will on top of the guitar), strings are an integral part of the whole system, and a guitar's entire design and structure revolves around making the strings ring out with a joyful noise.

♪ **Top.** The face of the guitar. On an acoustic, this piece is also the *sounding board*, which produces almost all the guitar's acoustic qualities. On an electric, the top is merely a cosmetic or decorative cap that overlays the rest of the body material.

> ♪ **Tuning machines.** Geared mechanisms that raise and lower the tension of the strings, drawing them to different pitches. The string wraps tightly around a post that sticks out through the top, or face, of the headstock. The post passes through to the back of the headstock, where gears connect it to a tuning key. Also known as tuners, tuning pegs, tuning keys, and tuning gears.
>
> ♪ **Volume and tone controls (electric only).** Knobs that vary the loudness of the guitar's sound and its bass and treble frequencies.

How Guitars Work

After you can recognize the basic parts of the guitar, you may also want to understand how those parts work together to make sound (in case you happen to choose the *parts of a guitar* category in *Jeopardy!* or get into a heavy argument with another guitarist about string vibration and string length). We present this information just so that you know why your guitar sounds the way it does, instead of like a kazoo or accordion. The important thing to remember is that a guitar makes the sound, but you make the music.

String vibration and string length

Any instrument must have some part of it moving in a regular, repeated motion to produce musical sound (a sustained tone, or *pitch*). In a guitar, this part is the vibrating string. A string that you bring to a certain tension and then set in motion (by a plucking action) produces a predictable sound — for example, the note A. If you tune the six strings of a guitar to different tensions, you get different tones. The greater the tension of a string, the higher the pitch.

You couldn't do very much with a guitar, however, if the only way to change pitches was to frantically adjust the tension on the strings every time you pluck a string. So guitarists resort to the other way to change a string's pitch — by shortening its effective vibrating length. They do so by fretting — pacing back and forth and mumbling to themselves. Just kidding; guitarists never do *that* kind of fretting unless they haven't held their guitars for a couple of days. In guitar-speak, *fretting* refers to pushing the string against the fretboard so that it vibrates only between the fingered fret (metal wire) and the bridge. This way, by moving the left hand up and down the neck (toward the bridge and the nut, respectively), you can change pitches comfortably and easily.

The fact that smaller instruments such as mandolins and violins are higher in pitch than are cellos and basses (and guitars, for that matter) is no accident. Their pitch is higher because their strings are shorter. The string tension of all these instruments may be closely related, making them feel somewhat consistent in response to the hands and fingers, but the drastic difference in string lengths is what results in the wide differences of pitch among them. This principle holds true in animals, too. A Chihuahua has a higher-pitched bark than a St. Bernard because its strings — er, vocal cords — are much shorter.

Using both hands to make a sound

The guitar normally requires two hands working together to create music. If you want to play, say, middle C on the piano, all you do is take your index finger, position it above the appropriate white key under the piano's logo, and drop it down: *donnnng*. A preschooler can sound just like Horowitz if playing only middle C, because you use just one finger of one hand pressing one key to make the sound.

The guitar is somewhat different. To play middle C on the guitar, you must take your left-hand index finger and *fret* the 2nd string (that is, press it down to the fingerboard) at the first fret. This action, however, does not itself produce a sound. You must then strike or pluck that 2nd string with your right hand to actually produce the note middle C audibly. *Music readers take note:* The guitar sounds an octave lower than its written notes. For example, playing a written, third-space C on the guitar actually produces a middle C.

Frets and half steps

The smallest interval (unit of musical distance in pitch) of the musical scale is the *half step*. On the piano, the alternating white and black keys represent this interval (except for the places where you find two adjacent white keys with no black key in between). To proceed by half steps on a keyboard instrument, you move your finger up or down to the next available key, white or black. On the guitar, *frets* — the horizontal metal wires (or bars) that you see embedded in the fretboard, running perpendicular to the strings — represent these half steps. To go up or down by half steps on a guitar means to move your left hand one fret at a time, higher or lower on the neck.

Pickups

Vibrating strings produce the different tones on a guitar. But you must be able to *hear* those tones, or you face one of those if-a-tree-falls-in-a-forest questions. For an acoustic guitar, that's no problem, because an acoustic instrument provides its own amplifier in the form of the hollow sound chamber that boosts its sound . . . well, acoustically.

But an electric guitar, on the other hand, makes virtually no acoustic sound at all. (Well, a tiny bit, like a buzzing mosquito, but nowhere near enough to fill a stadium or anger your next-door neighbors.) An electric instrument creates its tones entirely through electronic means. The vibrating string is still the source of the sound, but a hollow wood chamber isn't what makes those vibrations audible. Instead, the vibrations disturb, or *modulate,* the magnetic field that the *pickups* — wire-wrapped magnets positioned underneath the strings — produce. As the vibrations of the strings modulate the pickup's magnetic field, the pickup produces a tiny electric current that exactly reflects that modulation.

If you remember from eighth-grade science, wrapping wire around a magnet creates a small current in the wire. If you then take any magnetic substance and disturb the magnetic field around that wire, you create fluctuations in the current itself. A taut steel string vibrating at the rate of 440 times per second creates a current that fluctuates 440 times per second. Pass that current through an amplifier and then a speaker and — *voilà* — you hear the musical tone *A*. More specifically, you hear the A above middle C, which is the standard absolute tuning reference in modern music — from the New York Philharmonic to the Rolling Stones to Metallica (although we've heard that Metallica sometimes uses a tuning reference of 666 — just kidding, Metallica fans!). For more on tuning, see Chapter 2.

Guitars, therefore, make sound either by amplifying string vibrations acoustically, by passing the sound waves through a hollow chamber, or electronically, by amplifying and outputting a current through a speaker. That's the physical process anyway. How a guitar produces *different* sounds — and the ones that you want it to make — is up to you and how you control the pitches that those strings produce. Left-hand fretting is what changes these pitches. Your right-hand motions not only help produce the sound by setting the string in motion, but they also determine the *rhythm* (the beat or pulse), *tempo* (the speed of the music), and *feel* (interpretation, style, spin, magic, mojo, *je ne sais quoi,* whatever) of those pitches. Put both hand motions together, and they spell music — make that *guitar* music.

Chapter 2

Turn On, Tune In

● ●

In This Chapter

▶ Tuning the guitar relatively (to itself)

▶ Tuning to a fixed source

● ●

*T*uning is to guitarists what parallel parking is to drivers: an everyday and necessary activity that's nevertheless vexingly difficult to master. And the task is *never* fun. Unlike the piano, which a professional tunes and you never need to adjust until the next time the professional tuner comes to visit, the guitar is normally tuned by its owner — and it needs constant adjusting. One of the great injustices of life is that, before you can even play music on the guitar, you must endure the painstaking process of getting your instrument in tune.

Fortunately for guitarists, you have only six strings on a guitar instead of the couple hundred of a piano. Also encouraging is the fact that you can use several different methods to get your guitar in tune, as this chapter describes.

Everything's Relative, Einstein: Tuning the Guitar to Itself

Relative tuning is so named because you don't need any outside reference to which you tune the instrument. As long as the strings are in tune in a certain relationship with each other, you can create sonorous and harmonious tones. Those same tones may turn into sounds resembling those of a cat fight if you try to play along with a piano or flute; however, but as long as you tune the strings relative to one another, the guitar is in tune with itself.

To tune a guitar in a relative method, choose one string as the starting point — say, the 6th string (the fattest one, closest to the ceiling). The current tone of that string you leave as is. You then tune all the other strings relative to that 6th string.

You can tune from any string, including the 1st (skinniest, closest to the floor), but in *relative* tuning, where you tune each successive string according to the last, going from 6th to 1st is just better, because tuning *open* strings is easier than tuning fretted ones. (See the section "Tuning fork," later in this chapter, for more information on tuning fretted strings.) If you tune to another guitar, tuning from the 1st string to the 6th is usually easier, because the higher-pitched strings (1st, 2nd, and 3rd) come first and are easier to discern (for most ears, anyway).

The fifth-fret method

The *fifth-fret method* derives its name from the fact that you almost always play a string at the fifth fret and then compare the sound of that note to that of the next open string. You need to be careful, however, because the fourth fret (the fifth fret's jealous understudy) puts in a cameo appearance toward the end of the process. (*Fret* can refer to either the space where you put your left-hand finger or to the thin metal bar running across the fingerboard. Whenever you deal with guitar fingering, *fret* means the space in between the metal bars — where you can comfortably fit a left-hand finger.)

The first fret is the region between the nut (the thin, grooved, ivory-colored strip that separates the headstock from the neck) and the first metal bar. The fifth fret, then, is the fifth square up from the nut — technically, the region between the fourth and fifth metal fret bars. (Most guitars have a marker on the fifth fret, either a decorative design embedded in the fingerboard or a dot on the side of the neck, or both.)

Here's how you get your guitar in tune by using the fifth-fret method:

1. **Play the fifth fret of the 6th (low E) string (the fattest one, closest to the ceiling) and then play the open 5th (A) string (the one next to it).**

   Let both notes ring together. Their pitches should match exactly. If they don't seem quite right, determine whether the 5th string is higher or lower than the fifth-fretted 6th string. If the 5th string seems lower, or *flat,* use its tuning key to raise the pitch slightly. If the 5th string seems *sharp,* or higher-sounding, use its tuning key to slightly lower the pitch. You may go too far with the tuning key if you're not careful; if so, you need to reverse your motions. In fact, if you *can't* tell whether the 5th string is higher or lower, tune it flat or sharp intentionally (that is, tune it too far in one direction) and then come back to the desired pitch. If you do so, we recommend going way flat (below the desired pitch) and then tuning up.

2. **Play the fifth fret of the 5th (A) string and then play the open 4th (D) string.**

   Let both of these notes ring together. If the 4th string seems flat or sharp relative to the fretted 5th string, use the tuning key of the 4th string to adjust its pitch accordingly. Again, if you're not sure whether the 4th string is higher or lower, "overtune" it in one direction (flat, or lower, is best) and then come back.

3. **Play the fifth fret of the 4th (D) string and then play the open 3rd (G) string.**

   Let both notes ring together again. If the 3rd string seems flat or sharp relative to the fretted 4th string, use the tuning key of the 3rd string to adjust the pitch accordingly.

4. **Play the fourth (*not* the fifth!) fret of the 3rd (G) string and then play the open 2nd (B) string.**

   Let both strings ring together. If the 2nd string seems flat or sharp, use its tuning key to adjust the pitch accordingly.

5. **Play the fifth (yes, back to the fifth for this one) fret of the 2nd (B) string and then play the open 1st (high E) string.**

   Let both notes ring together. If the 1st string seems flat or sharp, use its tuning key to adjust the pitch accordingly. If you're satisfied that both strings produce the same pitch, you've now tuned the upper (that is, "upper" as in higher-pitched) five strings of the guitar relative to the fixed (untuned) 6th string. Your guitar's now in tune with itself.

Figure 2-1 shows a diagram outlining all five steps involved in tuning the guitar to itself.

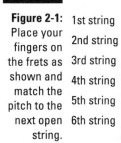

Figure 2-1: Place your fingers on the frets as shown and match the pitch to the next open string.

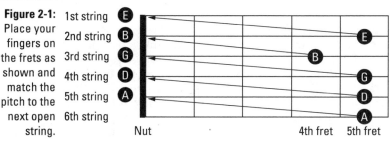

You may want to go back and repeat the process, as some strings may have slipped or the neck may have changed positions slightly in the tuning process. But tuning the guitar this way guarantees that it plays in tune with itself.

We recommend that you memorize the letter names of the open strings (E, A, D, G , B, E, from 6th to 1st) so that you're not limited to referring to them by number. An easy way to memorize the open strings in order is to remember the phrase "**E**ddie **A**te **D**ynamite; **G**ood **B**ye, **E**ddie."

Checking whether you're really in tune

Because you've just compared sets of adjacent strings to each other, a good idea is to check to make sure that you didn't get off track somewhere along the line. Tuning in pairs is sort of like the game of telephone: If one person gets the message wrong, that incorrect information gets passed on, along with any new errors that someone else introduces at each exchange. So here are a few tricks you can use to make sure that you're accurate across all six strings:

- ♪ **Play the two outside strings.** These strings are both E, two octaves apart, so they should sound in tune with each other, although one (the 6th) is low (in pitch) and one is high. If they aren't in tune, determine whether the high E of the 1st string is *relatively* (discounting the two-octave spread, of course) sharp or flat to the low E of the 6th string. That tells you in which direction you erred while tuning.

- ♪ **Match octaves of adjacent strings.** Play the open (low E) 6th string and then the 5th string fretted at the seventh fret. The two should sound exactly an *octave* (two notes with the same letter name but eight steps apart in different registers) apart, and hearing octaves that don't match is *very* easy. Continue up the strings: Match the open 5th (A) string to the 4th string, seventh fret; the open 4th (D) string to the 3rd (G) string, seventh fret; the open 3rd (G) string to the 2nd (B) string, eighth (not seventh!) fret; and the open 2nd (B) string to the 1st (high E) string, seventh fret.

- ♪ **Match octaves of every other string.** Instead of tuning in adjacent pairs, check the tuning of every other string relative to the lower string. Play the open 6th string, for example, and while letting it ring, play the 4th string on the second fret. This combination of notes should be an octave apart. Continue up the strings, matching the open 5th string with the 3rd string, second fret; the open 4th string with the 2nd string, third fret; and the open 3rd string with 1st string, third fret. In each case, make adjustments to the higher-pitched, fretted strings if they're flat or sharp to their open-string counterparts. One word of caution in using this method: You must make sure that the 6th, 5th, and 4th strings are in tune with each other, as this method ensures that the fretted, higher-pitched strings (strings 3, 2, 1) match their open, lower-octave counterparts.

- ♪ **Play a chord.** By themselves the open strings don't really add up to much. Strumming them all simultaneously creates mush. But play a nice E or G chord (see Chapter 4) slowly, one string at time (which is called *arpeggiating*), and you can hear all six strings acting in cooperation with each other. Then you can more easily hear whether a string is out of tune. Often, a string that seems out of tune in one chord sounds in tune in another. (No one said that tuning was simple, but it does get easier — we promise.)

In Deference to a Reference: Tuning to a Fixed Source

Getting the guitar in tune with itself through the relative method is good for your ear but isn't very practical if you need to play with other instruments or voices that are accustomed to standard tuning references, such as A-440. (See the section "Tuning fork," a little later in this chapter.) If you want to bring your guitar into the world of other people, you need to know how to tune to a fixed source, such as a piano, pitch pipe, tuning fork, or electronic tuner. Using such a source ensures that everyone is playing by the same tuning rules. Besides, your guitar and strings are built for optimal tone production if you tune to standard pitch.

The following sections describe some typical ways to tune your guitar by using fixed references. These methods not only enable you to get in tune, but also to make nice with all the other instruments in the neighborhood.

Piano

Because it holds its pitch so well (needing only biannual or annual tunings, depending on the conditions), a piano is a great tool that you can use for tuning a guitar. Assuming that you have an electronic keyboard or a well-tuned piano around, all you need to do is match the open strings of the guitar to the appropriate keys on the piano. Figure 2-2 shows a piano keyboard and the corresponding open guitar strings.

Pitch pipe

Obviously, if you're off to the beach with your guitar, you're not going to want to put a piano in the back of your woody, even if you're really fussy about tuning. So you need a smaller and more practical device that supplies standard-tuning reference pitches. Enter the *pitch pipe*. The pitch pipe evokes images of stern, matronly chorus leaders who purse their prunelike lips around a circular harmonica to deliver an anemic squeak that instantly marshals together the reluctant voices of the choir. Yet pitch pipes serve their purpose.

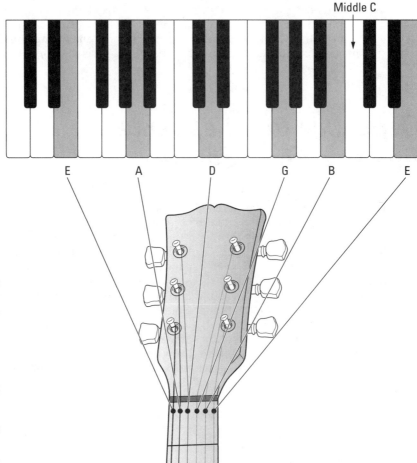

Figure 2-2:
A view of
the piano
keyboard,
highlighting
the keys
that
correspond
to the open
strings of
the guitar.

For guitarists, special pitch pipes exist consisting of pipes that play only the notes of the open strings of the guitar (but sounding in a higher register) and none of the in-between notes. The advantage of a pitch pipe is that you can hold it firmly in your mouth while blowing, keeping your hands free for tuning. The disadvantage to a pitch pipe is that you sometimes take a while getting used to hearing a wind-produced pitch against a struck-string pitch. But with practice, you can tune with a pitch pipe as easily as you can with a piano. And a pitch pipe fits much more easily into your shirt pocket than a piano does! Check out Chapter 15 for a picture of a pitch pipe.

Tuning fork

After you get good enough at discerning pitches, you need only one single-pitched tuning reference to get your whole guitar in tune. The tuning fork offers only one pitch, and it usually comes in only one flavor: *A* (the one above middle C, which vibrates at 440 cycles per second, commonly known as *A-440*). But that note's really all you need. If you tune your open 5th string (A) to the tuning fork's A (although the guitar's A sounds in a lower register), you can tune every other string to that string by using the relative tuning method that we discuss in the section "Everything's Relative, Einstein: Tuning the Guitar to Itself," earlier in this chapter.

Or you could fret the note A on each string and match that to the tuning fork. On the 4th string, for example, the seventh fret is an A. So is the 3rd string, second fret (which is the octave A to the open 5th string that we use in the section "Checking whether you're really in tune," also earlier in this chapter). And so are the 1st string, fifth fret, and the 6th string, fifth fret.

By fretting all your strings to the note A (except for the open 5th string, which is already A in its open state), you can check to see whether these pitches match your tuning fork's A. If a string is off, you need to tune it up or down accordingly, but you're now tuning a fretted string. That's a little trickier to *do* (but not to *hear*) because you must tune the string while fretting it. Most people reach their right hand *over* their left (which is holding down the string at the correct fret) to give the tuning peg a crank.

Using a tuning fork requires a little finesse. You must strike the fork against something firm, such as a tabletop or kneecap, and then hold it close to your ear or place the stem (or handle) — and *not* the tines (or fork prongs) — against something that resonates. This resonator can be the tabletop again or even the top of the guitar. (You can even hold it between your teeth, which leaves your hands free! It really works, too!) At the same time, you must somehow play an A note and tune it to the fork's tone. The process is kinda like pulling your house keys out of your pocket while you're loaded down with an armful of groceries. The task may not be easy, but if you do it enough, you eventually become an expert.

Electronic tuner

The quickest and most accurate way to get in tune is to employ an *electronic tuner*. This handy device seems to possess witchcraftlike powers. Newer electronic tuners made especially for guitars can usually sense what string you're playing, tell you what pitch you're nearest, and indicate whether you're flat or sharp. About the only thing these devices don't do is turn the tuning keys for you (although we hear they're working on that). Some older, graph-type tuners feature a switch that selects which string you want to tune. Figure 2-3 shows a typical electronic tuner.

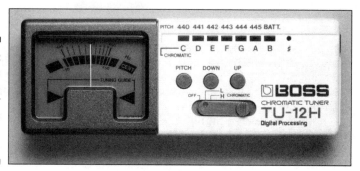

Figure 2-3:
An electronic tuner makes tuning a snap.

You can either plug your guitar into the tuner (if you're using an electric instrument) or you can use the tuner's built-in microphone to tune an acoustic. In both types of tuners — the ones where you select the strings and the ones that automatically sense the string — the display indicates two things: what note you're closest to (E, A, D, G, B, E) and whether you're flat or sharp of that note.

Electronic tuners are usually powered by 9-volt batteries or two AAs that can last for a year with regular usage (up to two or even three years with only occasional usage). Electronic tuners are not that expensive (as low as $20 or so) and are well worth the money. (For more on tuners, see Chapter 15.)

Using the CD

Lest we forget, you have at your disposal (although you should never toss it in the trash) one more fixed source as a tuning reference: your *Guitar For Dummies* CD.

For your tuning convenience, we play the open strings on Track 1 of the audio CD that comes with this book. Listen to the tone of each open string as they sound slowly, one at a time (from the 1st to the 6th, or skinniest to fattest) and tune your guitar's open strings to those on the CD. Use the track skip button on the CD player's remote control or front panel to go back to the beginning of Track 1 to repeat the tuning notes as often as necessary to get your strings exactly in tune with the strings on the CD.

Unlike a cassette tape — or any analog tape system, for that matter — a CD always plays back the exact pitch that it records and never goes sharp or flat, not even a little bit. So you can use your Dummies CD on any CD player at any time to get perfectly tuned notes.

Chapter 3

Ready, Set . . . Not Yet: Developing the Tools and Skills to Play

*G*uitars are user-friendly instruments. They fit comfortably into the arms of most humans, and the way your two hands fall on the strings naturally is the way you should pretty much play the guitar. In this chapter, you find out all about good posture techniques and how to hold your hands — just as if you were a young socialite at a finishing school.

We're just kidding about the last part, but you really need to remember that good posture and position, at the very least, prevent strain and fatigue and, at best, help develop good concentration habits and tone. Ready? Pinkies up, everyone.

Hand Position and Posture

You can either sit or stand while playing the guitar, and the position you choose makes virtually no difference whatsoever to your tone or technique. Most people prefer to practice while sitting but perform publicly while standing. The one exception involves the classical guitar, which you play on a nylon-string acoustic guitar with very strict approaches to right- and left-hand position. The orthodox practice is to play in a seated position only. This practice doesn't mean that you *can't* play a classical-style guitar or classical music while standing, however — just that the serious pursuit of the classical guitar requires that you sit while performing.

Sitting position

To hold the guitar in a sitting position, rest the *waist* of the guitar on your right leg. (The waist is the indented part between the guitar's upper and lower *bouts*, which are the protruding curved parts that look like shoulders and hips.) Place your feet slightly apart. Balance the guitar by lightly resting your right forearm on the bass bout, as shown in Figure 3-1. Don't use the left hand to support the neck. You should be able to take your left hand completely off the fretboard without the guitar dipping toward the floor.

Figure 3-1:
Typical
sitting
position.

Classical guitar technique, on the other hand, requires you to hold the instrument on your *left* leg, not on your right. This position puts the center of the guitar closer to the center of your body, making the instrument easier to play, especially with the left hand, because you can better execute the difficult fingerings of the classical-guitar music in that position. Chapter 13 shows the classical-guitar sitting position.

You must also elevate the classical guitar, which you can do either by raising the left leg with a specially made *guitar foot stool* (the traditional way) or by using a *support arm,* which goes between your left thigh and the guitar's lower side (the modern way). This device enables your left foot to remain on the floor and instead pushes the guitar up in the air.

Standing position

To stand and play the guitar, you first need to have a strap and then to make sure that it's securely fastened to both strap pins (or otherwise tied to the guitar). Then you can stand in a normal way and check out how cool you look in the mirror with that guitar slung over your shoulders. You may need to adjust the strap to get the guitar at a comfortable height. The higher the guitar is, the easier it is to play. Current rock 'n' roll fashion dictates a lower-is-cooler position, but playing that way is a little more difficult, especially for the left hand.

If your strap slips off a pin while you're playing in a standing position, you have about a 50-50 chance of catching your guitar before it hits the floor (and that's if you're quick and experienced with slipping guitars). So don't risk damaging your guitar by using an old or worn strap or one with holes that are too large for the pins to hold securely. Guitars aren't built to bounce, as Pete Townshend has demonstrated so many times.

Your body makes a natural adjustment in going from a sitting to a standing position. So don't try to overanalyze where your arms fall, relative to your sitting position. Just stay relaxed and, above all, *look cool.* (You're a guitar player now! Looking cool is just as important as knowing how to play . . . well, *almost.*) Figure 3-2 shows a typical standing position.

Figure 3-2:
Typical
standing
position.

Left-hand position

To get an idea of correct left-hand positioning on the guitar, extend your left hand, palm up, and make a loose fist, placing your thumb roughly between your first and second fingers. All your knuckles should be bent. That's about how your hand should look after you stick a guitar neck in there. The thumb glides along the back of the neck, straighter than if you were making a fist but not rigid. The finger knuckles stay bent whether they're fretting or relaxed. Again, the left hand should fall in place very naturally on the guitar neck — as if you were picking up a specially made tool that you've been using all your life.

To fret a note, press the tip of your finger down on a string, keeping your knuckles bent. Try to get the fingertip to come down vertically on the string rather than from the side. This position exerts the greatest pressure on the string and also prevents the sides of the finger from touching adjacent strings — which may cause buzzing or *muting* (deadening the string, or preventing it from ringing). Use your thumb from its position underneath the neck to help "squeeze" the fingerboard for a tighter grip.

Don't be tempted to try speeding up the process of strengthening your hands through artificial means. Building up the strength in your left hand takes time. You may see advertisements for hand-strength conditioners and believe that these devices may expedite your left-hand endurance. Although we can't unequivocally declare that these devices are ineffective (and the same goes for the home-grown method of squeezing a racquet ball or tennis ball), one thing's for sure: Nothing helps you build your left-hand fretting strength better or faster than simply playing guitar.

If playing electric

Electric necks are both narrower (from 1st string to 6th string) and shallower (from fingerboard to the back of the neck) than acoustics. Electric guitars are, therefore, easier to grip but are harder to keep adjacent strings ringing freely. (The space between each string on the fretboard is smaller, so you're more likely to touch and deaden one string with the finger you're using to fret another.) But the biggest difference between fretting on an electric and on a nylon or steel-string acoustic is the action.

A guitar's *action* refers to how high above the frets the strings ride and, to a lesser extent, how easy the strings are to fret. On an electric guitar, fretting strings is like passing a hot knife through butter. The easier action of an electric enables you to use a more relaxed left-hand position than you normally would on an acoustic, with the palm of the left hand facing slightly outward. Figure 3-3 shows a photo of the left hand resting on the fingerboard of an electric guitar, fretting a string.

Figure 3-3:
The electric guitar neck lies comfortably between the thumb and first finger as the first finger frets a note.

If playing classical

Because nylon-string guitars have a wide fingerboard and are the model of choice for classical music, their necks require a slightly more (ahem) *formal* left-hand approach. Try to get the palm-side of your knuckles (the joints that connect your fingers to your hand) to stay close to and parallel to the side of the neck so that the fingers run perpendicular to the strings and all the fingers are the same distance away from the neck. (If your hand isn't perfectly parallel, the little finger "falls away" or is farther from the neck than your index finger.) Figure 3-4 shows the correct left-hand position for nylon-string guitars.

Figure 3-4:
Correct left-hand position for a classical guitar.

Left-hand fretting requires strength, and other parts of your body may tense up to compensate. At periodic intervals, make sure that you relax your left shoulder, which has a tendency to rise up as you work on your fretting. Take frequent "drop-shoulder" breaks. Make sure as well that your left elbow doesn't stick out to the side, like that of some rude dinner guest. You want to keep your upper arm and forearm parallel to the side of your body. Relax your elbow so that it stays at your side.

The important thing to remember in maintaining a good left-hand position is that you need to keep it comfortable and natural. If your hand starts to hurt or ache, *stop playing and take a rest.* As with any other activity that requires muscular development, resting enables your body to catch up.

Right-hand position

If you hold a guitar in your lap and drape your right arm over the upper bout, your right hand, held loosely outstretched, crosses the strings at about a 60-degree angle. This position is good for playing with a pick. For fingerstyle playing, you want to turn your right hand more perpendicular to the strings. For classical guitar, you want to keep the right hand as close to a 90-degree angle as possible.

If you're using a pick

You do almost all your electric guitar playing with a *pick,* whether you're belting out rock 'n' roll, blues, jazz, country, or pop. You play most *rhythm* (chord-based accompaniment) and virtually all *lead* (single-note melodies) by holding the pick, or *plectrum* (the old-fashioned term), between the thumb and index finger. Figure 3-5 shows the correct way to hold a pick — with just the tip sticking out, perpendicular to the thumb.

If you're *strumming* (playing rhythm), you strike the strings with the pick by using wrist and elbow motion. The more vigorous the strum, the more elbow you must put into the mix. For playing lead, you use only the more economical wrist motion. Don't grip the pick too tightly as you play — and plan on dropping it a lot for the first few weeks that you use it.

Picks come in all varieties of *gauges,* which just indicate how stiff they are. Thinner picks are easier to manage for the beginner. Medium picks are the most popular, because they're flexible enough for comfortable rhythm playing, yet stiff enough for leads. Heavy-gauge picks may seem unwieldy at first, but they're the choice for pros, and eventually all skilled instrumentalists graduate to them (although a few famous holdouts exist, Neil Young being a prime example).

Figure 3-5:
Correct
pick-
holding
technique.

If you're using your fingers

If you eschew such paraphernalia as picks and want to go *au natural* with your right hand, you're *fingerpicking* (although you can fingerpick with special individual, wraparound picks that attach to your fingers — called, confusingly enough, *fingerpicks*). Fingerpicking means that you play the guitar by plucking the strings with the individual right-hand fingers. In fingerpicking, you use the tips of the fingers to play the strings, positioning the hand over the sound hole (if you're playing acoustic) and keeping the wrist stationary but not rigid. Maintaining a slight arch in the wrist so that the fingers come down more vertically on the strings also helps. Chapter 12 contains more information on fingerpicking style.

Because of the special right-hand strokes that you use in playing classical guitar (the *free stroke* and the *rest stroke*), you must hold your fingers almost perfectly perpendicular to the strings to execute the correct technique. A perpendicular approach enables your fingers to draw against the strings with maximum strength. See Chapter 13 for more information on the rest strokes and free strokes.

Music Notation: Not Just for Virtuosos Anymore

Although you don't need to read music to play the guitar, musicians have developed a few simple tricks through the years that aid in communicating such basic ideas as song structure, chord construction, chord progressions, and important rhythmic figures. Pick up on the shorthand devices for *chord diagrams, rhythm slashes,* and *tablature* (which we describe in the following sections), and you're sure to start coppin' licks faster than Roy Clark pickin' after three cups of coffee.

How to read a chord diagram

Don't worry — reading a chord diagram is *not* like reading music; it's far simpler. All you need to do is understand where to put your fingers to form a chord.

Figure 3-6 shows the anatomy of a chord chart, and the following list briefly explains what the different parts of the diagram mean:

- ♪ *The grid of six vertical lines and five horizontal ones* represents the guitar fretboard, as if you stood the guitar up on the floor or chair and looked straight at the upper part of the neck from the front.

- ♪ *The vertical lines* represent the guitar strings. The vertical line at the far left is the low 6th string, and the right-most vertical line is the high 1st string.

- ♪ *The horizontal lines* represent frets. The thick horizontal line at the top is the nut of the guitar, where the fretboard ends. So the first fret is actually the second vertical line from the top. (Don't let the words here confuse you; just look at the guitar.)

- ♪ *The dots* that appear on vertical string lines between horizontal fret lines represent notes that you fret.

- ♪ *The numerals* directly below each string line (just below the last fret line), indicate which left-hand finger you use to fret that note. On the left hand, 1 = index finger; 2 = middle finger; 3 = ring finger; and 4 = little finger. You don't use the thumb to fret, except in some unusual circumstances.

- ♪ *The X or O symbol* directly above some string lines indicate strings that you leave open (unfretted) or that you don't play. An *X* above a string means that you don't pick or strike that string with your right hand. An *O* indicates an open string that you do play.

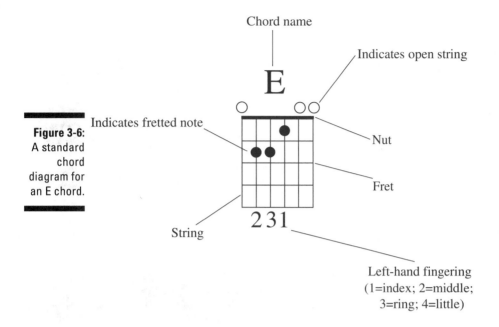

Figure 3-6:
A standard
chord
diagram for
an E chord.

If a chord starts on a fret *other* than the first fret (which you see a lot of in discussions on movable and barre chords in Chapter 8), a numeral appears to the right of the diagram, next to the top fret line, to indicate in which fret you actually start. (In such cases, the top line is *not* the nut.) In most cases, however, you deal primarily with chords that fall within only the first four frets of the guitar. Chords that fall within the first four frets typically use open strings and are referred to as *open* chords.

How to read rhythm slashes

Musicians use a variety of shorthand tricks to indicate certain musical directions. They use this shorthand because, although a particular musical concept itself is often simple enough, to notate that idea in standard written music form may prove unduly complicated and cumbersome. So they use a "cheat sheet" or a "road map" that gets the point across yet avoids the issue of reading (or writing) music.

Rhythm slashes are slash marks (/) that simply tell you *how* to play rhythmically but not *what* to play. The chord in your left hand determines what you play. Say, for example, that you see the diagram shown in Figure 3-7.

If you see such a chord symbol with four slashes beneath it, as shown in the figure, you know to finger an E chord and strike it four times. What you don't see, however, is a number of differently pitched notes clinging to various

Figure 3-7:
One
measure of
an E chord.

lines of a music staff, including several hole-in-the-center half notes and a slew of solid quarter notes — in short, any of that junk that you needed to memorize in grade school just to play "Mary Had a Little Lamb" on the recorder. All you need to remember on seeing this particular diagram is to "play an E chord four times." Simple, isn't it?

How to read tablature

Tablature (or just *tab*, for short) is a notation system that graphically represents the frets and strings of the guitar. Whereas chord diagrams do so in a static way, tablature shows how you play music over a period of time. For all the musical examples that appear in this book, you see a *tablature staff* (or *tab staff*, for short) beneath the standard notation staff. This second staff reflects exactly what's going on in the regular musical staff above it — but in *guitar language*. Tab doesn't tell you what *note* to play (such as C or F♯ or E♭). It does, however, tell you what *string* to fret and where exactly on the fingerboard to *fret* that string. Tab is actually guitar-specific — in fact, many call it simply *guitar tab*.

Figure 3-8 shows you the tab staff and some sample notes and a chord. The top line of the tab staff represents the 1st string of the guitar — high E. The bottom line of the tab corresponds to the 6th string on the guitar, low E. The other lines represent the other four stings in between — the second line from the bottom is the 5th string, and so on. A number appearing on any given line tells you to fret that string in that numbered fret — for example, if you see the numeral *2* on the second line from the top, you need to press down the 2nd string in the second fret above the nut. A zero on a line means that you play the open string.

Figure 3-8:
Three
examples of
tab staff.

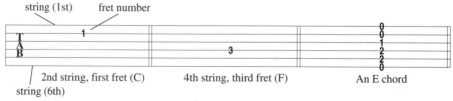

Getting the rhythm from listening to the CD

At the beginning of this book, we promise that you don't need to read music to play the guitar. And that's still true. With the help of chord diagrams, rhythm slashes, and tablature (which we explain in the previous section), plus *hearing what all this stuff sounds like* *through the magic of CD technology*, you can pick up on everything that you need to understand and play the guitar. Beginning in Chapter 4, listen closely to the CD and follow the corresponding written examples to make sure that you understand how the two relate.

How to Play a Chord

A chord is defined as the simultaneous sounding of three or more notes. You can play a chord several ways on the guitar — by strumming (dragging a pick or the back of your fingernails across the strings in a single, quick motion), plucking (with the individual right-hand fingers), or even smacking the strings with your open hand or fist. (Okay, that's rare, unless you're in some weird heavy-metal band.) But you can't just strike *any* group of notes; you must play a group of notes organized in some musically meaningful arrangement. For the guitarist, that means learning some left-hand chord forms.

Fingering a chord

After you think that you understand (somewhat) the guitar notation that we describe in the preceding sections, your best bet is to just jump right in and play your first chord. We suggest that you start with E major, as it's a particularly guitar-friendly chord and one that you use a lot.

After you get the hang of playing chords, you eventually find that you can move several fingers into position simultaneously. For now, however, just place your fingers one at a time on the frets and strings, as the following instructions indicate (you can also refer to Figure 3-6):

1. **Place your first (index) finger on the 3rd string, first fret, just *below* the metal fret wire on the fingerboard (actually between the nut and first fret wire but closer to the fret wire).**

   Don't press down hard until you have your other fingers in place. Apply just enough pressure to keep your finger from moving off the string.

2. **Place your second (middle) finger on the 5th string (skipping over the 4th string), second fret.**

   Again, apply just enough pressure to keep your fingers in place. You now have two fingers on the guitar, on the 3rd and 5th strings, with an as-yet unfretted string (the 4th) in between.

3. **Put your third (ring) finger on the 4th string, second fret.**

   You may need to wriggle your ring finger a bit to get it to fit in there between the first and second fingers. Make sure that it sits behind the fret wire and not on top of it. Figure 3-9 shows a photo of how your E chord should look after all your fingers are positioned correctly.

Figure 3-9:
Notice how the fingers curve and the knuckles bend on an E chord.

Avoiding buzzes

One of the hardest things to do in playing chords is to avoid *buzzing*. Buzzing results if you're not pressing down quite hard enough on a string or if one is hitting your fingertip in the wrong place. A buzz can also result if a finger that's fretting another string accidentally comes in contact with an adjacent string, preventing that string from ringing freely. Without removing your fingers from the frets, try "rocking and rolling" your fingers around on their tips to eliminate any buzzes when you strum the chord.

Part II
So Start Playing: The Basics

"This next piece is an intimate number I'd like to share one-on-one with you."

In this part . . .

This is the part of the book where things really start *happening,* in the way that Woodstock was a happening (in fact, if you want to nickname this part Woodstock, that's certainly okay with us). This is the part where you start actually playing the guitar. Chapter 4 presents you with some tools that will be your first and longest-lasting friends: open position major and minor chords. These puppies are the quickest, easiest way to start making recognizable music on the guitar, yet they're also a pretty constant part of guitar music. If you only work hard on one chapter in this book, let it be Chapter 4. Chapter 5 provides you with the basics of single-note melodies, so that you can inject some melody into your playing. Finally, the part winds up with a bit of spice, adding basic 7th chords to the mix.

Chapter 4

The Easiest Way to Play: Basic Major and Minor Chords

- -

In This Chapter

▶ Playing A-family chords

▶ Playing D-family chords

▶ Playing G-family chords

▶ Playing C-family chords

▶ Playing songs by using basic major and minor chords

▶ Sweatin' to the oldies

- -

*A*ccompanying yourself as you sing your favorite songs — or as someone else sings them if your voice is less than melodious — is one of the best ways to pick up basic guitar chords. If you know how to play basic chords, you can play lots of popular songs right away — from "Skip to My Lou" to "Louie Louie."

In this chapter, we organize the major and minor chords into *families*. A family of chords is simply a group of related chords. We say they're related because you often use these chords together to play songs. The concept is sort of like color-coordinating your clothing or assembling a group of foods to create a balanced meal. Chords in a family go together like peanut butter and chocolate (except that chords in a family are less messy).

Think of a family of chords as a plant. If one of the chords — the one that feels like home base in a song (usually the chord you start and end a song with) — is the plant's root, the other chords in the family are the different shoots rising up from that same root. Together, the root and shoots make up the family. Put 'em all together and you have a lush garden . . . er, make that a *song*. By the way, the technical term for a family is *key*. So you can say something like "This song uses A-family chords" *or* "This song is in the key of A."

Playing Chords in the A Family

The A family is a popular family for playing songs on the guitar because, like other families we present in this chapter, its chords are easy to play. That's because A-family chords contain *open strings* (strings that you play without pressing down any notes). Chords that contain open strings are called *open chords,* or *open-position chords.*

Listen to "Fire and Rain," by James Taylor, to hear the sound of a song that uses A-family chords.

Fingering A, D, and E chords

In fingering chords, use the "ball" of your fingertip, placing it just behind the fret (on the side toward the tuning pegs). Arch your fingers so that the fingertips fall perpendicular to the neck. And make sure that your left-hand fingernails are short so that they don't prevent you from pressing the strings all the way down to the fingerboard. *Don't* play any strings marked with an *X* (the 6th string on the A chord and the 5th and 6th strings on the D chord). If you play a string marked with an *X* and we catch you, we'll revoke your picking privileges on the spot.

Playing callusly

Playing chords can be a little painful at first. (We mean for you, not for people within ear-shot; c'mon, we're not *that* cruel.) No matter how tough you are, if you've never played the guitar before, your left-hand fingertips are *soft.* Fretting a guitar string, therefore, is going to feel to your fingertips almost as if you're hammering a railroad spike with your bare hand. (Ouch!)

In short, *pressing down the string hurts.* This situation is not weird at all — in fact, it's quite normal for beginning guitarists. (Well, it's weird if you *enjoy* the pain.) You must develop nice, thick calluses on your fingertips before playing the guitar can ever feel completely comfortable. You may take weeks or even months to build up those protective layers of dead skin, depending on how much and how often you play. But after you finally earn your calluses, you never lose them (completely, anyway). Like a Supreme Court justice, you're a guitar player *for life.*

You can develop your calluses by playing the basic chords in this chapter over and over again. As you progress, you also gain strength in your hands and fingers and become more comfortable in general while playing the guitar. Before you know it's happening, fretting a guitar becomes as natural to you as shaking hands with your best friend.

As with any physical-conditioning routine, make sure that you stop and rest if you begin to feel tenderness or soreness in your fingers or hands. Building up those calluses takes *time,* and you can't hurry time (or love, for that matter, as Diana Ross would attest).

Each of these chords is what's known as a *major* chord. A chord that's named by a letter name alone, such as these (A, D, and E), is always major. (See the sidebar "Chord qualities.") Figure 4-1 shows the fingering for the A, D, and E chords — the basic chords in the A family. (If you're unclear about reading the chord diagrams, check out the information in Chapter 3 on chord diagrams.)

Strumming A-family chords

Use your right hand to strum these A-family chords with one of the following:

♪ A pick

♪ Your thumb

♪ The back of your fingernails (in a brushing motion toward the floor)

Start strumming from the lowest-pitched string of the chord (the side of the chord toward the ceiling as you hold the guitar) and strum toward the floor.

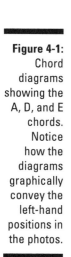

Figure 4-1: Chord diagrams showing the A, D, and E chords. Notice how the diagrams graphically convey the left-hand positions in the photos.

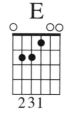

Chord qualities

Chords have different *qualities,* which has nothing to do with whether they're good or bad little chords. You can define *quality* as the *relationship* between the different notes that make up the chord — or simply, what the chord sounds like.

Besides the quality of being *major,* other chord qualities include *minor, 7th, minor 7th,* and *major 7th.* The following list describes each of these types of chord qualities:

♪ **Major chords:** These are simple chords that have a stable sound.

♪ **Minor chords:** These are simple chords that have a soft, sometimes sad sound.

♪ **7th chords:** These are bluesy, funky-sounding chords.

♪ **Minor 7th chords:** These chords sound mellow and jazzy.

♪ **Major 7th chords:** These chords sound bright and jazzy.

Each type of chord, or chord quality, has a different kind of sound, and you can often distinguish the chord type just by hearing it. Listen, for example, to the sound of a major chord by strumming A, D, and E. (For more information on 7th, minor 7th, and major 7th chords, check out Chapter 6.)

A *progression* is simply a series of chords that you play one after the other. Figure 4-2 presents a simple progression in the key of A and instructs you to strum each chord — in the order shown (reading from left to right) — four times. Use all *downstrokes* (dragging your pick across the strings toward the floor) as you play.

Listen to the example on the CD to hear the rhythm of this progression and try to play along with it.

Figure 4-2:
A simple chord progression in the key of A (using only chords in the A family).

TRACK 2, 0:00

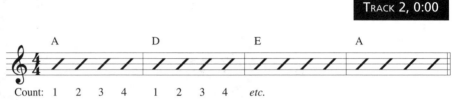

After strumming each chord four times, you come to a vertical line in the music that follows the four strum symbols. This line is a *bar line*. It's not something that you play. Bar lines visually separate the music into smaller sections known as *measures,* or *bars.* (You can use these terms interchangeably; they both mean the same thing.) Measures make written music easier to grasp, because they break up the music into little, digestible chunks. See Appendix A for more information on bar lines and measures.

Don't hesitate or stop at the bar line. Keep your strumming speed the same throughout, even as you play "between the measures" — that is, in the imaginary "space" from the end of one measure to the beginning of the next that the bar line represents. Start out playing as slowly as necessary to help you keep the beat steady. You can always speed up as you become more confident and proficient in your chord fingering and switching.

By playing a progression over and over, you start to develop left-hand strength and calluses on your fingertips. Try it (and try it . . . and try it. . . .).

If you want to play a song right away, you can. Skip to the section "Playing Songs with Basic Major and Minor Chords," at the end of this chapter. Because you now know the basic open chords in the A family, you can play "Kumbaya." Rock on!

Playing Chords in the D Family

The basic chords that make up the D family are D, Em (pronounced "E minor"), G, and A. The D family, therefore, shares two basic open chords with the A family (D and A) and introduces two new ones: Em and G. Because you already know how to play D and A from the preceding section ("Playing Chords in the A Family"), you need to work on only two more chords to add the entire D family to your repertoire: Em and G.

Listen to "Here Comes the Sun," by the Beatles, to hear the sound of a song that uses D-family chords.

Minor describes the quality of a type of chord. A minor chord has a sound that's distinctly different from that of a major chord. You may characterize the sound of a minor chord as *sad, mournful, scary,* or even *ominous.* Remember that the relationship of the notes that make up the chord determines a chord's quality.

Fingering D-family chords

Figure 4-3 shows you how to finger the two basic chords in the D family that aren't in the A family. You may notice that none of the strings in either chord diagram displays an *X* symbol, so you get to strike all the strings whenever

Figure 4-3:
The Em and
G chords.
Notice that
all six
strings are
available
for play in
each chord.

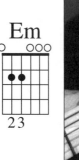

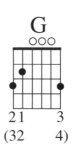

you play a G or Em chord. If you feel like it, go ahead and celebrate by dragging your pick or right-hand fingers across the strings in a big *keraaaang*.

Try the following trick to quickly pick up how to play Em and to hear the difference between the major and minor chord qualities: Play E, which is a major chord, and then lift your index finger off the 3rd string. Now you're playing Em, which is the minor-chord version of E. By alternating the two chords, you can easily hear the difference in quality between a major and minor chord.

Notice the alternative fingering for G (2-3-4 instead of 1-2-3). As your hand gains strength and becomes more flexible, you want to switch to the 2-3-4 fingering instead of the initially easier 1-2-3 fingering (the version shown in Figure 4-3). You can switch to other chords with greater ease and efficiency by using the 2-3-4 fingering for G.

Strumming D-family chords

In Figure 4-4, you play a simple chord progression using D-family chords. Notice the difference in the strum in this figure verses that of Figure 4-2. In Figure 4-2, you strum each chord four times per measure. Each strum is one pulse, or beat. Figure 4-4 divides the second strum of each measure (or the second beat) into two strums — up and down — both of which together take up the time of one beat, meaning that you must play each strum in beat 2 twice as quickly as you do a regular strum.

The additional symbol ⊓ with the strum symbol means that you strum down toward the floor, and ∨ means that you strum up toward the ceiling. (If you play your guitar while hanging in gravity boots, however, you must reverse these last two instructions.) The term *sim.* is an abbreviation of the Italian word *simile,* which instructs you to keep playing in a similar manner — in this case to keep strumming in a *down, down-up, down, down* pattern.

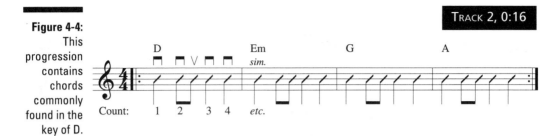

Figure 4-4:
This progression contains chords commonly found in the key of D.

If you're using only your fingers for strumming, play upstrokes with the back of your thumbnail whenever you see the symbol ∨.

Knowing the basic open chords in the D family (D, Em, G, and A) enables you to play a song in the key of D right now. If you skip to the section "Playing Songs with Basic Major and Minor Chords," later in this chapter, you can play the song "Swing Low, Sweet Chariot" right now. Go for it!

Playing Chords in the G Family

By tackling related chord families (as A, D, and G are), you carry over your knowledge from family to family in the form of chords that you already know from earlier families. The basic chords that make up the G family are G, Am, C, D, and Em. If you already know G, D, and Em (which we describe in the preceding sections on the A and D families), you can now try Am and C.

Listen to "You've Got a Friend," as played by James Taylor, to hear the sound of a song that uses G-family chords.

Fingering G-family chords

In Figure 4-5, you see the fingerings for Am and C, the new chords that you need to play in the G family. Notice that the fingering of these two chords is similar: Each has finger 1 on the 2nd string, first fret, and finger 2 on the 4th string, second fret. (Only finger 3 must change — adding or removing it — in switching between these two chords.) In moving between these chords, keep these first two fingers in place on the strings. Switching chords is always easier if you don't need to move all your fingers to new positions. The notes that different chords share are known as *common tones*. Notice the *X* over the 6th string in each of these chords. Don't play that string while strumming either C or Am. (We mean it!)

Figure 4-5:
The fingering for the Am and C chords.

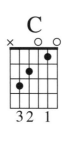

Strumming G-family chords

Figure 4-6 shows a simple chord progression that you can play by using G-family chords. Play this progression over and over to accustom yourself to switching chords and to build up those left-hand calluses. It *does* get easier after a while. We promise!

Notice that, in each measure, you play beats 2 *and* 3 as "down-up" strums. Listen to the CD to hear this sound.

TRACK 2, 0:43

Figure 4-6:
A chord progression that you can play by using only G-family chords.

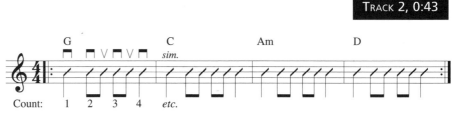

 Knowing the basic open chords in the G family (G, Am, C, D, and Em) enables you to play a song in the key of G right now. Skip to the section "Playing Songs with Basic Major and Minor Chords," later in this chapter, and you can play "Auld Lang Syne." As the relieved shepherd said after the mother sheep returned to the flock, "Happy, Ewe Near."

Playing Chords in the C Family

The last chord family that we need to discuss is C. Some people say that C is the easiest key to play in. That's because C uses only the white-key notes of the piano in its musical scale and, as such, is sort of the music-theory ground zero — the point at which everything (and, usually, everyone) begins in music.

We chose to place the C family last in this chapter because, heck, it's so easy that it has lots of chords in its family — too many to master all at once.

The basic chords that make up the C family are C, Dm, Em, F, G, and Am. If you practice the preceding sections on the A-, D-, and G-family chords, you know C, Em, G, and Am. (If not, check them out.) So in this section, you need to pick up only two more chords: Dm and F. After you know these two additional chords, you have all the basic major and minor chords that we describe in this chapter down pat.

Listen to "Dust in the Wind," by Kansas or "The Boxer," by Simon and Garfunkel to hear the sound of a song that uses C-family chords.

Fingering C-family chords

In Figure 4-7, you see the new chords that you need to play in the C family. Notice that both the Dm and F chords have the 2nd finger on the 3rd string, second fret. Hold this common tone down as you switch between these two chords.

Figure 4-7:
The Dm and F chords. Notice the indication (⌒) in the F-chord diagram that tells you to fret (or barre) two strings with one finger.

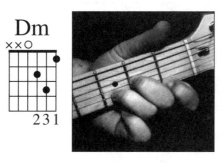
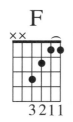

Many people find the F chord the most difficult chord to play of all the basic major and minor chords. That's because F uses no open strings, and it also requires a *barre*. A barre is what you're playing whenever you press down two or more strings at once with a single left-hand finger. To play the F chord, for example, you use your first finger to press down both the 1st and 2nd strings at the first fret simultaneously.

Tuning your way out of a jam

We've heard stories about people quitting the guitar just because the F chord was way too hard to play. But this nettlesome grain of sand in the chordal oyster may have produced at least one pearl. A famous story about Joni Mitchell says that, as she was first learning the guitar, she had so much trouble playing the F chord that she gave up and retuned her first string to avoid the barre.

As the legend goes, this classic example of F-avoidance is what led Joni to play in *open tunings* (alternate tunings in which the open strings form a chord such as G or D), a style in which she's considered a master. Her open stylings also produced some of Ms. Mitchell's biggest hits, such as "Big Yellow Taxi" and "Chelsea Morning." (See Chapter 10 for more information on alternate tunings.)

You must exert extra finger pressure to play a barre. At first, you may find that, as you strum the chord (hitting the top four strings only, as the *X*s in the chord diagram indicate), you hear some buzzes or muffled strings. Experiment with various placements of your index finger. Try adjusting the angle of your finger or try rotating your finger slightly on its side. Keep trying until you find a position for the first finger that enables all four strings to ring clearly as you strike them.

Strumming C-family chords

Figure 4-8 shows a simple chord progression that you can play by using C-family chords. Play the progression over and over to get used to switching among the chords in this family and, of course, to help build up those nasty little calluses.

Notice in the strumming notation the small curved line joining the second half of beat 2 to beat 3. This line is known as a *tie*. A tie tells you *not* to strike the second note of the two tied notes (in this case, the one on beat 3). Instead, just keep holding the chord on that beat (letting it ring) without restriking it with your right hand.

Listen to the CD to hear the sound of this strumming pattern. This slightly jarring rhythmic effect is an example of *syncopation*. In syncopation, the musician either strikes a note (or chord) where you don't expect to hear it or fails to strike a note (or chord) where you do expect to hear it.

You probably usually expect to strike notes on the beats (1, 2, 3, 4). In the example in Figure 4-8, however, you strike no chord on beat 3. That variation in the strumming pattern makes the chord on beat 2^1/$_2$ feel as if it's *accentuated* (or, as musicians say, *accented*). This accentuation disrupts the normal (expected) pulse of the music, resulting in the syncopation of the music. Syncopation breaks up the regular occurrence of beats and presents an element of surprise in music. The balance between expectation and surprise in music is what holds a listener's interest. (Well, that and the promise of free hors d'oeuvres at the intermission.)

Figure 4-8:
A simple chord progression that you can play by using C-family chords.

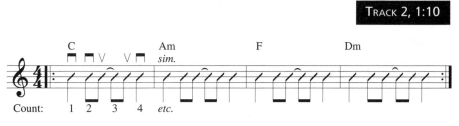

To play a song that uses C-family chords right now, skip to the song "Michael, Row the Boat Ashore," in the section "Playing Songs with Basic Major and Minor Chords," later in this chapter. Bon voyage.

Playing Songs with Basic Major and Minor Chords

This section is where the *real music* happens — you know, *songs*. If the titles here hearken back to those bygone campfire days in the distant recesses of your youth, fear not, young-at-heart campers. These songs, although seemingly simple, illustrate universal principles that carry over into the more — shall we say it? — *hipper* musical genres. Pick up on these songs first, and you're certain to be playing the music of your choice in no time — we promise!

You may notice that all the strumming examples that we provide in this chapter are only four measures long. Must all your exercises be limited this way, you may ask? No, but songwriters do very commonly write music in four-measure phrases. So the length of these exercises prepares you for actual passages in real songs. You may also notice that each strumming example is in 4/4 time, which means that each measure contains four beats. Any reason? Most popular songs contain four beats per measure, so the 4/4 time signature in the exercises also prepares you to play actual songs. (See Appendix A for more information on time signatures.)

In the examples that you find in earlier sections of this chapter, you play each chord for one full measure. But in this section of actual songs, you sometimes play a single chord for more than a measure, and sometimes you change chords within a single measure. Listen to the CD to hear the rhythm of the chord changes as you follow the beat numbers (1, 2, 3, 4) that appear below the guitar staff.

After you can comfortably play your way through these songs, try to memorize them. That way, you don't need to stare into a book as you're trying to develop your rhythm.

If you get bored with these songs — or with the way *you* play these songs — show the music to a guitar-playing friend and ask him to play the same songs by using the strumming patterns and chord positions that we indicate. Listening to someone else play helps you hear the songs objectively, and if your friend has a little flair, you may pick up a cool little trick or two. Work on infusing a bit of *personality* into all your playing, even if you're just strumming a simple folk song.

About the songs

Here's some special information to help you play the songs in this section:

♪ **Kumbaya.** To play "Kumbaya" (the ultimate campfire song), you need to know how to play A, D, and E chords (see the section "Fingering A, D, and E chords," earlier in this chapter); how to strum by using all downstrokes; and how to start a fire by using only two sticks and some dried leaves.

The first measure in this song is known as a *pickup* measure, which is incomplete; it starts the song with one or more beats missing — in this case, the first two. During the pickup measure, the guitar part shows a *rest,* or a musical silence. Don't play during the rest. Notice, too, that the last bar is missing two beats — beats 3 and 4. The missing beats in the last measure enable you to repeat the pickup measure in repeated playings of the song, and to make that measure, combined with the first incomplete measure, total the requisite four beats.

♪ **Swing Low, Sweet Chariot.** To play "Swing Low, Sweet Chariot," you need to know how to play D, Em, G, and A chords (see the section "Fingering D-family chords," earlier in this chapter); how to play down and down-up strums; and how to sing like James Earl Jones.

This song starts with a one-beat pickup, and the guitar rests for that beat. Notice that beat 2 of measures 2, 4, and 6 has two strums instead of one. Strum those beats down and then up (⊓ and ∨) with each strum twice as fast as a regular strum.

♪ **Auld Lang Syne.** To play "Auld Lang Syne," you need to know how to play G, Am, C, D, and Em chords (see the section "Fingering G-family chords," earlier in this chapter); how to play down and down-up strums; and what "Auld Lang Syne" means in the first place.

Measure 8 is a little tricky, because you play three different chords in the same measure. In the second half of the measure, you change chords on each beat — one stroke per chord. Practice playing only measure 8 slowly, over and over. Then play the song. *Note:* In changing between G and C, fingering G with fingers 2, 3, and 4 instead of 1, 2, and 3 makes the chord switch easier. If you finger the chord that way, the second and third fingers form a shape that simply moves over one string.

♪ **Michael, Row the Boat Ashore.** To play "Michael, Row the Boat Ashore," you need to know how to play C, Dm, Em, F, and G chords (see the section "Fingering C-family chords," earlier in this chapter); how to play a syncopated eighth-note strum (see the section "Strumming C-family chords," earlier in this chapter); and the meaning of the word *hootenanny*.

The strumming pattern here is *syncopated*. The strum that normally occurs on beat 3 is *anticipated*, meaning that it actually comes half a beat early. This kind of syncopation gives the song a Latin feel. Listen to the CD to hear the strumming rhythm. Remember that, on the Dm and F chords, you don't strum the lowest two strings (the 6th and 5th). For the C chord, don't strum the bottom string (the 6th).

Kumbaya

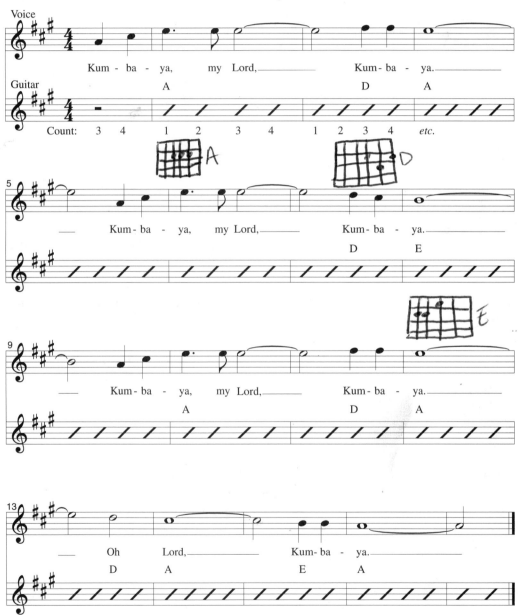

TRACK **4**

Swing Low, Sweet Chariot

Swing low, sweet char - i - ot,_____

Count: 4   1   2   3   4   1   2   3   4

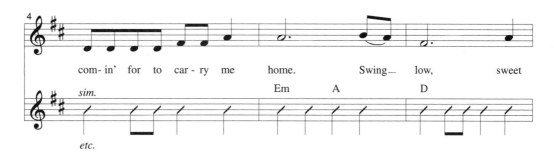

com - in' for to car - ry me home. Swing— low, sweet

sim.

etc.

char - i - ot,___ com - in' for to car - ry me home.

Auld Lang Syne

TRACK 6

Michael, Row the Boat Ashore

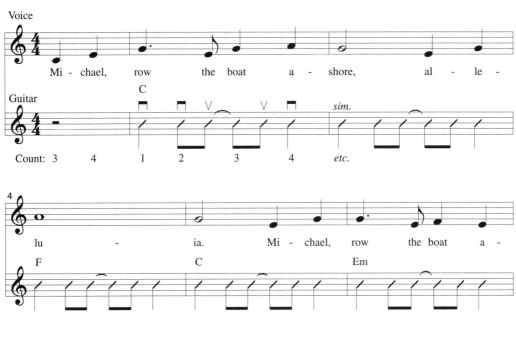

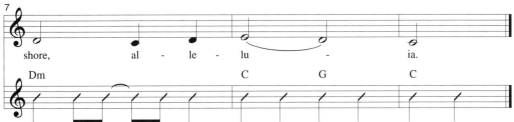

Having Fun with Basic Major and Minor Chords: The "Oldies" Progression

As we promise in the introduction to this chapter, you can play lots of popular songs right away if you know the basic major and minor chords. One cool thing that you can do right now is play *oldies* — songs from the late '50s and early '60s such as "Earth Angel" and "Duke of Earl." These songs are based on what's sometimes called the *oldies progression*. The oldies progression is a series of four chords; they're repeated over and over to form the accompaniment for a song.

You can play the oldies progression in any key, but the best guitar keys for the oldies progression are C and G. In the key of C, the four chords that make up the progression are C-Am-F-G. And in the key of G, the chords are G-Em-C-D.

Try strumming the progression in each key by playing four down-strums per chord. Play the four chords over and over, in the sequence given. If you need help with the fingerings for these chords, check out the sections "Playing Chords in the C Family" and "Playing Chords in the G Family," earlier in this chapter.

The fun begins as you sing oldies while accompanying yourself with the oldies progression. As you sing a particular song, you find that one of the keys (C or G) better suits your vocal range, so use that key. Playing oldies can become addicting, but the good news is that, if you can't stop, you build up your calluses very quickly.

For some songs, you play four one-beat strums per chord; for others, you play eight or two. Here are some songs you can play with the oldies progression. Next to each, we show you how many times you strum each chord. Don't forget to sing. Have fun!

Here are a few songs you can play right now using the oldies progression:

- ♪ **All I Have to Do Is Dream.** Two strums per chord.
- ♪ **Blue Moon.** Two strums per chord.
- ♪ **Breaking Up Is Hard to Do.** Two strums per chord.
- ♪ **Come Go with Me.** Two strums per chord.
- ♪ **Dream Lover.** Eight strums per chord.

♪ **Duke of Earl.** Four strums per chord.

♪ **Earth Angel.** Two strums per chord.

♪ **Heart and Soul.** Two strums per chord.

♪ **Hey Paula.** Two strums per chord.

♪ **In the Still of the Night.** (The one by the Five Satins, not the Cole Porter one.) Four strums per chord.

♪ **Little Darlin'.** Eight strums per chord.

♪ **Poor Little Fool.** Four strums per chord.

♪ **Runaround Sue.** Eight strums per chord.

♪ **Sherry.** Two strums per chord.

♪ **Silhouettes.** Two strums per chord.

♪ **Take Good Care of My Baby.** Four strums per chord.

♪ **Tears on My Pillow.** Two strums per chord.

♪ **Teenager in Love.** Four strums per chord.

♪ **What's Your Name.** Two strums per chord.

♪ **Why Do Fools Fall in Love?** Two strums per chord.

♪ **You Send Me.** Two strums per chord.

Chapter 5

Playing Melodies without Reading Music!

Most guitar books present melodies as a way to teach you to read music. In fact, the primary goal of most guitar books isn't to teach you to play guitar in the real world but to teach music reading through the guitar. The difference is significant.

If you pick up guitar playing through a book, you can eventually play nursery-rhyme ditties in perfect quarter and half notes. But if you learn to play as most guitar players do — through friends showing you licks or by using your ear — you can come away playing "Smoke on the Water," "Sunshine of Your Love," "Blackbird," and the entire repertoire of Neil Young. All of which means that *you don't need to read music to play guitar.*

Okay, so maybe reading music *is* a valuable skill. But the purpose of this chapter isn't to teach you to read; it's to get you to play. If we need to show you a lick, we use *tablature* — a special notation system designed especially for showing *how you play the guitar.* Or we refer you to the CD so that you can hear the lick. Or both.

We offer melodies in this chapter primarily so that you can accustom your hands to playing single notes. That way, whenever you decide that you want to play like a *real* guitarist — someone who combines chords, melodies, riffs, and licks into an integrated whole — you're ready to rock.

By the way, a *lick* is a short, melodic phrase, often made up on the spot and played only once. A *riff* is a short melodic phrase, often composed to be the main accompaniment figure in a song (as in "Can you play the 'Day Tripper' riff?").

Reading Tablature while Listening to the CD

Numbers on the tablature (or *tab*) staff tell you which frets on which strings to finger with your left hand. A zero indicates an open string. By listening to the CD, you can hear when to play these notes. And just to be safe, thorough, and completely redundant, we also include the standard notation for the following reasons:

- ♪ For people who read music already.
- ♪ For people who plan to read Appendix A (on how to read music) and apply what they read there.
- ♪ For people who want to gradually pick up the skill of music reading (at least by osmosis if not rigorous study) by listening to the CD and following along with the rhythm notation.
- ♪ For us, the authors, who get paid by the page.

Top or bottom

The music in this book contains a double staff: standard music notation on the top, tab on the bottom. The top staff is for music readers or for people interested in standard notation. The bottom staff shows the same info (minus the rhythm) but in tab numbers. Here's how the tab staff works.

The top line of the tab staff represents the *top* string of the guitar (high E). This positioning of the strings in the tab staff may momentarily confuse you, because the top string in the tab staff — the 1st — is actually the string closest to the floor as you hold the guitar in playing position. But trust us, the setup's more intuitive this way, and after you make the adjustment, you never think about it again. By the way, if you hold the guitar flat on your lap, with the neck facing the ceiling, the *1st* string is farthest away from you, just as the *top* line is when you see the tab staff on the page. Check out the cheat sheet at the beginning of the book to see a visual representation of this concept.

Moving on, the second tab line from the top represents the 2nd string (B) and so on down to the bottom tab line, which represents the 6th (low E) string on the guitar.

In guitar tab, lines represent strings and numbers represent frets. Tab does not, however, tell you which left-hand fingers to use. (Neither does standard notation, for that matter.) But more on fingering later.

Right or left?

Just as in reading text or music, you start from the left and proceed to the right in reading tab. Using Figure 5-1 as your example, begin with the first note, which you play on the first fret of the 2nd string. The placement of the tab number on the second line from the top tells you to play the B string — the one next to high E — and the number 1 tells you to place your finger on the first fret. Go ahead and play that note and then proceed to the next note, which is also on the 2nd string, first fret. Keep moving right, playing the notes in order, until you reach the end. (Don't worry about the symbols above the numbers for now; we explain them in the section "Alternate Picking," later in this chapter.) The vertical lines that appear on the staff after every few notes are *bar lines*. They divide the staff into small units of time, called *bars* or *measures*. Measures help you count beats and break up the music into smaller, more manageable units. In Figure 5-1, you see four measures of four beats each. See Appendix A for more information on beats and measures.

Figure 5-1:
A melody in standard notation and tab. Tab lines represent strings, and numbers on the lines represent fret numbers.

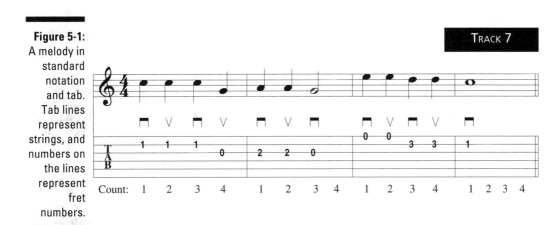

After you understand the concepts of top versus bottom and left versus right in the tab staff and also understand that the lines indicate strings and the numbers on the lines indicate fret position, you can listen to the CD and easily follow (and play) the tab. The two media, CD and print, serve to reinforce each other. If you didn't realize it yet, you're picking up guitar the multimedia way. (Mail us your proof-of-purchase and we even send you a secret decoder ring and virtual-reality goggles! Just kidding!)

Left-Hand Fingering

After you figure out how to read guitar tablature, you know what frets to press down, but you still may have no idea of which fingers to use to press down the frets. Usually, you don't need anyone to tell you which fingers to use, because you most often play in *position*. A position on the guitar is a group of four consecutive frets; for example, frets 1, 2, 3, 4 or 5, 6, 7, 8.

Each fret marks the beginning of a new position, and the index finger plays the note in the lowest fret of that position (*lowest* meaning toward the nut, of course). The easiest way to play melodies on the guitar is to play them in *first* or *second position* — that is, using frets 1 through 4 or frets 2 through 5 — because these positions are right next to the open strings (strings that you play without fretting). You can then utilize the open strings as well as the fretted notes in playing a melody.

Open position itself consists of the combination of all the open strings plus the notes in the first or second position — just as the chords that you play low on the neck using open strings (A, D, Em, and so on) are known as *open chords*. (For more information on open chords, check out Chapter 4.)

Imagine that you're playing five consecutive white keys on the piano. You use five fingers, one for each note. Using only one finger, such as just the thumb, to play all five notes is awkward and slow. The concept's the same on the guitar — use one finger per fret for ease and speed.

In any position, each finger plays the notes of a specific fret — and only of that fret. In first position, for example, the fret numbers correspond to the fingers — the first finger plays the notes in the first fret; the second finger plays the notes in the second fret; and so on. Using one finger per fret enables you to switch between notes quickly.

As you play the open-position melodies in this chapter, make sure that you press your left-hand fingers down correctly, as follows:

♪ Press down on the string with the tip of your finger just *before* the metal fret wire (toward the nut).

♪ Keep the last joint of the finger perpendicular (or as close to perpendicular as possible) to the fretboard.

Alternate Picking

As you play a song, you use both hands at once. After you figure out which notes to press with the left hand, you need to know how to strike the strings with the right.

You can use either a pick or the right-hand fingers to strike single notes; for now, use the pick, holding it firmly between the thumb and index finger (perpendicular to the thumb with just the tip sticking out). Check out Chapter 3 for more information on holding the pick. (We discuss playing with the fingers in Chapters 12 and 13.)

Alternate picking is the right-hand picking technique that uses both *downstrokes* (toward the floor) and *upstrokes* (toward the ceiling) to facilitate speed. Try the following experiment:

1. **Hold the pick between your thumb and index finger of your right hand.**

   Again, see Chapter 3 for more information on holding the pick.

2. **Using only downstrokes, pick the open 1st string repeatedly as fast as possible (down-down-down-down, and so on).**

   Try to play as smoothly and evenly as possible.

3. **Now try the same thing but alternating downstrokes and upstrokes (down-up-down-up, and so on).**

   This alternating motion feels much smoother, doesn't it? The advantage of alternate picking is that you can play rapid, successive notes in a smooth, flowing manner.

To play two successive downstrokes, you need to bring the pick back up above the E string *anyway*. But by actually striking the string with the pick on the way back up (using an upstroke) instead of avoiding the string, you can greatly increase your speed. Single notes that you need to play relatively fast almost always require alternate picking.

Check to make sure that you understand the concept of alternate picking by following the next two sets of steps.

To play a downstroke (the ⊓ symbol above the tab), follow these steps:

1. **Start with the pick slightly above the string (on the "ceiling" side).**

2. **Strike the string in a downward motion (toward the floor).**

To play an upstroke (the ∨ symbol above the tab), follow these steps:

1. **Start with the pick below the string (on the "floor" side).**

2. **Strike the string in an upward motion (toward the ceiling).**

The melody in the tab staff example that we show you in Figure 5-1 is actually that of "Old MacDonald Had a Farm." Try playing that melody to see how it sounds. First, play the tune slowly, using only downstrokes. Then play it faster by using alternating picking, as the symbols above the tab staff indicate. Here a pick, there a pick, everywhere a pick-pick. . . .

Playing Songs with Simple Melodies

In Chapter 4, all the songs that you play are in 4/4 time. The songs in this chapter, on the other hand, are in various *meters*. (The meter indicates how many beats per measure: 4, 3, 2, and so on; see Appendix A for more information on beats and measures.) You play all these songs in open position. (See the section "Left-Hand Fingering," earlier in this chapter.)

About the songs

You've probably known the songs in this chapter all your life, but never thought about them in a music sense — what meter they're in and what rhythms they use — and you almost certainly never thought of "E-I-E-I-O" as alternating downstrokes and upstrokes.

The fact that a bunch of supposedly simple folk songs — tunes you've never thought twice about before — now make you feel slow and clumsy as you try to play them may seem a bit deflating. But playing the guitar is a cumulative endeavor. Every technique you pick up, even if you practice it in "Little Brown Jug," applies to *all* songs that use those same techniques, from Van Morrison to Beethoven, from "Moondance" to the "Moonlight Sonata." Hang in there with the technical stuff and the rest follows.

Here is some useful information about the songs to help you along:

♪ **Little Brown Jug.** To play this song, you need to know how to count two beats per measure (see Appendix A and listen to the CD); how to finger notes in first position (see the section "Left-Hand Fingering," earlier in this chapter); and how to make a song about getting drunk sound suitable for small children.

This song has only two beats per measure (not four). The time signature (2/4) tells you this fact. Play all the fretted notes in the first position by using the same-numbered left-hand fingers as the fret numbers — that is, use the first finger for the first fret, the second finger for the second fret, and so on. Follow the ⊓ and ∨ indications above the tab numbers for downstrokes and upstrokes. The *sim.* means to continue the same picking pattern for the rest of the song.

♪ **On Top of Old Smoky.** To play this song, you need to know how to count three beats per measure (see Appendix A and listen to the CD); how to finger notes in first position (see the section "Left-Hand Fingering," earlier in this chapter); and how to make a song about infidelity sound childlike and whimsical.

This old favorite has three beats per measure, as the time signature (3/4) indicates. This song is in open position — the one that combines first position with the open strings. Use the same finger numbers for fretting as the indicated fret number. We don't indicate any symbols for up and down picking for you in this song; use your own judgment and pick out the notes of the song however feels most natural to you. Some of these notes you can play by using either up- or downstrokes.

♪ **Swanee River.** To play this song, you need to know how to count four beats per measure (see Appendix A and listen to the CD); how to finger notes in second position (see the section "Left-Hand Fingering," earlier in this chapter); and how to sound politically correct while playing a song about the old plantation.

This old tune of the South has four beats per measure, as its 4/4 time signature indicates. Play the song by using the open position that combines the *second position* with the open strings — that is, your first finger plays the notes on the second fret; your second finger plays the notes of the third fret; and your third finger plays the notes of the fourth fret. You can also play the song by using the *first position* with open strings, but playing it that way is a lot harder. (Fingers 1 and 3 are stronger than 2 and 4.) Try it if you don't believe us. See — we told you! (Oh, and see the section "Left-Hand Fingering," earlier in this chapter, if you don't know what positions you're playing here at all.) Notice the symbols for up and down picking above the tab staff. Play downstrokes (⊓) for the notes that fall on the beats and upstrokes (∨) for the notes that fall between the beats. Again, *sim.* means keep playing that same picking pattern to the end. By the way, this song's actual title is "Old Folks at Home," but most people just call it "Swanee River." (It's the song that stumped Ralph Kramden on the game show *The $99,000 Answer* on the old *Honeymooners* episode. The tune was written by Stephen Foster — not Ed Norton!)

TRACK 8

Little Brown Jug

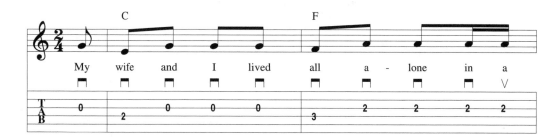

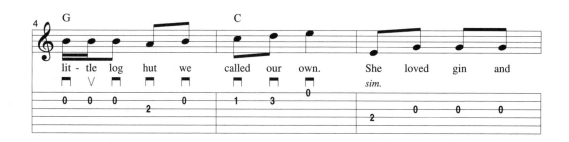

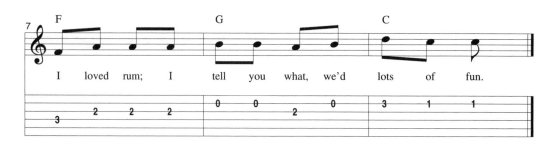

TRACK 9

On Top of Old Smoky

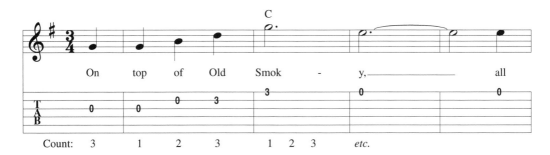

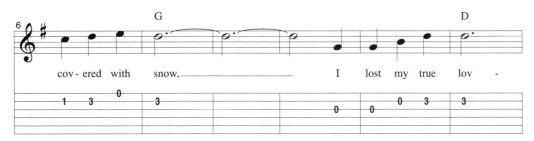

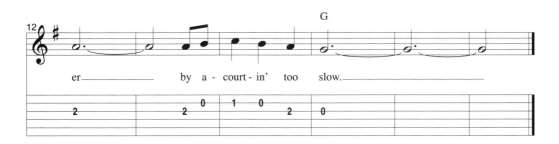

TRACK 10

Swanee River (Old Folks at Home)

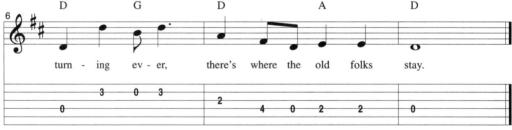
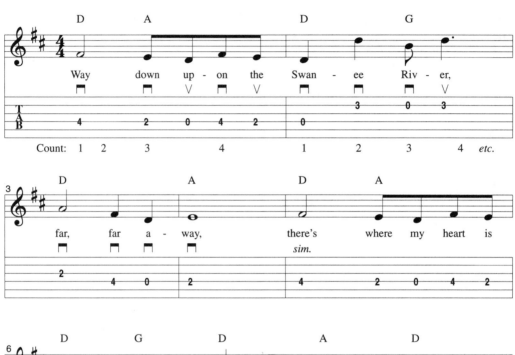

Chapter 6

Adding Some Spice: Basic 7th Chords

*I*n this chapter, we show you how to play what are known as open-position *7th chords*. Seventh chords are no more difficult to play than are the major or minor chords that we describe in Chapter 4, but their *sound* is more complex than that of major and minor chords (because they're made up of four different notes instead of three), and their usage in music is a little more specialized.

The situation's kind of like that of the knives in your kitchen. Any big, sharp knife can cut both a pizza and a pineapple, but if you spend a lot of time doing either, you figure out that you need to use the circular-bladed gizmo for the pizza and a cleaver for the pineapple. These utensils may not be as versatile or as popular as your general-purpose knives, but if you're making Hawaiian-style pizza, nothing beats 'em.

The more your culinary skills develop, the more you appreciate specialized cutlery. And the more your ear skills develop, the more you understand where to substitute 7th chords for the more ordinary major and minor chords. The different 7th chords can make the blues sound "bluesy" and jazz sound "jazzy."

Just as you have different types of three-note chords (major and minor, for example), you also have different types of 7th chords, and each type has a different sound, or quality. The following are the most important types of 7th chords that you encounter in playing the guitar:

♪ **Dominant 7th,** as in C7.

♪ **Minor 7th,** as in Am7.

♪ **Major 7th,** as in Dmaj7.

Dominant 7th Chords

Dominant seems a funny, technical name for a chord that's called a plain "seven" if you group it with a letter-name chord symbol. If you say just C7 or A7, for example, you're referring to a dominant 7th chord.

Actually, the term *dominant* refers to the 5th degree of a major scale — but don't worry about the theory. The important thing is that you call the chord "dominant 7th" merely to distinguish it from other types of 7th chords (minor 7ths and major 7ths). Note, too, that dominant has nothing whatsoever to do with leather and studded collars.

D7, G7, and C7

The D7, G7, and C7 chords are among the most common of the open dominant 7ths. Figure 6-1 shows you diagrams of these three chords that guitarists often use together to play songs.

If you already know how to play C (which we introduce in Chapter 4), you can form C7 by simply adding your pinky on the 3rd string (at the third fret).

Notice the *X*s above the 5th and 6th strings on the D7 chord. Don't play those strings as you strum. Similarly, for the C7 chord, don't play the 6th string as you strum.

Practice strumming D7, G7, and C7. You don't need written music for this exercise, so you're on the honor system to do it. Try strumming D7 four times, G7 four times, and then C7 four times. You want to accustom your left hand to the feel of the chords themselves and to switching among them.

If you want to play a song right now using these new chords, skip to the section "Playing Songs with 7th Chords," later in this chapter. You can play "Home on the Range" with the chords you know right now.

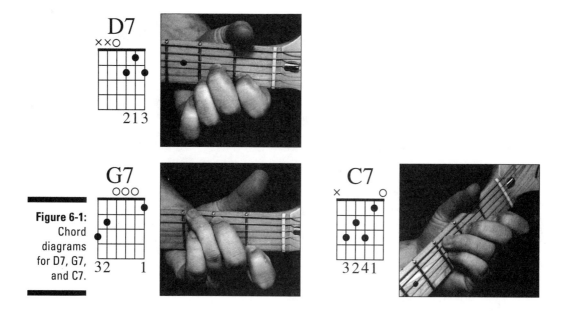

Figure 6-1:
Chord
diagrams
for D7, G7,
and C7.

E7 and A7

Two more 7th chords that you often use together to play songs are the E7 and A7 chords. Figure 6-2 shows how you play these two open 7th chords.

If you know how to play E (check out Chapter 4), you can form E7 by simply removing your 3rd finger from the 4th string. Remember to remove your watch before attempting this chord (just kidding!).

This version of the E7 chord, as the figure shows, uses only two fingers. You can also play an open position E7 chord with four fingers (as we describe in the following section). For now, however, play the two-finger version, because it's easier to fret quickly, especially if you're just starting out.

Practice E7 and A7 by strumming each chord four times, switching back and forth between them. Remember to avoid striking the 6th string on the A7 chord.

If you want to play a song that uses these two open 7th chords right now, skip to the section "Playing Songs with 7th Chords," later in this chapter, and play "All Through the Night."

Figure 6-2:
Chord
diagrams
for E7 and
A7.

E7 (four-finger version) and B7

Two more popular open-position 7th chords are the four-finger version of E7 and the B7 chord. Figure 6-3 shows you how to finger the four-finger E7 and the B7 chords. Most people think that this E7 has a better *voicing* (vertical arrangement of notes) than does the two-finger E7. You often use the B7 chord along with E7 to play certain songs. Remember to avoid striking the 6th string on the B7 chord.

If you already know how to play E (see Chapter 4), you can form this E7 by simply adding your pinky on the 2nd string (at the third fret).

Practice these chords by strumming each one four times, switching back and forth. As you do so, notice that your second finger plays the same note on the same fret in each chord — the one at the second fret of the 5th string. This note is a *common tone* (that is, it's common to both chords). In switching back and forth between the two chords, keep this finger down on the 5th string — doing so makes switching easier. Always hold down common tones whenever you're switching chords. They provide an anchor of stability for your left hand.

To use these chords in a song right now, skip to the section "Playing Songs with 7th Chords," later in this chapter, and play "Over the River and Through the Woods."

Figure 6-3:
Chord
diagrams
for E7 (the
four-finger
version)
and B7.

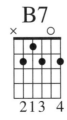

Minor 7th Chords — Dm7, Em7, and Am7

Minor 7th chords differ from dominant 7th chords in that their character is a little softer and jazzier. Minor 7th chords are the chords you hear in "Moondance," by Van Morrison, and the verses of "Light My Fire," by the Doors.

Figure 6-4 shows diagrams for the three open-position minor 7th (m7) chords. (See Chapter 8 for more minor 7th chords.)

Notice that the Dm7 uses a two-string *barre* — that is, you press down two strings with a single finger (the first finger, in this case) at the first fret. Angling your finger slightly or rotating it on its side may help you fret those notes firmly and eliminate any buzzes as you play the chord. The 6th and 5th strings have *X*s above them. Don't strike those strings while strumming.

 You finger the Am7 chord much like you do the C chord that we show you in Chapter 4; just lift your third finger off a C chord — and you have Am7. In switching between C and Am7 chords, remember to hold down the two common tones with your first and second fingers. This way, you can switch between the chords much more quickly. And if you know how to play an F chord (see Chapter 4), you can form Dm7 simply by removing your third finger.

Figure 6-4: Chord diagrams for Dm7, Em7, and Am7.

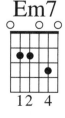

Major 7th Chords — Cmaj7, Fmaj7, Amaj7, and Dmaj7

Major 7th chords differ from dominant 7th chords and minor 7th chords in that their character is bright and jazzy. You can hear this kind of chord at the beginning of "Ventura Highway," by America, and "Don't Let the Sun Catch You Crying," by Gerry and the Pacemakers.

Figure 6-5 shows four open-position major 7th (maj7) chords. (For more major 7th chords, check out Chapter 8.)

Notice that the Dmaj7 uses a three-string barre with the first finger. Rotating the first finger slightly on its side helps make the chord easier to play. Don't play the 6th or 5th strings as you strike the Dmaj7 or Fmaj7 (see the *X*s in the diagrams in Figure 6-5). And don't play the 6th string on the Amaj7 or Cmaj7.

In moving between Cmaj7 and Fmaj7, notice that the second and third fingers move as a fixed shape across the strings in switching between these chords. The first finger doesn't fret any string in a Cmaj7 chord, but keep it curled and poised above the first fret of the 2nd string so that you can bring it down quickly for the switch to Fmaj7.

Cmaj7

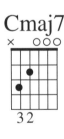

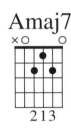

Amaj7

Figure 6-5:
Chord diagrams for Cmaj7, Fmaj7, Amaj7, and Dmaj7 chords.

Fmaj7

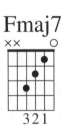

Dmaj7

Practice moving back and forth (strumming four times each) between Cmaj7 and Fmaj7 and between Amaj7 and Dmaj7.

Playing Songs with 7th Chords

Listen to the CD to hear the rhythm of the strums of these songs as you follow the *slash* notation in the guitar part. If you have difficulty remembering how to finger the chords, rip out the cheat sheet in the front of the book and consult the back side of it for some crib notes. Don't try to play the vocal line. It's there only as a reference.

About the songs

Here is some useful information about the songs to help you along:

♪ **Home on the Range.** To play "Home on the Range," you need to know how to play C, C7, F, D7, and G7 chords (see Chapter 4 for the C and F chords and the section "Dominant 7th Chords," earlier in this chapter, for the others); how to play a "bass-strum-strum" pattern (see the following paragraph); and how to wail like a coyote.

In the music, you see the words *Bass strum strum* over the rhythm slashes. Instead of simply strumming the chord for three beats, play only the lowest note of the chord on the first beat and then strum the remaining notes of the chord on beats 2 and 3. The *sim.* means to keep on playing this pattern throughout.

♪ **All Through the Night.** To play "All Through the Night," you need to know how to play D, E7, A7, and G chords (see Chapter 4 for the D and G chords and the section earlier in this chapter on the E7 and A7 chords); how to read repeat signs (see Appendix A); and how to stay awake during this intensely somnolent ditty.

In the music, you see *repeat signs,* which tell you to play certain measures twice. See Appendix A for more information on repeat signs. Use the two-finger E7 for this song.

♪ **Over the River and Through the Woods.** To play "Over the River and Through the Woods," you need to know how to play A, D, E7, and B7 chords (see Chapter 4 for the A and D chords and the section on the four-finger version of E7 and B7, earlier in this chapter); how to strum in 6/8 time (see the following paragraph); and the way to Grandma's house (in case your horse stumbles and you need to shoot it).

The 6/8 time signature has a lilting feel to it — sort of as though the music has a gallop or limp. "When Johnny Comes Marching Home Again" is another familiar song that you play in 6/8 time. (See Appendix A for more information on time signatures.) Count only two beats per measure — not six times (unless you want to sound like a rabbit that's had three cups of coffee). Use the four-finger E7 for this song.

♪ **It's Raining, It's Pouring.** To play "It's Raining, It's Pouring," you need to know how to play Amaj7 and Dmaj7 chords (see the section, "Major 7th Chords," earlier in this chapter) and how to sing in a really whiny, annoying voice.

This song is a jazzed-up version of the old nursery rhyme "It's Raining, It's Pouring," also known as the childhood taunt "Billy Is a Sissy" (or whichever personal childhood nemesis you plug in to the title). The major 7th chords that you play in this song sound jazzy and give any song a modern sound. Use all downstrokes on the strums.

♪ **Oh, Susanna.** To play "Oh, Susanna," you need to know how to play Cmaj7, Dm7, Em7, Fmaj7, Am7, D7, Dm7, G7, and C chords (see Chapter 4 for C and various sections earlier in this chapter for the different 7th chords) and how to balance a banjo on your knee while traveling the Southern United States.

This arrangement of "Oh, Susanna" uses three types of 7th chords: dominant 7ths (D7 and G7), minor 7ths (Dm7, Em7, and Am7), and major 7ths (Cmaj7 and Fmaj7). Using minor 7ths and major 7ths gives the song a hip sound. Lest you think this attempt to "jazz up" a simple folk song comes from out of the blue, listen to James Taylor's beautiful rendition of "Oh, Susanna" on the 1970 album *Sweet Baby James* to hear a similar approach. He actually says "banjo" without sounding corny. Use all downstrokes on the strums.

Home on the Range

TRACK 12

All Through the Night

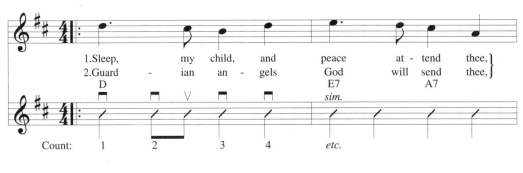

TRACK 13

Over the River and Through the Woods

It's Raining, It's Pouring

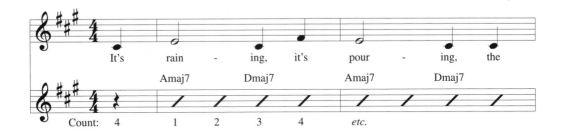

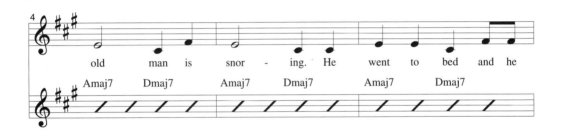

TRACK 15

Oh, Susanna

I—— come from Al - a - bam - a with a

Cmaj7   Dm7   Em7   Fmaj7

Count: 1   2   1   2

ban - jo   on   my   knee.   I'm—   goin'   to   Lou' - si -

Am7   D7   Dm7   G7   Cmaj7   Dm7

etc.

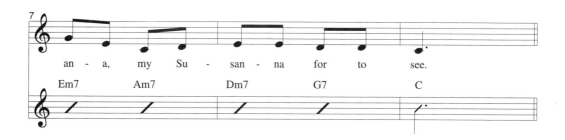

an - a,   my   Su - san - na   for   to   see.

Em7   Am7   Dm7   G7   C

Fun with 7th Chords: The 12-Bar Blues

Playing the guitar isn't all about folk songs and nursery rhymes, you know. Sometimes you can pick up something really cool. And what's cooler than the blues? By knowing a few dominant 7th chords and being able to strum four beats per measure, you already have the basics down pat for playing 99 percent of all blues songs ever written.

Ninety-nine percent?! That's right! The 12-bar blues follow a simple chord formula, or *progression,* that involves three dominant 7ths. In this progression, you don't need to know any new chords or techniques; you need to know only which three dominant 7th chords to play — and in which order.

Playing the 12-bar blues

Although you can play the 12-bar blues in any key, the key of E is probably the best "guitar key" for playing the blues. Figure 6-6 shows the chord progression to a 12-bar blues in E. Practice this pattern and become familiar with the way chords change in a blues progression.

TRACK 16

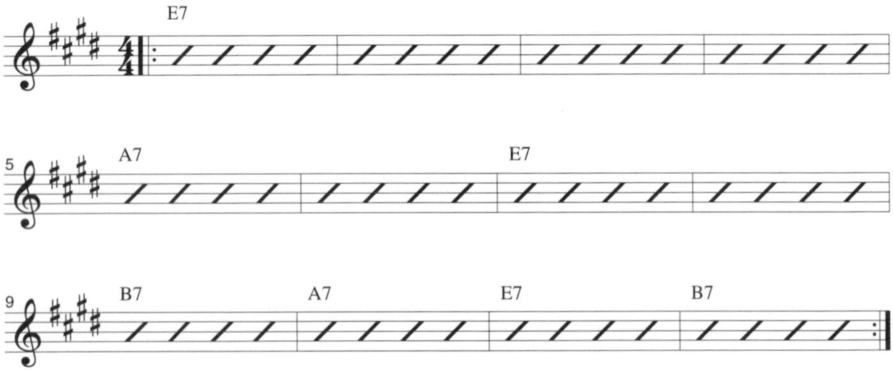

Figure 6-6:
A 12-bar blues progression in E.

All the songs that we list in the following paragraph are examples of 12-bar blues tunes. You can play any of these right now just by singing along and observing the 12-bar scheme in Figure 6-6. (For more information on 12-bar blues, see Chapters 10 and 11.)

Famous 12-bar blues songs include "Rock Around the Clock," "Blue Suede Shoes," "Roll Over Beethoven," "Long Tall Sally," "Kansas City," "The Twist," "The Peppermint Twist," and "Johnny B. Goode."

Writing your own blues song

Blues songs are simple to write lyrics for. (Just think of any Little Richard song.) Usually you repeat lines and then finish off with a zinger — for example:

My baby she done left me, and she stole my best friend Joe.
My baby she done left me, and she stole my best friend Joe.
Now I'm all alone and cryin', 'cause I miss him so.

Try composing some lyrics yourself, improvise a melody, and apply them to the blues progression that we outline here.

As a rule, a good blues song must include the following elements:

♪ A subject dealing with hardship or injustice.

♪ A locale or situation conducive to misery.

♪ Bad grammar.

Use the following table to find mix-and-match elements for your blues songs.

Song Element	Good Blues	Bad Blues
Subject	Treachery, infidelity, your mojo	Rising interest rates, an impending market correction, the scarcity of good help
Locale	Memphis, the Bayou, prison	Aspen, Rodeo Drive, Starbucks
Grammar	"My baby done me wrong."	"My life-partner has been insensitive to my needs."

Why not compose one yourself? Call it the "Left-Hand Callus Blues" and talk about how them bad ol' strings put a big hurtin' on your fingertips. Then see Chapter 11 for more info on the blues.

Part III
Beyond the Basics: Starting to Sound Cool

The 5th Wave   By Rich Tennant

"Frankly, I think anyone who can buy a blues guitar with a gold card doesn't deserve one."

In this part . . .

After you've got a pretty good handle on the basics of guitar playing and your fingers stop screaming in pain after a good practice session, you'll want to move into some more advanced territory. This is the place to look for it! Chapter 7 introduces you to position playing, in which you no longer pick or strum open strings; instead, they're all fretted. Chapter 8 tells you about barre chords, which are really useful because after mastering a finger position, you can move that position up and down the guitar neck to create new chords. Chapter 9 tells you about special licks that you can use to really strut your stuff!

Chapter 7

Up the Neck: Playing Melodies in Position and in Double-Stops

In This Chapter

▶ Playing single notes in position

▶ Playing double-stops as string pairs

▶ Playing double-stops across the neck

▶ Playing songs in position and in double-stops

---

*I*f you were in the United States during the '80s, you may remember Billy Crystal doing the Fernando skits on *Saturday Night Live:* "Darling, it is better to look good than to feel good, *and you look mahvelous.*" Many people pick up the guitar because they figure that playing is going to make them look marvelous (well, okay, way-cool). In playing the guitar, looking good may not actually be *better* than sounding good, but it's at least *as good.*

This chapter gives you equal parts of looking good and sounding good. In Chapters 4 and 5, you find out how to play perfectly acceptable songs on the guitar using only open-position chords and open-position melodies. But playing songs in this manner doesn't make you look *mahvelous.* (Your image in playing songs in this manner is closer to that of Gene Autrey than Eddie Van Halen.) In this chapter, you venture out of open-position base camp into the higher altitudes of position playing, waay up on the neck. You also pick up the technique of playing in double-stops along the way — another trick to help you sound *absolutely mahvelous.*

Playing in Position

As you listen to complicated-sounding guitar music played by virtuoso guitarists, you may imagine their left hands leaping around the fretboard with abandon. But usually, if you watch those guitarists on stage or TV, you're shocked to discover that their left hands hardly move at all.

Those guitarists are *playing in position*. Playing in position means that your left hand remains in a fixed location on the neck, with each finger more or less on permanent assignment to a specific fret, and that you fret every note — you don't use any open strings. If you're playing in *fifth position,* for example, your first finger plays the fifth fret, your second finger plays the sixth fret, your third finger plays the seventh fret, and your fourth finger plays the eighth fret. A position, therefore, gets its name from the fret that your first finger plays.

In addition to enabling you to play notes where they feel and sound best on the fingerboard — not just where you can most easily grab available notes (such as the open-string notes in open position), playing in position makes you look cool — like a nonbeginner! Think of it this way: A layup and a slam dunk are both worth two points in basketball, but only in the latter case does the announcer scream, "And the crowd goes wild!"

Playing in position versus playing with open strings

Why play in position? Why not use open position and open strings all the time? We can give you several key reasons, as the following list describes:

> ♪ You can't play music with high notes (higher than, say, those you can play on the fifth fret) in open position.

> ♪ In position playing, your left hand stays in a fixed place on the neck. If you try mixing low and high notes by playing the low ones in open position and higher ones in upper positions, your left hand is more prone to miss the higher notes because you need to move your hand to reach those notes. In position playing, your left hand doesn't jump; it stays in a fixed position. Hence, you face less risk of blowing any notes (unless you're playing harmonica at the same time).

> ♪ What you play by using position playing is *movable*. Any pattern or phrase that you know in position you can instantly transpose to another key simply by moving your hand to another position. If you know one major scale, you can play all 12 major scales just by moving your starting note to different frets and playing the same pattern. Or if you pick up a blues lick, a jazz line, or a rock riff, you can move that pattern to different starting frets, instantly and effortlessly transposing it to different keys.

People have the idea that playing guitar in lower positions is easier than playing in higher ones. The higher notes actually aren't harder to play; they're just harder to read in standard notation if you never get too far in a conventional method book (where reading high notes is usually saved till last). But here, you're not focusing on music reading but on guitar playing — so go for the high notes whenever you want.

Playing exercises in position

A good place to start practicing the skills you need to play in position is the major scale. Figure 7-1 shows a C major scale in second position. Although you can play this scale in open position, play it as the tab staff in the figure indicates, as you want to start practicing your position playing.

Figure 7-1:
A one-octave C-major scale in second position.

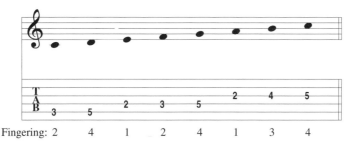

Fingering: 2   4   1   2   4   1   3   4

The most important thing about playing in position is the location of your left hand — in particular, the position and placement of the fingers of your left hand. The following list contains tips for positioning your left hand and fingers:

♪ Keep your fingers over the appropriate frets the entire time you're playing. Because you're in second position for this scale, keep your first finger over the second fret, your second finger over the third fret, your third finger over the fourth fret, and your fourth finger over the fifth fret at all times — *even if they're not fretting* any notes at the moment.

♪ Keep all your fingers close to the fretboard, ready to play. At first, your fingers may exhibit a tendency to straighten out and rise away from the fretboard. This tendency is natural, so work to keep them curled and to hold them down over the frets where they belong for the position.

♪ Relax! Although you may think that you need to intensely focus all your energy on performing this maneuver correctly or positioning that finger just so, that's not really the case. What you're actually working toward is simply adopting the most natural and relaxed approach to playing the guitar. (You may not think it all that natural right now, but eventually, you catch the drift. Honest!) So take things easy but remain aware of your movements. Is your left shoulder, for example, riding up like Quasimodo's? Check it periodically to make sure that it stays tension-free. And remember to take frequent deep breaths, especially if you feel yourself tightening up.

Notice that, in Figure 7-1, the score indicates left-hand fingerings under the tab numbers. These indicators aren't essential because the position itself dictates these fingerings. But if you want, you can read the finger numbers (instead of the tab numbers) and play the C scale that way (keeping an eye on the tab staff to check which string you're on). Then, if you memorize the fingerings, you have a *movable pattern* that enables you to play a major scale in any key.

Play the *one-octave scale* (one having a range of only eight notes) shown in Figure 7-1 by using both up- and downstrokes — that is, by using alternate (up and down) picking. (See Chapter 5 for more information on alternate picking.) This scale is not on the CD; you already know how it sounds — it's the familiar *do-re-mi-fa-so-la-ti-do*.

Figure 7-2 shows a two-octave C-major scale (one with a range of 15 notes) in the seventh position. Notice that this scale requires you to play on all six strings. Seventh position is the only position on the guitar that enables you to play a two-octave C scale.

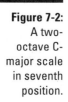

Figure 7-2:
A two-
octave C-
major scale
in seventh
position.

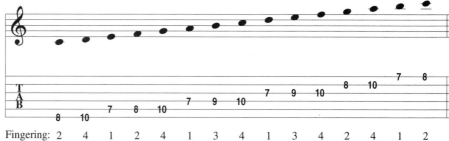

Fingering: 2   4   1   2   4   1   3   4   1   3   4   2   4   1   2

Remember to hold your fingers over the appropriate frets all the time, even if they're not playing at the moment, and to keep your fingers close to the fretboard. Here's a twist on an old expression to help you remember: Keep your friends close, your enemies closer, and your frets even closer than that.

Practice playing the scale shown in Figure 7-2 up and down the neck, using alternate picking (see Chapter 5). If you memorize the fingering pattern (shown under the tab numbers), you can play all 12 major scales simply by moving your pattern around. Try it. And then challenge the nearest piano player to a *transposing* (key-changing) contest using the major scale.

Shifting positions

Music isn't so simple that you can play it all in one position, and life would be pretty static if you could. In real-world situations, you must often play an uninterrupted passage that takes you through different positions. To do so successfully, you need to master the *position shift* with the aplumb of an old politician.

Andrés Segovia, legend of the classical guitar, devised fingerings for all 12 major and minor scales. (See Chapter 18 for more information on Segovia.) Figure 7-3 shows how Segovia played the two-octave C-major scale. It differs from the two scales in the preceding section in that it requires a position shift in the middle of the scale.

Play the first seven notes in second position and then shift up to fifth position by smoothly gliding your first finger up to the fifth fret (third string). As you play the scale downward, play the first eight notes in fifth position, and then shift to second postion by smoothly gliding your third finger down to the fourth fret (third string). The important thing is that the position shift sound seamless.

Someone listening shouldn't be able to tell that you shift positions. The trick is in the smooth gliding of the first (while ascending) or third (while descending) finger.

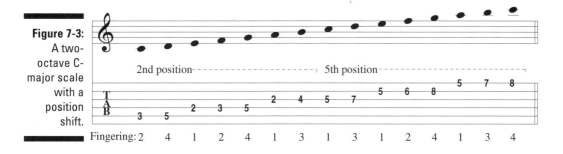

Figure 7-3: A two-octave C-major scale with a position shift.

You must practice this smooth glide to make it sound uninterrupted and seamless. Isolate just the two notes involved (3rd string, fourth fret, and 3rd string, fifth fret) and play them over and over as shown in the scale until you can make them sound as if you're making no position shift at all.

Building strength and dexterity by playing in position

Some people do all sorts of exercises to develop their position playing. They buy books that contain nothing but position playing exercises. Some of these books aim to develop sight-reading skills, and others aim to develop left-hand finger strength and dexterity. But you don't really need such books. You can make up your own exercises to build finger strength and dexterity. (And sight-reading doesn't concern you now anyway, because you're reading tab numbers.)

To create your own exercises, just take the two-octave major scale shown back in Figure 7-2 and number the 15 notes of the scale as 1 through 15. Then make up a few simple mathematical permutations that you can practice playing. Following are some examples:

- ♪ 1-2-3-1, 2-3-4-2, 3-4-5-3, 4-5-6-4, and so on. (See Figure 7-4a.)
- ♪ 1-3-2-4, 3-5-4-6, 5-7-6-8, 7-9-8-10, and so on. (See Figure 7-4b.)
- ♪ 15-14-13, 14-13-12, 13-12-11, 12-11-10, and so on. (See Figure 7-4c.)

Figure 7-4 four shows how these numbers look in music and tab. Remember these notes are just suggested patterns to memorize and help build dexterity.

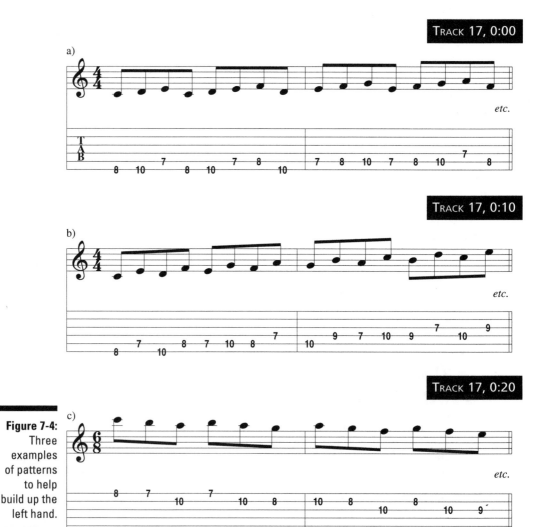

Figure 7-4: Three examples of patterns to help build up the left hand.

You get the idea. You can make up literally hundreds of permutations and practice them endlessly or until you get bored. Piano students have a book called *Hanon* that contains lots of scale permutations to help develop strength and independence of the fingers. You can check out that book for permutation ideas, but making up your own is probably just as easy.

If you know how to read music and if you're really interested in developing your position-playing sight-reading and technique, check out books of clarinet studies. The clarinet happens to have the same written range of notes as the guitar (about $3^1/_2$ octaves, starting from E below middle C). Because the clarinet does nothing but play single notes, books of clarinet studies contain lots of good examples in all keys. These examples translate to all *positions* on the guitar. Pick an example, find the best position for it according to the key of the example and the chart in the accompanying "Key positions" sidebar, which lists the best positions for each key, and play away.

Key positions

On the guitar, playing in certain keys happens to work well by also playing in certain positions. The best position for a key, therefore, is the one that enables you to play all the notes of that key within the four frets of that position.

The major scale of any key is simply all the notes of that key, in order, beginning from the root, or note 1. Each major scale has two really good positions on the guitar, as the following paragraphs describe:

✔ The first good position is the one in which your second finger starts the scale on the 6th string. In the key of C, for example, because C lies at the eighth fret of the 6th string, you'd play the scale in seventh position — so that your *second* finger plays at the *eighth* fret (C). This position is probably the best for playing in the key of C, because you can play a two-octave major scale in this position.

✔ The second good position for playing a major scale is the one in which your fourth finger starts the scale on the 5th string. In the key of C, for example, you'd play in 12th position — so that your fourth finger plays at the 15th fret (C). This position enables you to play all the notes in the key, but not as a two-octave scale — not that anything's wrong with that.

You don't always need to play in one of these "best" positions. Choose the position that enables you to play the melody with the most ease. Sometimes you may need to experiment to find that position. But starting your experimentation with one of these two "best" positions is usually a pretty good idea.

The following table provides you with a chart showing each of the 12 keys and which positions work best for each key. (The chart first shows the position in which your second finger starts the scale on the 6th string and then the one in which your fourth finger starts the scale on the 5th string.)

(continued)

(continued)

Key	First good position (two-octave scale)	Second good position (one-octave scale)
C	7th	12th
C♯/D♭	8th	1st
D	9th	2nd
D♯/E♭	10th	3rd
E	11th	4th
F	12th	5th
F♯/G♭	1st	6th
G	2nd	7th
G♯/A♭	3rd	8th
A	4th	9th
A♯/B♭	5th	10th
B	6th	11th

Double-Stops

The term *double-stop* doesn't refer to going back to the store because you forgot milk. *Double-stop* is guitar lingo for playing two notes at once — something the guitar can do with relative ease but that's impossible on woodwinds and only marginally successful on bowed string instruments. (Actually guitarists lifted the term from violin playing but quickly made double-stops truly their own.) By the way, you do nothing special in fretting the notes of a double-stop. Fret them the same way that you do chords or single notes.

You experience the guitar's capability to play more than one note simultaneously as you strum a chord, but you can also play more than one note in a melodic context. Playing double-stops is a great way to play in harmony with yourself. So adept is the guitar at playing double-stops, in fact, that some musical forms — such as '50s rock 'n' roll, country, and Mariachi music (you know, the music that Mexican street bands play) — use double-stops as a hallmark of their styles.

Understanding double-stops

A double-stop is nothing more that two notes that you play at the same time. It falls somewhere between a single note (one note) and a chord (three or more notes). You can play a double-stop on adjacent strings or on nonadjacent strings (by skipping strings). The examples and songs that you find in this chapter, however, involve only adjacent-string double-stops, because they're the easiest to play.

If you play a melody in double-stops, it sounds sweeter and richer, fuller and prettier than if you play it by using only single notes. And if you play a *riff* in double-stops, it sounds gutsier and fuller — the double-stops just create a bigger sound. Check out some Chuck Berry riffs — "Johnny B. Goode," for example — and you can hear that he uses double-stops all the time.

Playing exercises in double-stops

You can play double-stop passages on *one* pair of strings (the first two strings, for example) — moving the double-stops up and down the neck — or in one area of the neck by using *different* string pairs and moving the double-stops across the neck (first playing the 5th and 4th strings, for example, and then the 4th and 3rd, and so on).

Playing double-stops up and down the neck

Start with a C-major scale that you play in double-stop *thirds* (notes that are two letter names apart, such as C-E, D-F, and so on), exclusively on the first two strings, moving up the neck. This type of double-stop pattern appears in Figure 7-5. The left-hand fingering doesn't appear below the tab numbers in this score, but that's not difficult to figure out. Start with your first finger for the first double-stop. (You need only one finger to fret this double-stop because the 1st string remains open.) Then, for all the other double-stops in the scale, use fingers 1 and 3 if the notes are two frets apart (the second and third double-stops, for example) and use fingers 1 and 2 if the notes are one fret apart (the fourth and fifth double-stops, for example).

Playing double-stops across the neck

Playing double-stops *across* the neck is probably more common than playing up and down the neck on a string pair. Figure 7-6 shows a C-major scale that you play in thirds in open position, moving across the neck.

What's especially common in rock and blues songs is playing double-stops across the neck where the two notes that make up the double-stop are on the same fret (which you play as a two-string barre). Check out Chapters 10 and 11 for more information on rock and blues.

Figure 7-5:
A C-major
scale that
you play in
double-
stops,
moving up
the neck on
one pair of
strings.

TRACK 18, 0:00

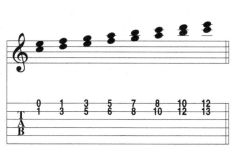

Again, the example in Figure 7-6 doesn't show the fingerings for each double-stop. But you can use fingers 1 and 2 if the notes are one fret apart and fingers 1 and 3 if the notes are two frets apart.

Figure 7-6:
A C-major
scale that
you play in
double-
stops,
moving
across the
neck in
open
position.

TRACK 18, 0:11

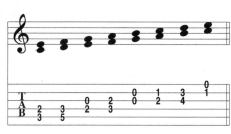

TIP

To hear double-stops in action, listen to the opening of Jimmy Buffett's "Margaritaville," Leo Kottke's version of the Allman Brothers' "Little Martha," Van Morrison's "Brown-Eyed Girl," Chuck Berry's "Johnny B. Goode," and the intros to Simon and Garfunkel's "Homeward Bound" and "Bookends."

Playing Songs in Position and in Double-Stops

Scales, which are based on keys, fall well into certain positions on the guitar, as earlier sections of this chapter describe. Similarly, songs, which are also based on keys, benefit from position playing, too. You can see the importance of position playing in crystal clarity in the various chapters in Part IV of this book. Rock, jazz, blues, and country lead playing all virtually scream for certain positions to render an authentic sound.

Telling you that the melody of a song sounds best if you play it in one position rather than another may seem a bit arbitrary to you. But trust us on this one — playing a Chuck Berry lick in A is almost impossible in anything *but* fifth position. Country licks that you play in A, on the other hand, fall most comfortably in second position, and trying to play them anywhere else is just making things hard on yourself.

That's one of the great things about the guitar: The best position for a certain style not only sounds best to your ears, but also feels best to your hands. And that's what makes playing the guitar so much fun.

About the songs

Play these song by reading the tab numbers and listening to the CD; notice how cool playing up the neck feels instead of playing way down in open position, where those beginners play.

Whenever you're playing in position, remember to keep your left hand in a fixed position, perpendicular to the neck, with your first finger at a given fret and the other fingers following in order, one per fret. Hold the fingers over the appropriate frets, very close to the fretboard, even if they're not fretting notes at the moment.

Here is some useful information to help you play the songs:

♪ **Simple Gifts.** To play this song, you need to know how to play in fourth position (see the section "Playing in Position," earlier in this chapter) and what *'tis* and *'twill* mean.

This song is in the key of A, making fourth position ideal, because you find all the notes between the fourth and seventh frets. Because you play no open strings in this song, memorize the fingering and then try playing the same melody in other positions and keys. The fingering is the same in every position, even though the tab numbers change. Go on — try it.

♪ **Turkey in the Straw.** To play this song, you need to know how to play in seventh position (see the section "Playing in Position," earlier in this chapter) and what saying "day-day" to a wagon tongue means.

Remember that each key has two good positions in which to play (to cover all the notes of the key within four frets). "Simple Gifts" uses the scale position where the *second* finger plays the root on the *6th* string. "Turkey in the Straw," on the other hand, uses the scale position where the *fourth* finger plays the root on the *5th* string. (See the sidebar "Key positions," earlier in this chapter.)

♪ **Aura Lee.** To play this song, you need to know how to play double-stops up and down the neck on the 1st and 2nd strings (see the section "Playing double-stops up and down the neck," earlier in this chapter) and how to gyrate your pelvis while raising one side of your upper lip.

You play this arrangement of "Aura Lee" — a song made famous by Elvis Presley as "Love Me Tender" — exclusively on the first two strings, moving up and down the neck. In the double-stop scales that you practice in Figures 7-5 and 7-6, the two notes of the double-stop move up or down together. In "Aura Lee" the two notes of the double-stop sometimes move in the same direction and sometimes in opposite directions. Other times, one of the notes moves up or down while the other remains stationary. Mixing directions makes an arrangement more interesting. Play and listen to "Aura Lee" and you see what we mean.

Notice that the left-hand fingerings appear under the tab numbers. If the same finger plays successive notes, but at different frets, a slanted line indicates the position shift (as in measures 5, 7, and 9). For your right-hand picking, use all downstrokes. Remember to repeat the first four bars (as the repeat signs around them indicate) before continuing to bar 5. (Check out Appendix A for more information on repeat signs.) And make the song tender, just as Elvis did. Uh-thank yew verrah much.

♪ **The Streets of Laredo.** To play this song, you need to know how to play double-stops across the neck (see the section "Playing double-stops across the neck," earlier in this chapter) and how to sound light-hearted while playing a song about a conversation with a corpse.

In this arrangement, you play double-stops across the strings, near the bottom of the neck. The double-stops give the song a sweet, pretty sound — just the thing for a tête-à-tête between a passerby and a mummified cowboy. The tab doesn't indicate fingering, but you can use fingers 1 and 2 for double-stops that are one fret apart and 1 and 3 for double-stops that are two frets apart. For right-hand picking, use all downstrokes.

TRACK 19

Simple Gifts

TRACK 20

Turkey in the Straw

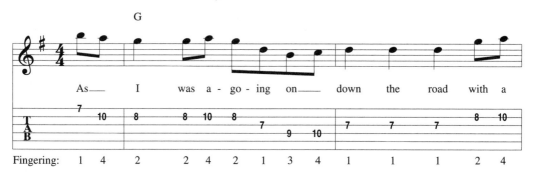

As— I was a-go-ing on— down the road with a

Fingering: 1 4 2 2 4 2 1 3 4 1 1 1 2 4

ti - red team— and a heav-y load, I— cracked my— whip— and the

1 1 1 4 2 4 1 4 4 1 4 2 2 4 2 1 3 4

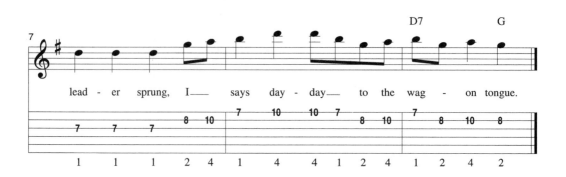

lead - er sprung, I— says day - day— to the wag - on tongue.

1 1 1 2 4 1 4 4 1 2 4 1 2 4 2

Aura Lee

TRACK 22

The Streets of Laredo

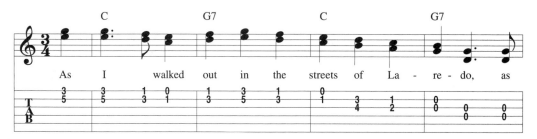

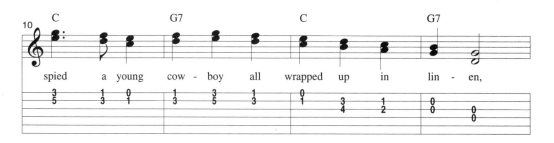

Chapter 8

Stretching Out: Barre Chords

. . . .

In This Chapter

▶ Playing barre chords based on E

▶ Playing barre chords based on A

▶ Playing power chords

▶ Playing songs with barre chords and power chords

. . . .

*I*n this chapter, we show you how to play chords that you can move all around the neck — unlike those open-position ones that we show you in Chapters 4 and 6. In most of these movable chords, you play what's called a *barre* (pronounced "bar"), a term coined from the Spanish word for *bar*.

As you play a barre, one of your left-hand fingers (usually the index) presses down all or most of the strings at a certain fret, enabling the remaining fingers to play a chord form immediately above (toward the body of the guitar) the barre finger. Think of your barre finger as a sort of movable nut or capo and your remaining fingers as playing certain open-position chord forms directly above it. (See Chapter 12 if you're not sure how a capo works.)

A movable barre chord contains no open strings — only fretted notes. You can slide these fretted notes up or down the neck to different positions to produce other chords of the same quality.

Playing Major Barre Chords Based on E

One of the most useful movable barre chords is the one based on the open E chord. (See Chapter 4 if you're not sure how to finger an open E chord.) The best way to get a grip on this barre chord is to start out with an open-position E chord. Follow these steps (as shown in Figure 8-1):

1. **Play an open E chord, but instead of using the normal 2-3-1 left-hand fingering, use fingers 3-4-2.**

   This fingering leaves your first (index) finger free, hovering above the strings.

2. **Lay your first finger down across all six strings *on the other side of the nut* (the side toward the tuning pegs).**

   Placing your index finger across the strings at this location doesn't affect the sound of the chord because the strings don't vibrate on that side of the nut. Extending your first finger across the width of the strings, however, helps you get the "feel" of a barre chord position. But don't press too hard with any of your fingers, because you're going to move the chord.

3. **Take the entire left-hand shape from Step 2 and slide it up (toward the body of the guitar) one fret so that your first finger is barring the first fret and your E-chord fingers have all advanced up a fret as well.**

   You're now in an F-chord position (because F is one fret higher than E), and you can press down across all the strings with your index finger.

4. **Try playing the notes of the chord one string at a time (from the 6th string to the 1st) to see whether all the notes ring out clearly.**

   The first few times you try this chord, the chances are pretty good that some of the notes aren't going to ring clearly and that your left-hand fingers are going to start to hurt.

Figure 8-1:
The insidious F barre chord.

Having difficulty at first in creating a barre F is normal (discouraging maybe, but normal). So before you give up on the guitar and take up the sousa-phone, here are some tips to help you nail this vexing chord:

♪ Make sure that you line up your left-hand thumb on the back of the guitar neck under the spot between your first and second fingers. This position gives you maximum leverage while exerting pressure.

♪ Instead of holding your first finger totally flat, rotate it a little onto its side.

♪ Move the elbow of your left arm in close to your body, even to the point that it's touching your body at the waist. As you play open-position chords, you find that you usually hold your elbow slightly away from your body. Not so with full barre chords.

♪ If you hear muffled strings, check to see that your left-hand fingers are touching only the appropriate strings and not preventing adjacent ones from ringing. Try exerting more pressure with the fingers. Calluses and experience help you get a clear sound from a barre chord.

You need to exert more pressure to fret at the bottom of the neck (at the first fret) than you do at, say, the fifth fret. Try moving your F chord up and down the neck to different frets on the guitar to prove to yourself that playing the chord gets easier as you move up the neck. Remember that the essence of this chord form is that it's *movable*. Unlike what your elementary school teachers may have told you, don't sit so still! Move around already!

Playing barre chords on an electric guitar is easier than playing them on an acoustic guitar. The *string gauges* (the thickness of the strings) are lighter on an electric guitar and the *action* (distance of the strings to the fretboard) is lower than on an acoustic. If you're using an acoustic and you're having trouble with barre chords, try playing them on an electric (but not one of those el-cheapo ones from the pawn shop) and take note of the difference. Doing so may inspire you to keep at it.

Finding the right fret

Because you can play an F chord as a barre chord, you can now, through the miracle of movable chords, play *every major chord* — all 12 of them — simply by moving up the neck. Knowing the name of each chord is simply a matter of knowing what note name you're playing on the 6th (low E) string — because all E-based barre chords get their name from the 6th string (just as the open E chord does).

Remember that each fret is a half step away from each adjacent fret. So if a first-fret barre chord is F, the second-fret barre chord is F♯; the third-fret chord is G; the fourth fret is G♯; and so on through to the 12th fret. Check out Appendix A for a listing of the names of the notes on the A string.

After you reach the 12th fret, the notes — and thus the barre chords that you play at those frets — repeat: The 13th-fret barre chord is the same as the first (F); the 14th is the same as the second (F♯); and so on. The frets work sort of like a clock: 13 equals 1, 14 equals 2, and so on.

Playing progressions using major barre chords based on E

A good way to build your comfort and confidence in playing barre chords is by practicing a *progression,* which is nothing more than a series of chords. Listen to the CD to hear what a four-measure progression using E-based major barre chords sounds like. Figure 8-2 shows the exercise. Below the staff, you see the correct first-finger fret for each chord.

Figure 8-2: A progression using E-based major barre chords.

TRACK 23, 0:00

Use only barre chords for this exercise (and for all the exercises in this chapter), even if you know how to play these chords as open-position chords. Play the C chord, for example, by barring at the eighth fret. Then play A at the fifth fret, G at the third fret, and F at the first fret. Use the F-chord fingering for all these chords.

Trying to make all six strings ring out clearly on each chord can get a little tiring. You can give your left-hand fingers a break by releasing pressure as you slide from one chord to the next. This action of "flexing and releasing" can help you develop a little finesse and keep you from tiring so easily. You don't need to keep a Vulcan Death Grip on the neck all the time — only while you're strumming the chord.

Although you can stop altogether if your hand starts to cramp, try to keep at it; as with any physical endeavor, you eventually build up your strength and stamina. Without question, barre chords are the triathlon of guitar playing, so strap on your best Ironman regalia and feel the burn.

To demonstrate the versatility of barre-chord progressions, here's an example that has a syncopated strum and sounds a little like the music of the Kinks. (The Kinks, in case you don't recall, were *the* English proto-punk band of the '60s, who gave us such classic hits as "You Really Got Me," "So Tired," and "Lola.") Figure 8-3 shows you how to play this progression by using major barre chords. Because the two chords move back and forth so quickly, the *release time* (the period during which you can relax your fingers) is very short. Check out the CD to hear how this exercise should sound before you get ready to sub for Ray Davies on a world tour.

Track 23, 0:13

Figure 8-3:
A syncopated progression using E-based major barre chords.

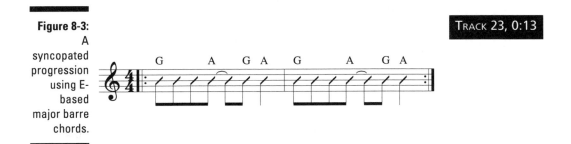

Playing Minor, Dominant 7th, and Minor 7th Barre Chords Based on E

After you're familiar with the basic feel and movement of the major barre chords, you want to start adding other chord qualities into your *repertoire* (which is a fancy French word for "bag of tricks" that musicians frequently use in discussing their music).

The good news is that everything you know about moving chords around the neck — getting a clear, ringing tone out of the individual notes in the chord (you are practicing, aren't you?) and the flex-and-release action that you use in playing major barre chords — carries over to the other forms of barre chords. Playing a minor, a 7th, or a minor 7th barre form is no more physically difficult than playing a major barre, so as you practice all the various barre chords, you should start to notice things getting a little easier.

Minor chords

Forming an E-based *minor* barre chord is similar to forming a major barre chord, as we explain in the steps in the section "Playing Major Barre Chords Based on E," earlier in this chapter. You can follow that set of steps, starting with an open Em chord but fingering it with fingers 3-4 (instead of how you usually finger the chord, as we describe in Chapter 4). Next, lay your first finger across all the strings on the other side of the nut and then slide the shape up one fret, producing an Fm chord.

You can use this "sliding up from an open-position chord" technique to form all the barre chords in this chapter. But you don't need to go through all that. The following simple steps, for example, describe another way to approach the Fm barre chord:

F

Fm

1. **Play an F major barre chord.**

   See the section "Playing Major Barre Chords Based on E," earlier in this chapter.

2. **Remove your second finger from the 3rd string.**

   The first-finger barre, which is already pressing down all the strings, now frets the new note on the 3rd string.

That's all you need to do. You instantly change a major barre chord to a minor barre chord by removing just one finger. Now, by using the low-E string chart in Appendix A again as the reference, you can play any of the 12 minor chords by moving the Fm chord to the appropriate fret. To play an Am barre chord, for example, you just move the barre to the fifth fret.

If you're not sure whether you're playing a barre chord on the correct fret, try alternating the chord with its open-position form, playing first the barre and then the open form. Play the two versions in rapid succession several times. You can then hear whether the two chords are the same or different.

Try playing the simple progression shown in Figure 8-4, which uses both major and minor barre chords.

Figure 8-4:
A
progression
using both
major and
minor barre
chords.

TRACK 23, 0:27

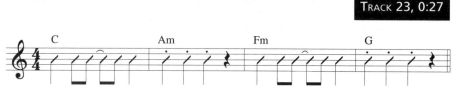

The dots above the slashes in bars 2 and 4 of Figure 8-4 are called *staccato* marks. They tell you to cut the notes short. (Instead of playing *daahh-daahh-daahh*, play *di-di-di*.) The best way to cut these notes short is to slightly release your left-hand finger pressure right after you strum the chord.

Now try playing the progression shown in Figure 8-4 two frets higher than the figure indicates. This two-fret variation gives you a D-Bm-Gm-A progression. You've just *transposed* (changed the key of) the progression quickly and easily — through the magic of movable chords!

Dominant 7th chords

Dominant 7th chords have a sharper, more complex sound than do straight major chords. (See Chapter 6 for more information on dominant 7ths.) Switching to a barre dominant 7th chord from a major barre chord, however, is just as easy as switching from a major to a minor barre chord — you just lift a single (although different) finger.

To change an F major barre chord into an F7 barre chord, follow these steps:

1. **Finger an F major barre chord, as we describe in the section "Playing Major Barre Chords Based on E," earlier in this chapter.**

2. **Remove your fourth finger from the 4th string.**

   The first-finger barre now frets the chord's new note.

Try playing the simple progression shown in Figure 8-5 using major and dominant 7th barre chords.

TRACK 23, 0:41

Figure 8-5:
A progression using major and 7th barre chords.

Playing the progression in Figure 8-5 in different keys is as simple as starting in a different location from the third fret and moving the same distance. From wherever you start, simply move up two frets for the second chord, up three more frets for the third chord, and then up two more frets for the fourth and last chord.

Say the names of the chords you play out loud to help you associate their names with their locations. Although movable chords make transposing on the guitar a snap, memorizing just the pattern of the hand movement instead of the actual chord names you're playing is far too easy. So say the names of the chords as you play them. After enough times through, you instinctively come to know that you play a B7 chord at the seventh fret.

Minor 7th chords

Minor 7th chords have a softer, jazzier, and more complex sound than straight minor chords do. (Check out Chapter 6 for more information on minor 7th chords.) You can form a minor 7th E-based barre chord by simply combining the actions you take to change major to minor and major to dominant 7th.

To change an F major barre chord into an Fm7 barre chord, follow these steps:

1. **Play an F major barre chord, as we describe in the section "Playing Major Barre Chords Based on E," earlier in this chapter.**

2. **Remove your second finger from the 3rd string and your fourth finger from the 4th string.**

   The first-finger barre, which is already pressing down all the strings, frets the new notes on the 3rd and 4th strings.

To help you get accustomed to minor 7th barre chords, we put together the exercise shown in Figure 8-6. Listen to the CD to hear what it sounds like.

Figure 8-6: A progression using major and minor 7th barre chords.

TRACK 23, 0:54

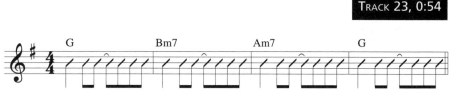

You can play this progression, as you can the other progressions in this section, in different keys simply by starting from chords other than G and moving the same relative number of frets to make the next chord. After the first chord, simply move up four frets for the second chord and then down two for the third chord; then move down another two for the last chord.

Say the names of the chords as you play them. Say them out loud. We're not kidding. You want to get so sick of hearing your own voice say the names of these chords at their correct locations that you can *never* forget that you play Am7 — the third chord of this progression — at the fifth fret.

What's that we hear? It must be the pitter-patter of little reindeer feet. In the next exercise, as shown in Figure 8-7, you can practice lots of E-based barre chords all over the neck by playing the chord progression to the song "We Wish You a Merry Christmas." To help you out in this exercise, we indicate the fret number your first finger barres for each chord.

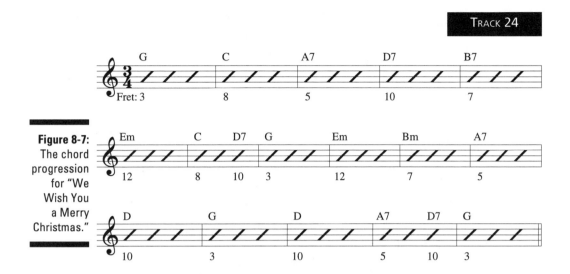

TRACK 24

Figure 8-7: The chord progression for "We Wish You a Merry Christmas."

If you're playing a nylon-string acoustic guitar, you can't play the Em chord at the 12th fret — the body of the guitar gets in the way. (Even on a steel-string acoustic, this chord is almost unplayable.) Substitute an open-position Em chord, but play it with fingers 3 and 4 to keep your hand in the barre formation.

In the section "Playing Songs with Barre Chords and Power Chords," later in this chapter, you find another version of this song, with melody and lyrics — but don't jump there until after you master your *A-based* barre chords!

Playing Major Barre Chords Based on A

In the preceding sections, we introduce barre chords based on the E chord, but now we shift gears and introduce another major group of barre chords, the *A-based* barre chords. The A-based major barre chord looks like an open A chord (but with different fingering, which we give you in the following section) and takes its letter name from the fret on the *5th* string at which you place your first-finger barre.

The theory seems simple enough, but you may find this chord a little more difficult to play than you do the E-based major barre chord. Don't worry, however, as we have a substitute waiting for you that involves only two fingers. But for now, humor us and create the A-based barre chord according to the directions in the following section.

Fingering the A-based major barre chord

To finger an A-based major barre chord, follow these steps:

1. **Finger an open A chord but, instead of using the normal fingering of 1-2-3, use 2-3-4.**

   This fingering leaves your first (index) finger free and ready to act as the barre finger. (If you're not sure how to finger an open A chord, see Chapter 4.)

2. **Lay your first finger down across all six strings, *just above the nut* (the side toward the tuning pegs).**

   Because you strum only the top five strings for A-based barre chords, you *could* lay your finger down across just five strings. But most guitarists cover all six strings with the barre because it feels more comfortable and it prevents the open 6th string from accidentally sounding.

   Placing your index finger across the strings at this point doesn't affect the sound of the chord because the strings don't vibrate on this side of the nut. Right now, you're just getting the feel of the chord position. Don't press too hard with any of your fingers because you're going to move the chord.

3. **Take the entire left-hand shape from Step 2 and slide it up one fret so that your first finger barres the first fret, producing a B♭ chord, as shown in Figure 8-8.**

After you finger the B♭ chord, try playing the notes of the chord one string at a time (from the 5th string to the 1st) to see whether all the notes ring out clearly. If you encounter any muffled notes, check to see that your left-hand fingers are touching only the appropriate strings and aren't preventing adjacent ones from ringing. If the sound is still muted, you need to exert more pressure with your fingers.

Figure 8-8:
The barre
B♭ chord.

Finding the right fret

Because you can play a B♭ chord as a barre chord, you can now play all 12 A-based major barre chords — but only if you know the names of all the notes on the fifth string. All A-based barre chords get their name from the fifth string (just as the open A chord does). Check out Appendix A for the names of the notes on the 5th string.

The notes and frets work sort of like a clock. After you get past 12, they repeat, so the 13th fret is the same as the first (B♭); the 14th is the same as the second (B); and so on.

Progressions using A-based major barre chords

Before playing any progressions using A-based major barre chords, you need to know that most guitarists don't finger them as we describe earlier (refer to Figure 8-8). Take a look at Figure 8-9 to see another way to finger this chord (using the B♭ chord at the first fret as an example). Use your ring finger to barre the three notes at the third fret.

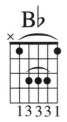

Figure 8-9:
Alternative fingering for the A-based major barre chord.

The tricky thing about the fingering in Figure 8-9 is that, for the 1st string to ring, you need to engage in a mean contortion with your third finger, elevating the middle knuckle out of the way (see photo). Some people can accomplish this position and some can't — it's kind of like wiggling your ears. The people who can't (lift their finger, not wiggle their ears) can use the fingering shown in Figure 8-10.

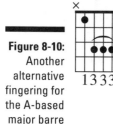

B♭

Figure 8-10:
Another
alternative
fingering for
the A-based
major barre
chord.

1 3 3

If you play the B♭ barre chord as shown in Figure 8-10 (with the 1st string not played), make sure that the 1st string doesn't accidentally sound, either by not striking it with the right hand or by *muting* it (deadening it by lightly touching it) with the third finger. Experiment with all three fingerings and pick one that feels best for you, but we bet that you decide on the form shown in Figure 8-10.

The exercise shown in Figure 8-11 uses A-based major barre chords and has a light, early rock sound. You can give your left-hand fingers a break by releasing pressure as you slide from one chord to the next. Don't forget that you can (and should) transpose this progression to other keys by moving the entire pattern to a new starting point. Do so for all the exercises in this chapter. Notice, too, the staccato marks in measure 4 (play it di-di-di).

TRACK 25, 0:00

Figure 8-11:
A pro-
gression
using
A-based
major barre
chords.

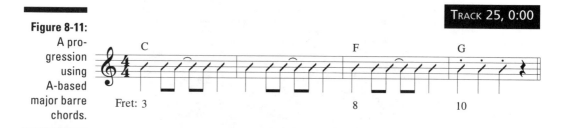

Fret: 3   8   10

Playing Minor, Dominant 7th, Minor 7th, and Major 7th Barre Chords Based on A

We admit that the A-based major barre chord is something of an oddball with respect to left-hand fingering. But all the other A-based forms are much more logical and comfortable in terms of left-hand fingering.

For the rest of the A-based forms, you don't encounter any weird hand contortions or new techniques. All you do is pick up a variety of different forms to enrich your chord vocabulary.

Minor chords

To form an A-based minor barre chord you *could* follow steps similar to the ones that we describe in the section "Playing Major Barre Chords Based on A," earlier in this chapter: Play an open Am chord by using a 3-4-2 fingering instead of 2-3-1 (see Chapter 4 if you need help with the open Am chord); lay your first finger down across all the strings on the other side of the nut; and then slide the shape up one fret and press down firmly, producing a B♭m chord.

But if you want, you can form the B♭m chord by skipping the "sliding up from an open chord" process and just placing your fingers directly on the frets, as indicated by the first chord diagram in Figure 8-12. Check your strings individually to see that they're clear and buzz-free. (Notice that we've gone ahead and also given you the fingerings for B♭7, B♭m7, and B♭maj7 in Figure 8-12. More on these in the following sections.)

Figure 8-12:
B♭m, B♭7,
B♭m7, and
B♭maj7
barre
chords.

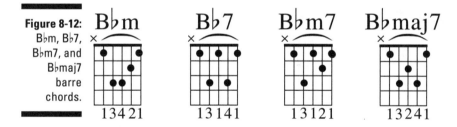

The progression in Figure 8-13 is typical of a rock, folk, or country song and uses both major and minor A-based barre chords. Refer to Appendix A if you need the appropriate fret for each chord along the A string.

Figure 8-13:
A
progression
using both
major and
minor A-
based barre
chords.

TRACK 25, 0:12

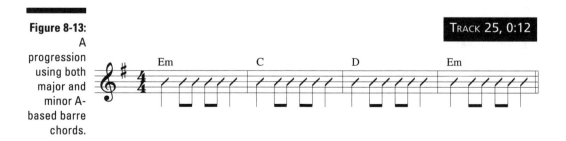

Dominant 7th chords

Dominant 7th chords sound bluesy and funky compared to major chords. Refer to Figure 8-12 to see the fingering for the B♭7 barre chord (A-based). Remember that you can "slide up" to this chord from a two-finger, open-position A7 chord (but only if you use a 3-4 fingering for the A7).

Now, using the A-String chart in Appendix A to find the appropriate fret for any A-based barre chord, try playing the simple progression shown in Figure 8-14, which uses major, minor, and dominant 7th A-based barre chords.

Figure 8-14: A progression using major, minor, and dominant 7th barre chords.

TRACK 25, 0:26

Minor 7th chords

Minor 7th chords sound soft and jazzy compared to major chords. You can form the B♭m7 chord by "sliding up" from an open-position Am7 chord (using a 3-2 fingering), or you can refer to the example shown in Figure 8-12 and place your fingers directly on the frets for the B♭m7.

The simple progression that Figure 8-15 shows uses A-based minor 7th chords exclusively. If you need to, use Appendix A to find the appropriate fret for each chord.

TRACK 25, 0:42

Figure 8-15: A progression using minor 7th barre chords.

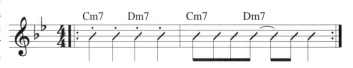

Major 7th chords

Major 7th chords have a bright and jazzy sound compared to major chords. (You may notice that, in the section on E-based barre chords earlier in this chapter, we don't include the major 7th chord. That's because you don't play such chords in a barre form.)

You can form the B♭maj7 chord by "sliding up" from an open-position Amaj7 chord (using a 3-2-4 fingering), or you can refer to the example shown in Figure 8-12 and place your fingers directly on the frets for the barre chord, as the figure shows you.

The simple progression shown in Figure 8-16 uses A-based minor 7th and major 7th barre chords. Use Appendix A to find the appropriate fret for each chord, if necessary.

Figure 8-16: A progression using minor 7th and major 7th barre chords.

TRACK 25, 0:55

The exercise shown in Figure 8-17 uses the chord progression for the song "We Wish You a Merry Christmas." Play this progression by using only A-based barre chords. To help you out in this exercise, we indicate at which fret to place your first-finger barres for each chord. You may notice that the chords are different from those in the other "We Wish You a Merry Christmas" example (refer to Figure 8-7), but that's only because we use a different starting chord here.

If you're playing a nylon-string acoustic guitar, you're going to have trouble playing the Am chord at the 12th fret — the body of the guitar gets in the way. (And playing the chord's no picnic on a steel-string acoustic either.) Substitute an open-position Am chord but use a 3-4-2 fingering to keep your hand in the barre position.

You may notice, in playing the exercises in this chapter — and especially in the "We Wish You a Merry Christmas" exercises — that your left hand leaps around in sudden, jerky movements. That's because you're playing all the required chords by using only one chord form — either the E-based form or the A-based form. If you combine forms, you base your chord selection on economy of movement. The F and B♭ chords are five frets away from each other if you use the same barre form, but they're at the same fret (the first) if you use the E-based form of F and the A-based form of B♭. Playing songs actually gets easier as you add additional chords to your arsenal.

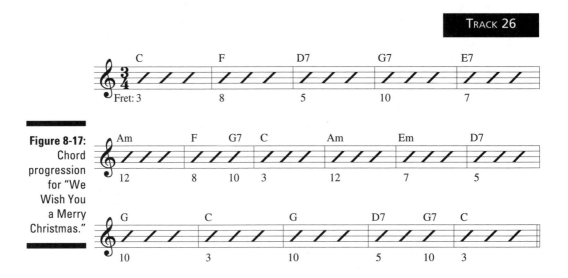

Figure 8-17: Chord progression for "We Wish You a Merry Christmas."

To see how much easier playing "We Wish You a Merry Christmas" is if you use both A-based barre chords and E-based barre chords together, check it out in the section "Playing Songs with Barre Chords and Power Chords," later in this chapter.

Wailing on Power Chords

A *power chord* — not to be confused with a power *cord* (the cable that provides electricity to your motorized shoe buffer) — is usually nothing more than the lowest two or three notes of a regular open-position or barre chord. Guitarists often used power chords in rock music to create a big sound. Power chords are easier to play than are their full-version counterparts and don't contain a major or minor quality to them, so they can stand in for either type of chord. Plus they're loads of fun to play!

Fingering power chords

A power chord consists of only two different notes that are always five steps apart, such as A–E or C–G. (Count letter names on your fingers to confirm that A to E and C to G are five steps apart.) But the actual chord that you play may involve more than two strings, because you may be *doubling* each of the notes that makes up the power chord — that is, playing the same notes in different octaves (and on different strings).

As do most other chords, power chords come in two varieties: *open-position* and *movable*. We show you the most common open-position power chords — E5, A5, and D5 — in Figure 8-18. These chords are merely the two or three lowest notes of the simple open-position E, A, and D chords that we describe in Chapter 4.

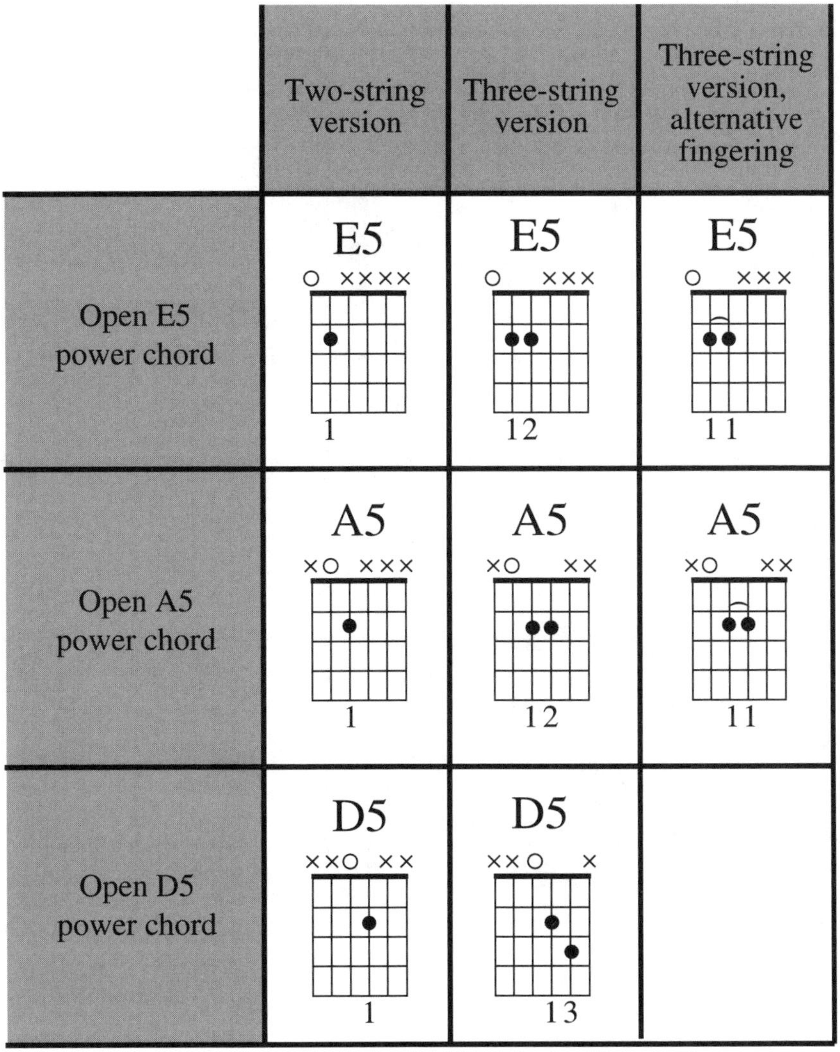

	Two-string version	Three-string version	Three-string version, alternative fingering
Open E5 power chord			
Open A5 power chord			
Open D5 power chord			

Figure 8-18: E5, A5, and D5 power chords.

Movable power chords are simply the two or three lowest notes of the movable barre chords that we describe in the preceding sections of this chapter. As is the case with movable barre chords, movable power chords are either E-based, getting their names from the notes that you play on the 6th (low E) string, or A-based, getting their names from the notes that you play on the 5th (A) string. Figure 8-19 shows the F5 and B♭5 power chords that you play at the first fret, but you can move these chords to any fret, determining their names from the charts in Appendix A on the low-E string and A string. Or, better yet, you can determine the power-chord names by memorizing the names of the notes on the 6th and 5th strings — and not resort to the Appendix at all! (Hint, hint.)

For the most part, the two- and three-string power chords are interchangeable. For some situations, such as in playing the Chuck-Berry–style figures that we present in Chapter 10, the two-string version is preferable.

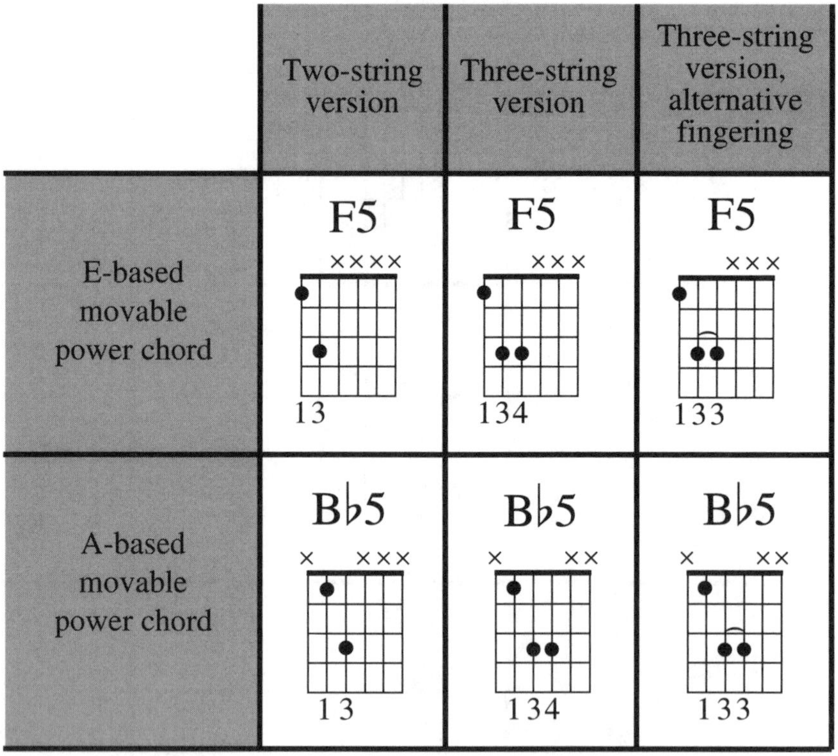

	Two-string version	Three-string version	Three-string version, alternative fingering
E-based movable power chord	F5 ×××× 1 3	F5 ××× 1 3 4	F5 ××× 1 3 3
A-based movable power chord	B♭5 × ××× 1 3	B♭5 × ×× 1 3 4	B♭5 × ×× 1 3 3

Figure 8-19: F5 and B♭5 (movable) power chords.

How you use power chords

In straight-ahead rock music (and even in some pop music), guitarists often substitute power chords for full chords to give the accompaniment (specifically, the rhythm guitar part) a sparser, leaner sound than what you'd get with full chords. This course is sometimes taken to enable the vocal part to stand out more from the music. You can hear this kind of power chord sound in old songs such as "Johnny B. Goode" and "Peggy Sue." The progression shown in Figure 8-20 illustrates the power chords that you use to produce this kind of sound. Play this progression by using either two- or three-string power chords.

TRACK 27, 0:00

Figure 8-20: A power-chord progression in D.

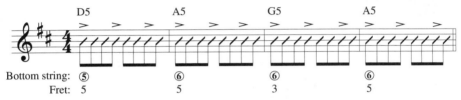

Bottom string ⑥ means chord is E-based; bottom string ⑤ means chord is A-based

The > symbol is called an *accent*. It tells you to play the accented notes a little louder than the other notes — to accentuate them. Sometimes accents form a rhythmic pattern that gives a song a certain flavor, such as a Latin flavor, a Bo Diddley flavor, a polka flavor, or even a rocky road flavor.

In hard-rock and heavy-metal music, guitarists often like to use a heavy or ominous sound in their chords. They achieve this mood by playing low notes with *distortion* — a fuzzy-sounding signal that results if the signal is too powerful for the amp's circuitry and the speakers to handle effectively.

Hard-rock and heavy-metal guitarists love to play power chords instead of full chords right off the bat, because power chords sound lower (mainly because they don't include the higher strings). In addition, the distorted tone really limits them to power chords, because full chords (chords with more than two different notes in them) can sound like mud with heavy distortion.

The progression shown in Figure 8-21 illustrates a typical heavy-metal riff using both movable and open-position power chords. If you have an electric guitar and an amp or effect device that enables you to *overdrive* it (see Chapter 15), use distortion while practicing this progression, as you hear on the CD. You can use either the two- or three-string version of the power chords, but the two-string version is what you hear on the CD.

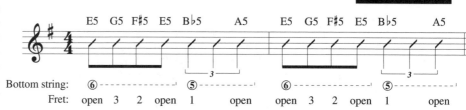

Figure 8-21:
A heavy-metal power-chord progression to bang your head to.

Bottom string ⑥ means chord is E-based; bottom string ⑤ means chord is A-based

To play a song with power chords right away, check out "Power Play" in the following section, "Playing Songs with Barre Chords and Power Chords."

Playing Songs with Barre Chords and Power Chords

Now the fun begins. You revisit a song that you may have already played at some point (refer to Figures 8-7 and 8-17, earlier in this chapter), but we show you in this section how playing a song is easier if you combine different chord forms.

About the songs

Here is some useful information about the songs to help you along:

♪ **We Wish You a Merry Christmas.** To play "We Wish You a Merry Christmas," you need to know how to play E-based barre chords (see the sections "Playing Major Barre Chords Based on E" and "Playing Minor, Dominant 7th, and Minor 7th Barre Chords Based on E," earlier in this chapter); how to play A-based barre chords (see the sections "Playing Major Barre Chords Based on A" and "Playing Minor, Dominant 7th, Minor 7th, and Major 7th Barre Chords Based on A," earlier in this chapter); and how to play guitar dressed in a stuffy costume with a pillow strapped to your belly.

Chord progressions for this song appear twice in exercises in this chapter, first in the exercise in Figure 8-7, as practice for E-based barre chords, and then again in the exercise for Figure 8-17, as practice for A-based barre chords. In each of those exercises, your left hand must jump all over the fingerboard. By combining both kinds of barre chords (E-based and A-based), you can play this song with much less left-hand movement. Minimizing left-hand movement enables you to play both faster and more smoothly as well as to achieve better *voice leading,* or smoothness of motion between the individual notes of the changing chords. (Good voice leading produces a pleasing sound.)

♪ **Power Play.** To play "Power Play" (a four-bar rock progression using only power chords), you need to know how to finger and play the A5, G5, and D5 power chords (see the section "Fingering power chords," a bit earlier in this chapter) and how to crank your amp up to 11 (à la Spinal Tap).

This "song" is a four-bar rock progression using only power chords. Countless rock songs use this progression, including the classic "Takin' Care of Business," by Bachman-Turner Overdrive (known as BTO to their friends).

Remember that power chords are well-suited to a heavier, distorted sound, and you can use them in place of full versions of chords because they usually contain the same bottom two or three notes. So if you're feeling a bit rebellious, a bit wicked, crank up your amp and play "We Wish You a Merry Christmas" with power chords, a distorted sound, and a *really* bad attitude.

Power Play

Chapter 9

Special Articulation: Making the Guitar Talk

*A*rticulation refers to how you play and connect notes on the guitar. If pitches and rhythms are *what* you play, articulation is *how* you play. Articulation gives your music expression and enables you to make your guitar talk, sing, and even cry. From a technical standpoint, such articulation techniques as *hammer-ons, pull-offs, slides,* and *bends* enable you to connect notes together smoothly, giving your playing a little "grease" (a good thing, especially in playing the blues). *Vibratos* add life to sustained (or held) notes that otherwise just sit there like a dead turtle, and *muting* shapes the sound of individual notes, giving them a tight, clipped sound.

As you start to incorporate articulation in your playing, you begin to exercise more control over your guitar. You're not merely playing "correctly" — you're playing with individual *style*.

This chapter shows you how to play all the articulation techniques you need to get your guitar talking. After we explain each technique, we present some *idiomatic licks* (musical phrases that naturally suit a particular technique or style) so that you can play the technique in context.

Rockin' On with Hammer-ons

A *hammer-on* doesn't refer to playing the guitar while wearing a tool belt; a hammer-on is a left-hand technique that enables you to play two consecutive ascending notes by picking only the first note. The hammer-on derives its name from the action of your left-hand finger, which acts like a hammer striking the fretboard, causing the note of that fret to sound out. This technique makes the connection between the notes sound smooth — far more smooth than if you simply pick each note separately. In the tab (and standard) notation in this book, the letter *H* with a *slur* (a curved line) indicates a hammer-on. (The slur connects the first fret number [or note] of the hammer-on with the last, and the *H* appears centered over the slur. If two *H*s appear over the slur, the hammer-on involves three notes.)

Playing a hammer-on

An open-string hammer-on (or just *hammer,* for short) is the easiest kind to play. Following are the steps for the open-string hammer-on, as shown in Figure 9-1a:

1. **Pick the open G string (the 3rd string) as you normally do.**

2. **While the open string is still ringing, use a finger of your left hand (say, the first finger) to quickly and firmly strike (or slam or smack, as you prefer) the second fret of the same string.**

   If you bring your finger down with enough force, you hear the new note (the second fret *A*) ringing. Normally, your left hand doesn't *strike* a fret; it merely *presses* down on it. But to produce an audible sound without picking, you must hit the sting pretty hard, as though your finger's a little hammer coming down on the fretboard.

Figure 9-1b shows a hammer-on from a fretted note on the 3rd string. Use your first finger to fret the first note at the fourth fret and strike the string; then, while that note's still ringing, use your second finger to hammer down on the fifth fret.

Figure 9-1c shows a *double hammer-on* on the 3rd string. Play the open string and hammer the second fret with your first finger; then, while that note's still ringing, hammer the string again (at the fourth fret) with your third finger, producing a super-smooth connection between all three notes. Don't rush the notes together; rushing is a tendency as you first work with hammer-ons.

Figure 9-1d shows a double hammer-on on the same string using three fretted notes. This type of hammer-on is the most difficult to play and requires some practice. Play the note at the fourth fret, fretting with your first finger; hammer-on the fifth-fret note with your second finger; then hammer the seventh-fret-note with your fourth finger.

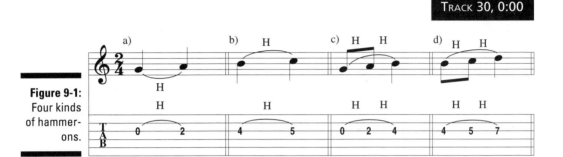

Figure 9-1:
Four kinds
of hammer-
ons.

You can also play hammer-ons as double-stops. The most common double-stop hammer-ons — and the ones that are the easiest to play — are the ones where both double-stop notes lie on the same fret, enabling you to barre them (play them with one finger). (See Chapter 7 for more information on double-stops.)

Figure 9-2a shows a *double-stop hammer-on* from open strings (the 2nd and 3rd). After striking the two open strings with the pick, and while the open strings are still ringing, slam down your first finger at the second-fret, across both strings at the same time.

Next, try a double-stop hammer-on from the second fret to the fourth fret, also on the 2nd and 3rd strings, as shown in Figure 9-2b. Use your first finger to barre the second fret and your third finger to barre the fourth fret. Now, to get really fancy, try a *double double-stop hammer-on,* on the same strings, as shown in Figure 9-2c. Start with the open strings; hammer the second-fret barre with your first finger; then hammer the fourth-fret barre with your third finger.

Figure 9-3 shows what's known as a *"hammer-on from nowhere."* It's not a typical hammer-on in that the hammered note doesn't follow an already-ringing lower note. In fact, the hammered note is on an entirely different string than the previous note. Sound the hammered note by fretting it very hard ("hammering" it) with a left-hand finger — hard enough that the note rings out without your striking it with the pick.

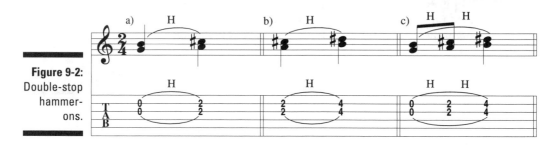

TRACK 30, 0:27

Figure 9-2:
Double-stop hammer-ons.

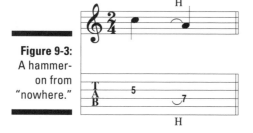

TRACK 30, 0:48

Figure 9-3:
A hammer-on from "nowhere."

Why would you even use this type of hammer-on? Sometimes, in fast passages, your right-hand picking pattern just doesn't give you time for that one extra pick attack when you need it. But you can sound the note anyway by fretting it hard enough with a finger of the left hand — hammering it from nowhere.

Getting idiomatic with hammer-ons

In Figures 9-4 through 9-7, you see some idiomatic licks using hammer-ons. (The little numbers in the standard notation indicate fingerings.) The lick in Figure 9-4 uses single-note hammer-ons from open strings. You may hear this kind of lick in a rock, blues, or country song. Try it out for a bit more practice with hammer-ons.

Another cool trick is to strum a chord while hammering one of the notes. Figure 9-5 shows this technique — which James Taylor often employs — in the context of a musical phrase.

Figure 9-6 shows single-note hammer-ons involving only fretted notes. You can hear this kind of lick in many rock and blues songs. Down-picks are indicated by the ⊓ symbol and up-picks are indicated by the ∨ symbol. (The *sim.* means to keep playing in a similar manner — here referring to the picking pattern indicated.)

Figure 9-4:
Single-note
hammer-
ons from
open
strings.

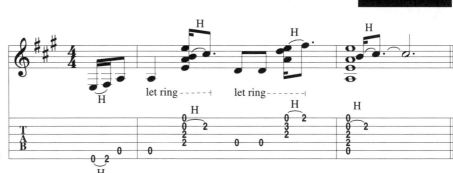

Figure 9-5:
Strumming
a chord
while
hammering
one of the
notes, in the
context of a
musical
phrase.

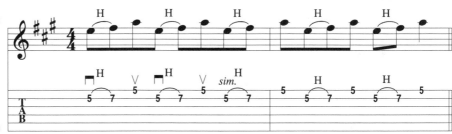

Figure 9-6:
Single-note
hammer-
ons from
fretted
notes.

Keep your first finger barring the fifth fret for this lick as you play it. You get a smoother sound, and you find that it's easier to play, too.

Figure 9-7 combines a double-stop hammer-on with a hammer-on from nowhere in fifth position. (See Chapter 7 for more information on playing in position.) Try picking that last note, and you can easily see that the hammer-on from nowhere feels more comfortable than the picked version of the note.

TRACK 34

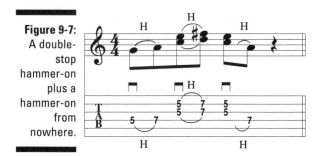

Figure 9-7:
A double-stop hammer-on plus a hammer-on from nowhere.

Pullin' Off Pull-offs

A *pull-off* is another technique that enables you to connect notes smoothly. It enables you to play two consecutive descending notes by picking only once with the right hand and, as the first note rings, pulling your finger off that fret. As you pull your finger off one fret, the next lower fretted (or open) note on the string then rings out instead of the first note. You can sort of think of a pull-off as the opposite of a hammer-on, but that particular contrast doesn't really tell the whole story. A pull-off also requires that you exert a slight sideways pull on the string where you're fretting the picked note and then release the string from your finger in a snap as your pull your finger off the fret — something like what you do in launching a tiddly-wink. The tab (and standard) notation in this book indicates a pull-off by showing the letter *P* centered over a slur (short curved line) connecting the two tab numbers (or notes).

Playing pull-offs

A pull-off (or *pull,* for short) to an open string is the easiest kind to play. Following are the steps for the open-string pull-off shown in Figure 9-8a:

1. **Press down the 3rd string at the second fret with your first or second finger (whichever is more comfortable) and pick the note normally with your right hand.**

2. **While the note is still ringing, pull your finger off the string in a sideways motion (toward the 2nd string) in a way that causes the open 3rd string to ring — almost as if you're making a left-hand finger pluck.**

   If you're playing up to speed, you can't truly pluck the string as you remove your finger — you're half lifting and half plucking . . . or somewhere in between. Experiment to find the left-hand finger motion that works best for you.

Figure 9-8b shows a pull-off involving only fretted notes. The crucial factor in playing this kind of pull-off is that *you must finger both pull-off notes ahead of time*. We put that last part in italics because it's so important. This requirement is one of the big differences between a hammer-on and a pull-off. You must anticipate, or set up, a pull-off in advance. Following are the steps for playing the fretted pull-off shown in Figure 9-8b:

1. **Press down both the second fret of the 3rd string with your first finger and the fourth fret of the 3rd string with your third finger *at the same time*.**

2. **Strike the 3rd string with the pick and, while the fourth-fret note is still ringing, pull your third finger off the fourth fret (in a half pluck, half lift) to sound the note of the second fret (which you're already fingering).**

   Try to avoid accidentally striking the 2nd string as you pull off. You can see that, if you aren't already pressing down that second-fret note, you end up pulling off to the open string instead of the second fret!

Figure 9-8c shows a *double pull-off* to the open 3rd string. Start by simultaneously fretting the first two notes (with your first and third fingers). Pick the string and then pull off with your third finger to sound the note at the second fret; then pull off with your first finger to sound the open string. (Notice that two *P*s appear over the slur connecting the three notes; these indicate that you're pulling off two notes and not just one.)

Figure 9-8d shows a double pull-off on the 3rd string using only fretted notes. Start with all three notes fretted (using your first, second, and fourth fingers). Pick the string and then pull off with your fourth finger to sound the fifth-fret note; then pull off with your second finger to sound the fourth-fret note.

You can also play pull-offs as double-stops. As is true with hammer-ons, the double-stop pull-offs that are the most common and are the easiest to play are those where both double-stop notes lie on the same fret, enabling you to barre them. (See Chapter 7 for more information on double-stops.)

TRACK 35, 0:00

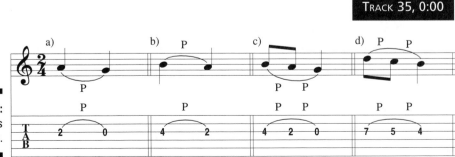

Figure 9-8:
Four kinds
of pull-offs.

Figure 9-9a shows a double-stop pull-off to open strings on the 2nd and 3rd strings. After striking the notes at the second fret, and while the strings are still ringing, pull off your first finger (in a half pluck, half lift) from both strings at the same time (in one motion) to sound the open strings.

Next, try a double-stop pull-off from the fourth fret to the second fret, as shown in Figure 9-9b. Place your first finger at the second fret, barring the 2nd and 3rd strings, and place your third finger at the fourth fret (also barring the 2nd and 3rd strings) *at the same time.* Pick the strings and then pull your third finger off the fourth fret to sound the notes at the second fret of both strings.

Now try a *double double-stop pull-off,* on the same strings, as shown in Figure 9-9c. This type of pull-off is similar to what you play in the example shown in Figure 9-9b except that, after the notes on the second fret sound, you pull your first finger off the second fret to sound the open strings.

TRACK 35, 0:27

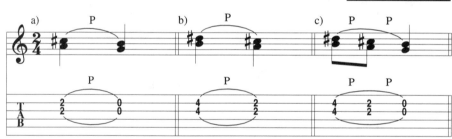

Figure 9-9:
Double-stop
pull-offs.

Getting idiomatic with pull-offs

In Figures 9-10 and 9-11, you see two idiomatic licks using pull-offs. Figure 9-10 involves single-note pull-offs to open strings. You can hear this kind of lick in many rock and blues songs.

TRACK 36, 0:00

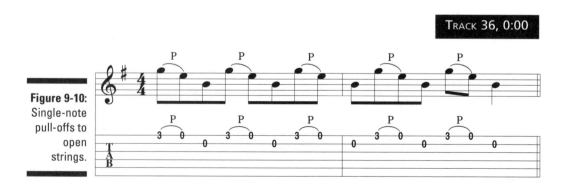

Figure 9-10:
Single-note
pull-offs to
open
strings.

Figure 9-5, in the section "Getting idiomatic with hammer-ons," earlier in this chapter, shows you how to strum a chord while hammering on a note of that chord. Figure 9-11 shows the opposite technique: strumming a chord while pulling off one note. The passage in this figure leads off with two single-note pull-offs, just to get you warmed up.

TRACK 36, 0:19

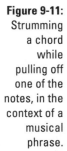

Figure 9-11: Strumming a chord while pulling off one of the notes, in the context of a musical phrase.

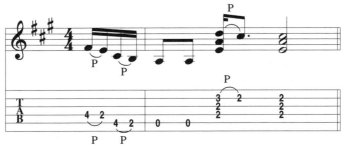

Getting Down with Slides

A *slide* is an articulation technique in which you play a note and then move your left-hand finger along the string to a different fret. This technique enables you to connect two or more notes smoothly and quickly. It also enables you to change positions on the fretboard seamlessly.

Many different types of slides are possible. The most basic are as the following list describes:

- ♪ Slides between two notes where you pick only the first note.

- ♪ Slides between two notes where you pick both notes.

- ♪ Slides from an indefinite pitch a few frets above or below the target note. (The pitch is indefinite because you begin the slide with very little finger pressure, gradually increasing it till you land on the target fret.)

- ♪ Slides to an indefinite pitch a few frets above or below the starting note. (The pitch is indefinite because you gradually release finger pressure as you move away from the starting fret.)

- ♪ Slides into home plate.

In the tablature (and standard) notation, we indicate a slide by the letters *sl.* centered over a slanted line.

Playing slides

The name of this technique, *slide,* gives you a pretty good clue about how to play it. You slide a left-hand finger up or down a string, maintaining contact with it, to arrive at a new note. Sometimes you connect two notes of definite pitch (for example, you slide from the seventh fret to the ninth), and sometimes you connect a definite pitch with an indefinite pitch (you produce indefinite pitches by picking a string while you gradually add or release finger pressure as you're sliding).

Figure 9-12a shows a slur (small curved line) along with the slanted line. The slur indicates that this is a *legato* slide, which means that you *don't pick the second note.* Play the first note at the ninth fret normally, holding the note for one beat. At beat 2, while the string is still ringing, quickly slide your left-hand finger to the 12th fret, keeping full finger pressure the whole time. This action causes the note at the 12th fret to sound without you picking it.

In Figure 9-12b, which notates a slide *without* a slur, you *do* pick the second note. Play and hold the ninth-fret note for a beat; then, at beat two, slide up to the 12th fret — maintaining full finger pressure as you go — and strike the note with the pick just as you arrive at the 12th fret.

TRACK 37, 0:00

Figure 9-12:
Two types
of slides:
one with
the second
note
unpicked
and the
other with it
picked.

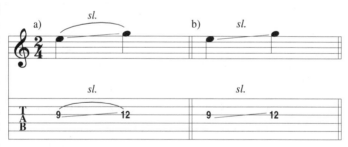

If you play the slide in Figure 9-12b slowly enough, you produce what's known as a *glissando.* A glissando is an effect that you hear on harps, pianos, and guitars, wherein all the notes between the two principal notes sound.

An *ascending immediate slide* serves to decorate only one note and isn't something that you use to connect two different notes of definite pitch. In the example shown in Figure 9-13a, you slide into the ninth fret from a few frets below. Follow these steps:

1. **Start the slide from about three frets below the target fret (the sixth fret if the ninth fret is your target), using minimal finger pressure.**

2. **As your finger slides up, gradually increase your finger pressure so that, as you arrive at the target fret, you exert full pressure.**

3. **Strike the string with the pick while your left-hand finger is in motion, somewhere between the starting and target frets (the sixth and ninth frets, in this example).**

The slide shown in Figure 9-13b is a *descending immediate slide.* This kind of slide usually occurs after you hold a note for a while. It gives a long note a fancy ending. Follow these steps:

1. **Pick the note that the tab indicates (the one on the twelfth fret in this case) in the normal manner.**

2. **After letting the note ring for the indicated duration, slide your left-hand finger down the string, gradually releasing finger pressure as you go, to cause a fading-away effect.**

   After a few frets, you should lift your finger completely off the string — unless you want to play what's known as a *long slide.* In that case, you can slide your finger all the way down the neck, releasing finger pressure (and finally removing your finger from the string) toward the end of the neck, as near to the nut as you want to go.

TRACK 37, 0:10

Figure 9-13: Immediate ascending and descending slides.

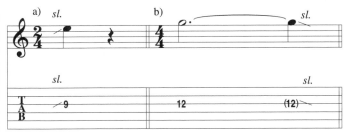

Playing idiomatic licks using slides

Figures 9-14 and 9-15 show two idiomatic licks using slides. Figure 9-14 shows immediate ascending slides, including a barred double-stop slide. Use your first finger to play the barred double-stop at the fifth fret, sliding into it from only one or two frets below. This lick has a Chuck Berry-ish sound.

TRACK 38

Figure 9-14:
Some
Chuck
Berry-ish
slides.

Figure 9-15 (which also contains a hammer-on and pull-off) shows how you can use slides to smoothly change positions. (The small numbers in the standard notation indicate left-hand fingering.) Here you move from third position to fifth position and back to third position. Notice that the tab indicates the slides with slurs — so don't pick the second note of each slide. And follow the up- and downstroke picking indications on the tab (∨ and ⊓) — you pick notes only five times, even though you actually play nine notes!

TRACK 39

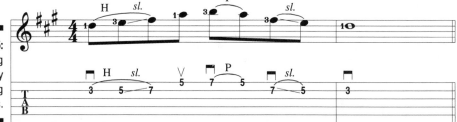

Figure 9-15:
Changing
positions by
using
slides.

Getting the Bends

More than any other type of articulation, the *string bend* is what makes your guitar talk (or sing or cry), giving the instrument almost vocal-like expressive capabilities. Bending is nothing more than using a left-hand finger to push or pull a string out of its normal alignment, stretching it across the fingerboard toward the 6th or 1st string. (More later on how to tell in which direction to stretch the string.)

As you bend a string, you raise its pitch by stretching that string. This rise in pitch can be slight or great, depending on exactly how far you bend the string. Between the slightest and greatest bends possible are infinite degrees of in-between bends. It's those infinite degrees that make your guitar sing.

The tab notation in this book indicates a bend by using a curved arrow and either a number or a fraction (or both) or the word *Full* at the peak of the arrow. The fraction *1/2,* for example, means that you bend the string until the pitch is a half step (the equivalent of one fret) higher than normal. The word *Full* above a bend arrow means that you bend the string until the pitch is a full step, or whole step (the equivalent of two frets), higher than normal. You may also see fractions such as 1/4 and 3/4 or bigger numbers such 1 1/2 or 2 above a bend arrow. These fractions or numbers all tell you how many (whole) steps to bend the note. But 1/2 and Full are the most common bends that you see in most tab notation.

You can check to see that you're bending in tune by fretting the target note normally and comparing that to the bent note. If the bend indicates a whole step (Full) on the seventh fret of the 3rd string, for example, play the ninth fret normally and listen carefully to the pitch. Then try bending the seventh-fret note to match the ninth-fret pitch in your head.

Although nearly all publishers of printed guitar music use curved arrows and numbers to indicate bends in tablature, not all publishers use these indications on the standard notation staff as well. Some publishers instead show the pitch of both the unbent and bent notes, with one of them in parentheses or one of them very small. To avoid confusion, make sure that you establish how each system treats the issue of bent notes before you start playing that music.

Playing bends

Take the photo at the left of Figure 9-16 as a starting point for playing a bend. You play this bend on the 3rd string with the third finger, which represents a very common bending situation — probably the most common. Follow these steps:

1. **Place your third finger at the seventh fret but *support* the third finger by placing the second finger at the sixth fret and the first finger at the fifth fret, all at the same time (see Figure 9-16 left).**

   The first and second fingers don't produce any sound, but they add strength to your bend. Supporting your bends with any other available fingers is always a good idea.

2. **Pick the 3rd string with your right hand.**

3. **Immediately after picking, use all three fingers together to push the string toward the 6th string, raising the pitch a whole step (to the pitch you normally get at the ninth fret — see Figure 9-16 on the right).**

Figure 9-16:
Before bending (left) and bending (right).

You can refer to this type of bend as an *immediate bend,* because you bend the string immediately after picking it. Figure 9-17a shows what this bend looks like in music and tab.

Squeezing the neck of the guitar a little from behind with your thumb may help as you're playing a bend. This technique gives you added leverage and thus makes bending easier. Some people prefer to rotate their hand by turning their wrist, pushing up the string that way instead of merely moving their finger(s) to do so. Try both ways to see which is most comfortable for you. Using *light-gauge,* or thin, strings on your guitar also makes bending easier.

Strings are measured in *gauges,* with that term referring to the diameter of the string in millimeters. You don't normally do a lot of string bending on acoustic guitars, because the typical string gauges are too heavy. A light-gauge set of acoustic strings starts with the diameter for the 1st string at .012 mm, which is generally considered unbendable by all except the most dedicated masochists. (Guitarists refer to the entire set in shorthand as *twelves.*) In electric guitar playing, where string bending is an integral technique, the most common gauges start with sets that use a .009 or .010 mm gauge for the top string ("nines" and "tens," to use the vernacular). You can bend with .011's and .012's ("elevens" and "twelves") on your guitar, but doing so isn't much fun unless you're seriously into pain.

Figure 9-17b is called a *bend and release.* Pick the note; then bend it (without repicking), and unbend it (release it without repicking) to its normal position. Unlike the bend in Figure 9-17a, this bend is not immediate; instead, you see it notated in a specific rhythm (that you can hear on the CD). You can refer to this type of bend as a *bend in rhythm,* or a *measured bend.*

Figure 9-17c shows a *prebend* and release. You *prebend* the note, or bend it *before* you strike it with the pick. Bend the note as you do in Figure 9-17a but don't pick the string until after you bend it. After you pick the note, unbend (release without repicking) the string to its normal position.

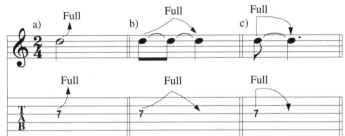

Figure 9-17:
Three types
of bends.

Most often, as the examples in Figure 9-17 show, you push the string toward the 6th string (or toward the ceiling). But if you bend notes on the bottom two strings (the 5th and 6th strings), you *pull* the string toward the 1st string (or toward the floor) — otherwise the string slides right off the fretboard.

You may wonder just how you know which notes to bend and how much to bend them. You can find out more about that in Chapters 10 and 11.

Getting idiomatic with bends

Figure 9-18 shows a very common bend figure that you can use in rock soloing. Notice the fingering that the standard notation staff indicates to use. Your left hand hardly moves — it's locked in fifth position (see Chapter 7 for more information on positions), with the first finger barring the 1st and 2nd strings at the fifth fret. The second note of the figure (fifth fret, 2nd string) happens to be the same pitch (E) as your target bend, so you can use that second note to test the accuracy of your bend. Soon, you start to feel just how far you need to bend a string to achieve a whole-step or half-step rise in pitch. All the bends in this example are immediate bends.

After you play each 3rd-string bend, just before you pick the 2nd-string note, reduce your finger pressure from the bent note. This action causes the 3rd string to stop ringing as you pick the 2nd string.

TRACK 41

Figure 9-18:
Bending the
3rd string in
a classic
rock 'n' roll
lead lick.

In Figure 9-19, you bend the 2nd string, once as an immediate bend and once as a bend in rhythm. Listen to the CD to hear how this example sounds. Strictly speaking, because you're in 12th position, you should be using your fourth finger to play the 15th fret. But we indicate for you to use the third finger, because if you're up at the 12th fret, the frets are closer together, so your third finger can easily make the reach and is stronger than your fourth finger.

TRACK 42

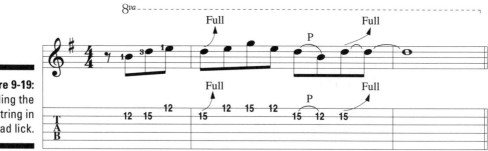

Figure 9-19:
Bending the
2nd string in
a lead lick.

You play the examples shown in Figures 9-18 and 9-19 in what lead guitarists call a *"box" pattern* — a group of notes in one position that vaguely re-sembles the shape of a box. You can use this pattern for improvising lead solos. (For more information on box patterns and soloing, see Chapters 10 and 11.)

Figure 9-20 uses a small box pattern in the eighth position. This example features an immediate bend of the 1st string with a measured (in rhythm) release. Listen to the CD to get this rhythm.

TRACK 43

Figure 9-20:
Bending
and
releasing a
note in a
lead lick.

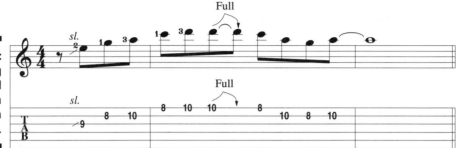

Although you bend most notes by pushing a string toward the 6th string, you may sometimes need to bend a string the other way, even on a middle or upper string (but *not* on the 1st string because it slides off the neck if you do). You need to use this type of opposite-direction bend if the note that follows a bend is on a string that's adjacent to the bent string. You need to bend *away* from the upcoming string; otherwise, your bending finger may accidentally touch it, inadvertently muting it.

Figure 9-21 shows two first-finger, half-step bends on the 3rd string. The first one bends toward the 6th string because the following note is on the 2nd string. (Remember that you're bending *away* from the following note.) The second one, however, bends toward the floor because the following note is on the adjacent 4th string. Again, you're bending away from the next note.

TRACK 44

Figure 9-21:
Bending the
same string
in two
different
directions.
The aste-
risks and
footnotes
tell you
in which
direction to
bend.

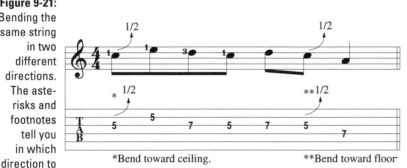

*Bend toward ceiling.   **Bend toward floor

You can create an interesting effect by bending a note, letting it ring in its bent state, striking a note on another string, and then restriking the bent string and releasing it. Many southern-rock and country-rock guitarists are fond of this kind of bend. Figure 9-22 shows this "held-bend" technique. In the notation, the dotted line after the arrow indicates that you hold the bend not only as you strike the 2nd string, but also as you restrike the 3rd string; the downward-curved solid line shows the release of the bend. Make sure that you bend the 3rd string toward the ceiling so that your bending finger is out of the way of the 2nd string. Listen to the CD to hear how this lick sounds.

TRACK 45

Figure 9-22:
Bending and holding a note while striking another string and then restriking and releasing the bent note.

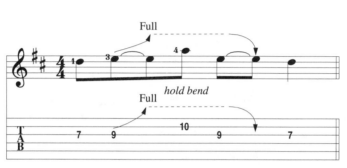

You can also play bends as double-stops — you just bend two strings at the same time, usually by barring the two strings with one finger. (See Chapter 7 for more information on double-stops.) Figure 9-23 shows a double-stop bend of the 2nd and 3rd strings in the box pattern at the fifth fret. Use your first finger to play the fifth-fret double-stop; then use your third finger to play the double-stop bend and release at the seventh fret. The double arrow in the notation tells you to bend both notes. By the way, it's shown as a single arrow on the release of the bend only to avoid messiness in the notation — so go ahead and release both notes.

TRACK 46

Figure 9-23:
A double-stop bend and release.

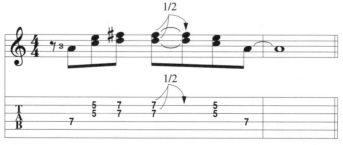

Vibrato

Think of the term *vibrato,* and you may imagine a singer's wavering voice or a violinist's twitching hand. On the guitar, however, *vibrato* is a steady, even (and usually slight) fluctuation of pitch, most often achieved by rapidly bending and releasing a note a slight degree. A vibrato can add warmth, emotion, and life to a held, or sustained, note.

How do you know when to apply vibrato to a note? The most obvious time is whenever you hold a note for a long time. That's when you can add some emotion to the note by using vibrato. Vibrato not only gives the note more warmth, but it also increases the sustain period of the note. Some guitarists, such as blues great B.B. King, are renowned for their expressive vibrato technique. Both the tab and standard notation indicate a vibrato by placing a wavy line at the top of the staff over the note to which you apply the technique.

You can produce a vibrato in several ways, as the following list describes:

♪ You can slightly bend and release a note over and over again, creating a wah-wah-wah effect. The average pitch of the vibrato is slightly higher than the unaltered note. The left-hand technique for this method is the same as the technique for bending — you move a finger back and forth, perpendicular to the string, creating a fluctuation of pitch.

♪ You can very rapidly slide your finger back and forth along the length of a string, within one fret. Although you're not actually moving your finger out of the fret, the pitch becomes slightly sharper as you move toward the nut and slightly flatter as you move toward the bridge. Consequently, the average pitch of the vibrato is the same as the unaltered note. This type of vibrato you reserve almost exclusively for playing classical guitar with nylon strings. (See Chapter 13 for more information on playing classical guitar.)

♪ If your electric guitar has a whammy bar mounted on it, you can move the bar up and down with your right hand, creating a fluctuation in pitch. In addition to giving you greater rhythmic flexibility and pitch range, the whammy bar enables you to add vibrato to an open string.

The first type of vibrato that we mention in the preceding list, the bend-and-release type, is the most common, by far, and is the one shown in the examples in this chapter. Support your vibrato finger with other available fingers by placing them all on the string at the same time. You can either move your whole hand by rotating it at the wrist and keeping the finger fixed, or you can move just your finger(s). Try both ways and see which feels most comfortable.

TIP

You may find that playing a vibrato is easier if you anchor your left hand on the neck as you play. Squeeze the neck a little between the side of your thumb and the part of your palm that's about half an inch below your first finger. This action gives you better leverage and helps you control the evenness of the fluctuation.

Figure 9-24a shows a vibrato at the ninth fret of the 3rd string. Anchor your hand as we describe in the preceding paragraph and slightly bend and release the note over and over. Try the vibrato with each finger. Try it at different frets and on different strings. The notation for a vibrato never tells you how fast or slowly to bend and release — that's up to you. But whether you play a fast vibrato or a slow one, make sure that you keep the fluctuations steady and even. The notation *does* tell you, however, whether to make the vibrato *narrow* (that is, you bend the string only slightly — less than a half step — for each pulsation) or *wide* (you bend the string to a greater degree — about a half step or more). Figure 9-24a shows a regular (narrow) vibrato, and Figure 9-24b shows a wide vibrato, indicating the latter by using an exaggerated wavy line (with deeper peaks and valleys). Try playing a wide vibrato with each finger. Try it at different frets and on different strings.

TRACK 47

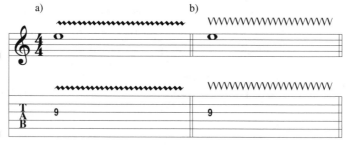

Figure 9-24: Narrow and wide vibratos.

If the note that you're holding is a bent note (see the section "Getting the Bends," earlier in this chapter), you create the vibrato by *releasing and bending* (instead of bending and releasing) — because the note's already bent as you start the vibrato. This action makes the average pitch lower than the held (bent) note, which itself produces the highest pitch in the vibrato.

After a long vibrato, guitarists often play a descending slide, gradually releasing finger pressure as they go, to give the vibrato a fancy little ending. Another trick is to play a long note without vibrato for a while and then add some vibrato toward the end of the note. This "delayed vibrato" is a favorite technique that singers often use.

To practice playing vibratos, play the examples shown in Figures 9-19, 9-20, and 9-23 again, but add vibrato to the final note of each figure. Be careful with the example in Figure 9-19 — the last note is bent, so you need to unbend (release) and bend the note to produce the vibrato. If you want, finish off each vibrato with a little slide-off. (See the section "Getting Down with Slides," earlier in this chapter, for more information on this technique.)

Muting

To *mute* notes or chords on the guitar, you use your right or left hand to touch the strings so as to partially or completely deaden the sound. You apply muting for one of following reasons:

♪ To create a thick, chunky sound as an effect.

♪ To prevent unwanted noises from strings that you're not playing.

♪ To silence annoying commercials on TV.

Creating a thick, chunky sound as an effect

To use muting to create percussive effects, lightly lay your left hand across all six strings to prevent the strings from ringing out as you strike them. Don't press them all the way down to the fretboard (which would cause the fretted notes to sound), but press them hard enough to prevent the strings from vibrating. Then strike the strings with the pick to hear the muted sound. The tab notation indicates this type of muting by placing little *X*s on the string lines (and in place of the actual notes on the standard staff), as shown in Figure 9-25a.

Although *left-hand muting* deadens the strings completely, *right-hand muting* deadens them only partially — to whatever degree you desire. With partial muting, you can still discern the strings' pitches. To accomplish this technique, place the heel of your right hand (the side of your hand) against the bridge as you play. It may seem a little awkward at first, but don't worry. With a little practice, you can keep your hand on the bridge and still strike the strings with the pick. As you move your right hand toward the fretboard, you increase the amount of muting. That way, you can vary the degree of muting. The tab notation indicates this type of muting by placing the letters *P.M.* (for *palm mute*) above the tab staff, with a dotted line indicating how long to continue the muting, as shown in Figure 9-25b.

Figure 9-25:
Muting with
the left hand
produces a
dead thud.
Muting with
the right
hand gives
the notes
a thick,
chunky
sound.

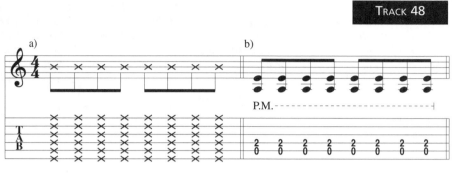

TRACK 48

Preventing unwanted string noise

As a beginner, you don't normally worry too much about preventing unwanted string noises — you're too involved in just getting your hands into a
comfortable position on the instrument. But as an experienced guitarist, you
prevent unwanted string noises all the time, sometimes without even being
aware of it. Following are some examples of how you do so:

♪ If you finger, say, the seventh fret of the 3rd string with your third finger,
your third finger leans slightly against the 2nd string, preventing it from
ringing. And as you pick the string with your right hand, your pick also
lands against the 2nd string, further preventing it from ringing.

♪ If you play an open-position D chord, and you don't want to strike the
6th string because it doesn't belong in the chord, you can bring your
left thumb up around the neck ever so slightly to touch the 6th string,
ensuring that it doesn't ring.

♪ If you play a chord that omits a middle string, you need to mute that
string with a finger of the left hand. A lot of people, for example, just
because they think it sounds better, like to omit the 5th string if they
play the open-position G chord (even though you normally fret that
string for the chord). The finger that's playing the 6th string leans
against the 5th, muting it completely.

Playing idiomatic licks by using muting

If you strum the same chord over and over, especially a barre chord in a
steady eighth-note pattern, you can create additional interest by sometimes
lifting your left hand slightly to mute out the strings. The alternation of the
normally fretted chord and the muted strings can create some interesting
syncopation effects (effects where the normal, expected accentuation of notes
is intentionally altered or disrupted). Figure 9-26 demonstrates this technique.

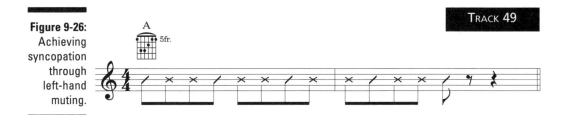

Figure 9-26:
Achieving
syncopation
through
left-hand
muting.

TRACK 49

Figure 9-27 demonstrates how to use right-hand muting in a typical hard rock or heavy-metal rhythm-guitar figure. Keep the heel of your right hand against or near the bridge as you play the notes for which the tab indicates a palm mute (*P.M.*). Don't deaden the notes so much, however, that you can't discern their pitches. Lift your hand for the accented notes (indicated by the symbol >).

TRACK 50

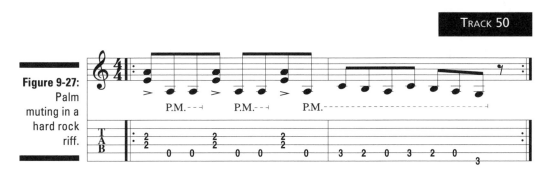

Figure 9-27:
Palm
muting in a
hard rock
riff.

On Johnny Cash records and other classic country records, you can hear the sound of muted country guitars. Figure 9-28 is based on a simple C chord, but the palm muting gives the riff a country sound.

TRACK 51

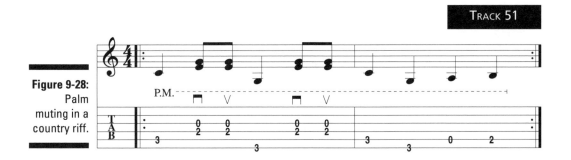

Figure 9-28:
Palm
muting in a
country riff.

Playing a Song with Varied Articulation

"The Articulate Blues" is a short solo piece, in the form of a 12-bar blues, that employs all the articulations that we discuss in this chapter. (See Chapters 6, 10, and 11 for more on the 12-bar blues form.) It combines single notes, chords, and riffs. It's an integrated style of playing that real-life guitarists use. Looking at the song's notation, you see slides, pull-offs, bends, vibratos, and a hammer-on. The tab doesn't indicate any muting, but you can use that technique any time that you want to avoid unwanted noises; in measure 5, for example, you can lean your left thumb lightly against the 6th string to prevent it from ringing while you play the A7 chord.

TRACK 52

The Articulate Blues

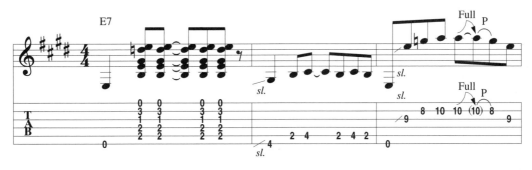

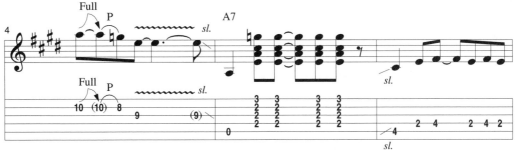

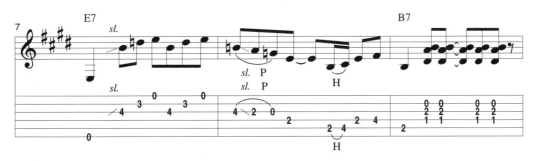

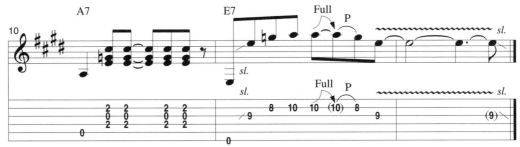

Part IV
A Cornucopia of Styles

The 5th Wave   By Rich Tennant

Elena Mendoza – master of the ostrich, penguin and flamingo guitars.

In this part . . .

Maybe you grew up with a poster of Jimi Hendrix on your wall, or maybe your tastes run more to Roy Clark. Whether your guitar hero is Stevie Ray Vaughan, Joni Mitchell, B.B. King, Bonnie Raitt, George Benson, or Andres Segovia, one thing's for sure: The guitar is a versatile instrument. In this part, you can sample some of the techniques that allow the same instrument to make so many different kinds of music.

Chapter 10

Rock

*P*laying rock 'n' roll guitar is arguably the most fun that you can have with an inanimate object in your hands. With the volume turned up and your adrenaline flowing, nothing's quite like laying down a chunking rhythm or ripping through a searing lead to screaming, adoring fans — or even to your own approving smile coming back at you from the mirror. All you need to do is figure out how to play a couple of simple patterns and you can be gyrating like Elvis, duck-walking like Chuck Berry, and windmilling like Pete Townshend in no time.

Stripped of all its bravado and showmanship, rock guitar is just like any other guitar style. You can absorb it in simple, easy steps and then practice, practice, practice until it comes naturally. After you pick up some rhythm and lead passages and get the techniques down, the real work begins: standing in front of a mirror and perfecting your moves.

Classic Rock 'n' Roll

Classic rock 'n' roll is defined here as the straightforward style pioneered by Chuck Berry and heard in the music of the early Beatles, the Rolling Stones, the Who, the Beach Boys, and others who based their sound on a solid, chord-based rhythm guitar groove. It also includes the sound of the blues-based rockers, such as Jimi Hendrix, Led Zeppelin's Jimmy Page, and Cream's Eric Clapton.

Rhythm guitar

About 99 percent of all rock guitar playing involves what's known as *"rhythm-guitar"* playing. To a guitarist, *playing rhythm* means supplying the accompaniment or backing part to a vocalist or other featured instrument. Mostly, this accompaniment involves strumming chords and, to a lesser extent, playing single-note or double-stop (two notes played at once) riffs in the lower register (on the bass strings). Listen to the verses of Chuck Berry's "Johnny B. Goode" or the Beatles' "I Saw Her Standing There" for some good, unadulterated rhythm guitar, and check out the Beatles' "Day Tripper" for low-note riffing. Listen also to almost anything by the Who's Pete Townshend, who's (no pun intended) the quintessential rock rhythm guitarist and who immortalized the "windmill" technique — the sweeping circular motion of the right hand that you can use for strumming chords. And although he's mostly known for his innovative lead work, Eddie Van Halen is one of the best rhythm guitarists in the modern-rock genre.

Open-position accompaniment

The *Chuck Berry style,* a simple *rhythm figure* (accompaniment pattern) in open position (using open strings), gains its name from the fact that almost all of Berry's songs use this pattern. Figure 10-1 shows the pattern for this style. The pattern features a movement within the chord between two notes, the fifth and sixth *degrees* (steps) of the scale (that is, of the major scale that corresponds to whatever key you're playing in). (You know the major scale; it's what you get when you play all the white keys from C to C on a piano — the familiar *do-re-mi-fa-so-la-ti-do.*) Knowing the degrees isn't important, except that musicians sometimes refer to this figure as the *5-to-6* pattern.

To play this rhythm effectively, use the following techniques:

- ♪ Anchor the first finger (at the second fret) and add the third finger (at the fourth fret) as you need it.
- ♪ Pick the notes using all downstrokes.
- ♪ Don't lift the first finger while adding the third finger.

Notice that all three chords, A, D, and E, use the exact same fingering and that the open strings make the pattern easy to play.

The 12-bar blues pattern

The 5-to-6 pattern sounds great, but to make it work for you, you need to put it into a progression. Figure 10-2 shows what's known as a *12-bar blues progression,* a common chord progression in tons of rock songs: "Johnny B. Goode," "Roll Over Beethoven," "Tutti Fruity," "At the Hop," and "Blue Suede Shoes," to name but a few. (See Chapters 6 and 11 for more information on the 12-bar blues.)

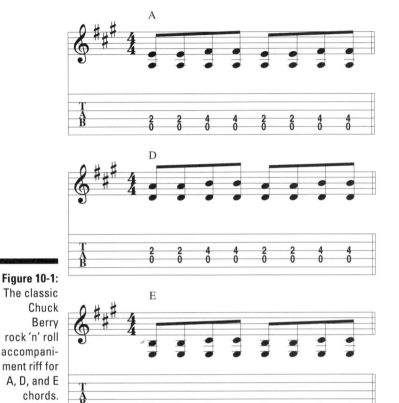

Figure 10-1:
The classic
Chuck
Berry
rock 'n' roll
accompani-
ment riff for
A, D, and E
chords.

Lead guitar

After you gain a solid feel for a basic rock 'n' roll rhythm, you may want to
try some lead guitar, which simply involves playing single notes over an
underlying accompaniment. You can play memorized *licks*, which are short,
self-contained phrases, or you can improvise by making up melodies on the
spot.

What's behind Box 1? The pentatonic minor scale

You can play lead right away by memorizing a few simple patterns on the
guitar neck, known as *boxes,* that produce instant results. Basically, guitarists memorize a finger pattern that vaguely resembles the shape of a box —
hence the term *box position* — and use notes from that pattern (in various
orders) over and over pretty much throughout a solo or a section of a solo.
In soloing over a basic chord progression, you can keep using this one
pattern even if the chords change.

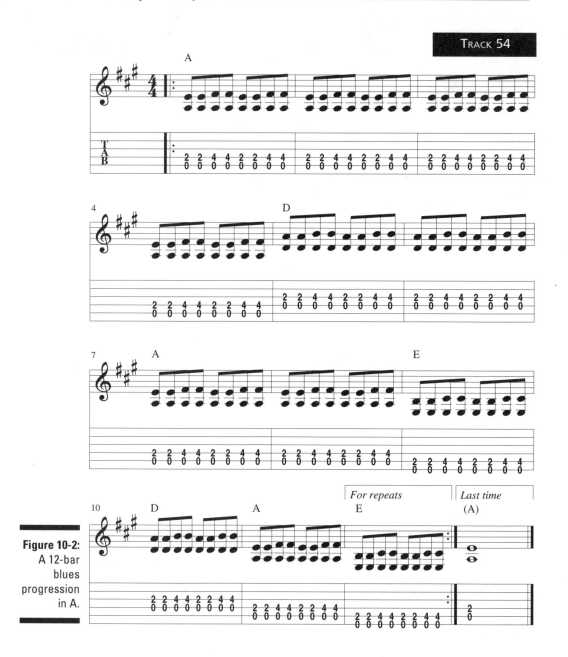

Figure 10-2:
A 12-bar
blues
progression
in A.

The first box we're going to show you is made up of notes of what's known as the *pentatonic minor scale,* and it's the most useful box for rock music (and is also the daddy of the blues boxes — see Chapter 11). You don't need to think about theory, scales, or chords — only the fingering, which you memorize. These patterns contain no "wrong notes," so by virtue of just moving your fingers around in time to a rhythm track, you can play instant rock 'n' roll lead guitar. You don't even need to add water (which is especially hazardous if you're playing an electric guitar).

The pentatonic minor scale is a five-note scale; its formula, in scale degrees (in comparison to a major scale that starts from the same note) is: 1, ♭3, 4, 5, ♭7. If the notes of a C major scale, for example, are numbered 1 – 7 — as follows: C(1), D(2), E(3), F(4), G(5), A(6), B(7) — the notes of the C pentatonic minor scale are C(1), E♭(♭3), F(4), G(5), B♭(♭7). That's the theory anyway, but for now, you're just going to memorize a pattern and use your ear — not your brain — to guide your fingers.

Figure 10-3 shows a two-octave A pentatonic minor scale in fifth position. (See Chapter 7 for more information about positions.) This example is your first "box," here called *Box I*. Notice that in the figure we show you (beneath the notes in the standard notation) the scale degree (not so important) and (beneath the tab numbers) the fingering (very important) for each note; we also show you which notes are good for bending. Memorize the fingering until you can play it in your sleep. This pattern is *essential* to know if you want to play rock guitar. Memorize it. Really do it. Play it over and over, up and down. Really. (We mean it. Honest!)

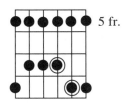

Box I

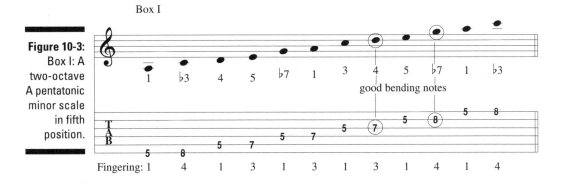

Figure 10-3:
Box I: A
two-octave
A pentatonic
minor scale
in fifth
position.

By the way, although other keys are possible, we use the key of A for all the examples in this section because the backing chords (as shown in Figure 10-2) are easy to play and the soloing notes fall around the middle of the neck, where they're comfortable to play.

Having a box to use in improvising lead guitar is what makes playing classic rock 'n' roll (or blues) so much fun; you don't need to think — you just gotta *feel*. Of course, you can't just play the five notes of the scale up and down, over and over — that would get boring very fast. You use your creativity to create licks by using the scale and adding *articulations* such as bends, slides, and hammer-ons until you have a complete solo. (See Chapter 9 for more information on articulation techniques.) We show you how to add these articulations in the following section.

Adding articulations

The box pattern shows you what to play, but articulations show you *how* to play. Articulations include *hammer-ons, pull-offs, slides, bends,* and *vibrato.* These elements are what make a solo sound like a solo, give the solo expression, and personalize it. Chapter 9 explains each articulation step by step, but we tell you how to *use* articulations to make some righteous rock 'n' roll right here.

Figure 10-4 shows a four-bar lick using notes of the pentatonic minor scale in ascending and descending order that you connect by using hammer-ons and pull-offs. Notice how much smoother and more flowing the sound is, as opposed to what you hear if you pick every note separately.

TRACK 55

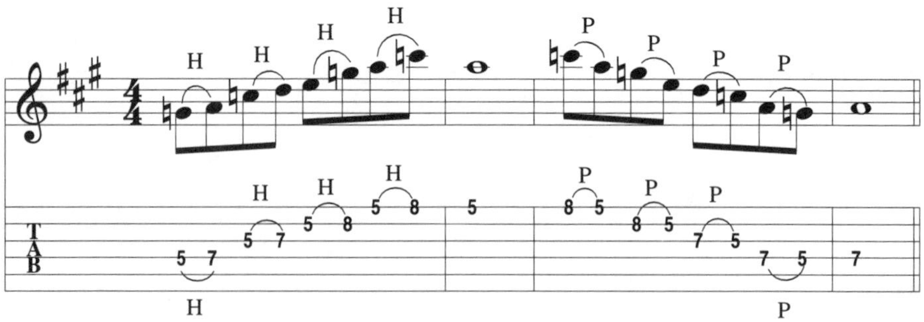

Figure 10-4: Using hammer-ons and pull-offs in Box I.

Bending notes is probably the coolest sound in lead soloing, but the trick is knowing which notes to bend and when to do so. You don't really need to think about this theoretically — it's part of the fingering pattern. Start off by bending the third-finger note on the 3rd string and the fourth-finger on the 2nd string. (See Chapter 9 for more information on how to bend a note.)

That Box I is the mother of all boxes — the grand-prize winner of the Most Popular Box contest — is no coincidence. Besides the fact that, at the fifth fret, the first finger plays every string (which provides a sturdy, anchored feel), the good notes for bending in this box all happen to fall in the right places, too.

Guitarists really like to bend notes on the 2nd and 3rd strings because the tension feels right, and they get to bend toward the ceiling — their favorite direction. And bending with the third or fourth finger enables you to add support to the bend by placing your other fingers behind the bending note (on the lower adjacent frets on the same string, as we describe in Chapter 9).

Figure 10-5 shows a typical four-bar phrase featuring the bend on the 3rd string and the bend on the 2nd string of Box I.

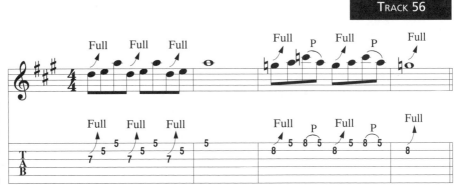

TRACK 56

Figure 10-5:
Bending the
3rd and 2nd
strings in
Box I.

Figure 10-6 shows a typical two-bar phrase featuring a double-stop bend in Box I. The note that's on the seventh fret of the 2nd string isn't part of the A pentatonic minor scale, but it sounds good anyway, and of course, you can't beat that fingering — the hands-down favorite third finger barres both notes of the double-stop.

TIP

Add some vibrato to the final note to give it some expression.

Figure 10-6:
A double-
stop bend in
Box I.

Building a solo using Box I

An improvised solo is something that you create, and nobody can show you exactly what to play. But we can show you the tools for soloing so that you can practice and get a feel for it. Beyond that, however, your personality does the talking.

For now, start out by getting the feel of playing lead over the 12-bar blues accompaniment pattern that we show you in Figure 10-2, which is incorporated into the rhythm track on the CD.

Notice that each of the phrases (in Figures 10-4, 10-5, and 10-6) that we show you in the preceding section, "Adding articulations," alternates one *active* measure (containing lots of notes) with one *static* measure (containing just one note). This alternation between activity and rest prevents monotony. Play these phrases in the order that we describe in the following instructions, and you have a ready-made 12-bar solo. (If you want, you can play the solo over and over.) To play such a solo, just follow these steps:

1. **For the first four bars of the solo, play the double-stop lick, shown in Figure 10-6 twice.**

2. **For the next four bars of the solo, play the hammer-on/pull-off lick, as shown in Figure 10-4.**

3. **For the last four bars of the solo, play the "bending the 3rd and 2nd strings" lick (refer to Figure 10-5).**

We notate the preceding steps in Figure 10-7. Playing this example gives you the feel of playing lead . . . your little solo sounds like a series of phrases — as it should.

TRACK 58

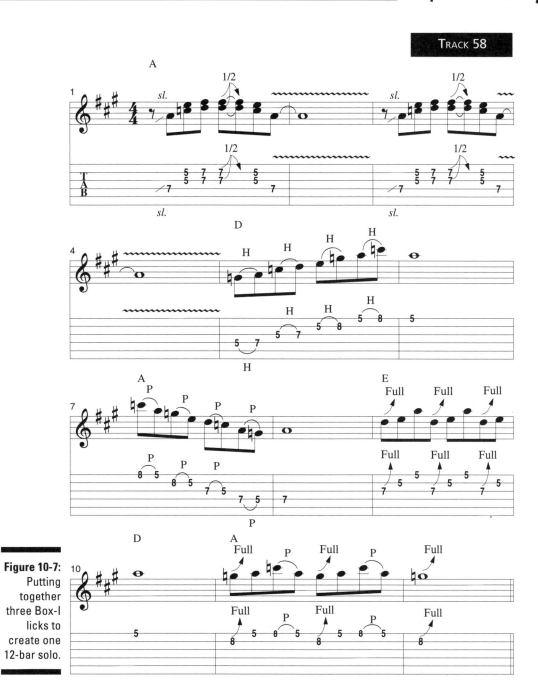

Figure 10-7:
Putting together three Box-I licks to create one 12-bar solo.

Boxes II and III

The next two boxes, which we name here *Box II* and *Box III,* don't generally use all six strings as Box I does, so you play only the notes on the top two or three strings.

Box II consists of five notes, as shown in Figure 10-8. Notice that the two notes at the top of this box (at the eighth fret) are also part of Box I, but in Box I, you play them with the pinky or third finger. This box shows notes from the A pentatonic minor scale in eighth position. Again, in the figure, we show you the scale degree and fingering for each note, and we show you which note is good for bending.

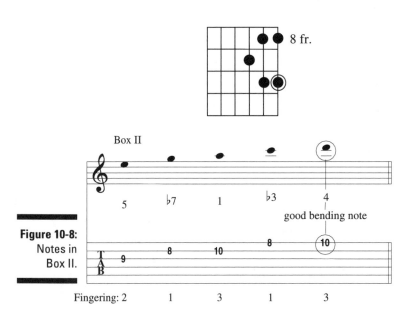

Figure 10-8: Notes in Box II.

Box II is popular because it features a good note for bending under the third finger, and that note also happens to be the highest note in the box. In playing lead, *high* is good. You can play the highest note in the box and then make it even higher by bending it up a step. This technique produces quite a dramatic effect. Try it.

In Figure 10-9 you see a typical lick using Box II notes that features a bend on the highest note of the box.

Figure 10-9:
A typical lick using Box II notes, featuring a bend on the highest note of the box.

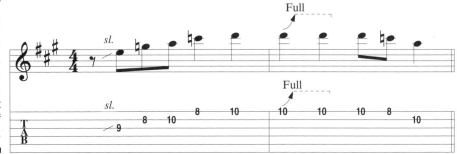

Box III is a funny one because some of its notes aren't in the A pentatonic minor scale — but guitarists use this box a lot anyway. The following list tells you all the stuff that Box III has going for it:

♪ Box III's easy to play and memorize — it's exactly like Box II but lies two frets higher on the neck.

♪ The fact that Box III has two notes — F♯ (the sixth degree) and B (the second degree) — that don't fall in the A pentatonic minor scale is a good thing. These two notes are borrowed from the parent major scale, and sometimes guitarists like to add them to the pentatonic minor scale for variety and spice. The *predominance* of notes from the pentatonic minor scale is what gives classic rock 'n' roll (and blues) its flavor — not the total exclusion of all other notes.

♪ The good note for bending in Box III falls under the third finger.

♪ The first degree of the scale, the note on which you often end a phrase, is under the first finger on the 2nd string in this box. You tend to apply vibrato to the ending note of a phrase (especially if you hold it), and this note provides an ideal finger and string on which to vibrato.

Figure 10-10 shows Box III (in 10th position for the key of A). Again we show you the scale degree and fingering for each note — and the note that's good for bending we circle again.

Often, guitarists concentrate on the 2nd and 3rd strings of Box III, as shown in Figure 10-11, which depicts a typical Box III phrase. Don't forget to vibrato that last note!

If you want to play a song in classic rock 'n' roll style right now, skip ahead to "Chuck's Duck" in the section "Playing Songs in the Rock Style," later in this chapter.

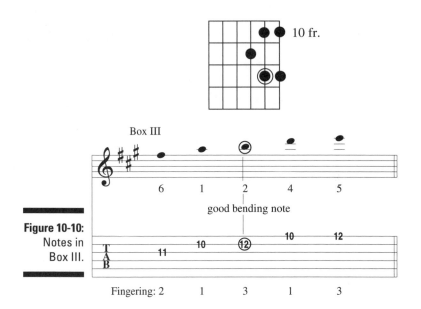

Figure 10-10:
Notes in
Box III.

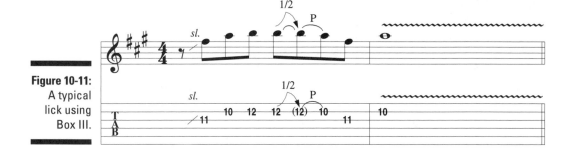

Track 60

Figure 10-11:
A typical
lick using
Box III.

Building a solo by using Boxes I, II, and III

This section simply puts together licks from the three boxes that we describe in the preceding sections. You don't need any new information; you just need to piece together what you know if you read the information we give in those sections. (If you haven't yet, we suggest that you do so now, before you try out the solo we describe here.) In other words, *after* you make the bricks, you can put them together to make a house.

Next, we show you how to build a ready-made 12-bar solo consisting of six two-bar phrases (using three boxes) that we show you in the preceding sections. Follow these steps:

1. **Play the Box I double-stop lick, as shown in Figure 10-6.**

2. **Play the Box I "bending the 3rd string" lick, as shown in the first half of Figure 10-5.**

3. **Play the Box III lick, as shown in Figure 10-11.**

4. **Play the Box I "bending the 2nd string" lick, as shown in the second half of Figure 10-5.**

5. **Play the Box II lick, as shown in Figure 10-9.**

6. **Play the Box I double-stop lick again, as shown in Figure 10-6.**

Figure 10-12 shows you the music to the preceding steps. Listen to the CD to hear how this solo sounds.

As you play this solo over and over, you get a feel for soloing with the three boxes over a 12-bar blues progression. The fun begins after you start making up your own solos. Following are some guidelines for creating your own leads:

♪ Think in terms of short phrases strung together. You can even play just one short phrase over and over, even though the backing chords change. A good way to make up a phrase is to make it a singable one. Sing a short phrase in your mind but use notes from the box.

♪ Add some articulation — especially bends, because they sound the coolest. Add vibrato to long notes that end a phrase, sometimes sliding down at the very end.

♪ Alternate between activity (lots of notes) and rest (a few notes or just one note or even silence for a few beats).

♪ Move from box to box to give your solo some variety.

Don't be inhibited or worry about making a mistake. First of all, you can't really make a mistake, because all the notes in the boxes sound good against all the chords in the backing progression. The biggest mistake that you can make is not to try soloing for fear of sounding lame. Soloing takes practice, but you gradually build confidence. If you're too shy to solo in front of people, start out by doing it along with the CD, where no one can hear you. Pretty soon, no one can stop you.

Listen to recordings to get new ideas as you become more confident in your playing. As you hear a recording, you practically already know what the guitarist is playing, because most guitarists use the same boxes, bends, vibratos, and so on that you do. Some good people to listen to for ideas are Chuck Berry, Jimi Hendrix, Eric Clapton, and Eddie Van Halen.

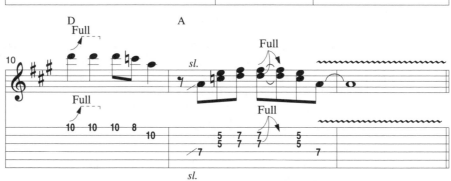

Modern Rock

Whereas classic rock 'n' roll uses simple chords, *modern-rock* music makes use of chords other than basic major, minor, and 7th chords. *Sus chords, add chords, slash chords,* and unusual chords that result from retuning your guitar are all part of the modern-rock lexicon.

Alternate tunings enable you to create entirely new colors and textures that aren't possible in standard tuning, and this sound is an especially important component of the '90s alternative movement.

Also in this section we describe another approach to lead playing in which you use the pentatonic *major* scale — a scale that's different from the bluesier pentatonic minor scale that you play mainly in classic rock 'n' roll and blues. You can use the pentatonic major scale for Southern- and country-rock leads, as well as for adding variety to blues-based leads.

"Sus" and "add" chords

Chords are often built by taking every other note of a major scale. For example, if you build a three-note chord by taking every other note of the C major scale (C-D-E-F-G-A-B), you get C-E-G (a C major chord). The chord *members* (the individual notes that make up the chord) are labeled according to their scale degrees: C is "1" (or the *root* of the chord); E is "3" (or the *third* of the chord); and G is "5" (or the *fifth* of the chord).

In *"sus"* chords, you replace the third of a chord with the fourth, as in *sus4* (which you pronounce *"suss-four"*) or sometimes with the second, as in *sus2.* The resulting sound is incomplete or unresolved but creates an interesting sound that's neither major nor minor.

An *"add"* chord is simply a basic chord (such as a major chord) to which you add an extra note. If you take a C chord and add a D note to it, for example, you have a *Cadd2* chord (with notes C-D-E-G). This chord is different from *Csus2,* which has no E. (The D took its place.)

Open-position sus chords

Although you can play sus chords as movable barre chords, the open-position ones are the easiest to play and are the ones guitarists most commonly use. Figure 10-13 shows the fingerings for a progression that uses Dsus4, Dsus2, Asus4, and Asus2 chords.

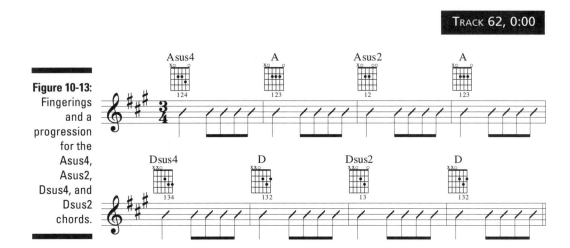

TRACK 62, 0:00

Figure 10-13: Fingerings and a progression for the Asus4, Asus2, Dsus4, and Dsus2 chords.

Open-position add chords

You can play add chords as movable barre chords, but the open-position add chords are the most common and the easiest to play. Add chords include notes in addition to the ones that you use to create basic chords. A Cadd9, for example, adds a D note (the ninth degree of the C scale) to the three notes that make up the basic C major chord.

Figure 10-14 shows the fingerings and a progression for the Cadd9 and "four-fingered" G chords. (The "four-fingered" G chord isn't an add chord, but you almost always use this G fingering before or after a Cadd9 chord.)

TRACK 62, 0:15

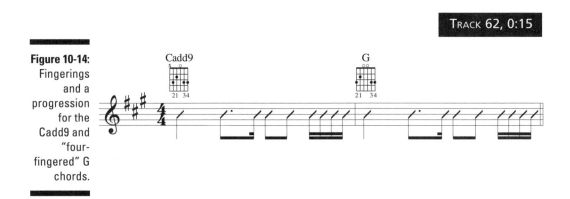

Figure 10-14: Fingerings and a progression for the Cadd9 and "four-fingered" G chords.

"Slash" chords

Slash chords are colorful, interesting chords that add spice and flavor to modern rock music. A slash chord is, simply, a chord with a slash (/) in its name, as in Am/C (which you pronounce as "A minor over C"). To the left of the slash is the chord itself. To the right of the slash is the *bass* note for that chord. Often, the lowest-pitched note of a chord — the bass note — is the *root* of the chord (the note that gives the chord its name). So if you see a chord name such as Am, you assume that the bass note is A. But the root isn't always the lowest note of a chord. In fact, any note can serve as a bass note, be it a chord tone other than the root (such as the third or fifth of the chord) or a note that isn't even a member of the chord at all. If you do have such a nonroot bass note, you indicate that bass note by placing it to the right of the slash. So Am/C means that you're playing an A minor chord — but with a C as the lowest note.

Guitarists often use slash chords in progressions where the bass line forms an ascending or descending scale. This sort of bass pattern gives interest and unity to a progression. You can hear a progression such as this one in the song "Whiter Shade of Pale," by Procol Harum. Figure 10-15 shows another progression using slash chords in this manner. To bring out the bass line, in each measure, play only the bottom note of the chord on beat 1 and then strum the chord on beats 2 and 3 (what "Bass strum strum" means).

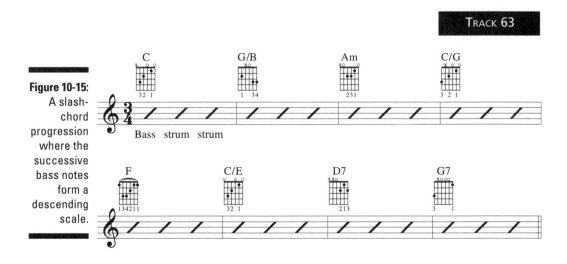

TRACK 63

Figure 10-15: A slash-chord progression where the successive bass notes form a descending scale.

The chords in Figure 10-15 show *X*s in the chord diagrams, which tell you which strings *not* to play. To keep a string from sounding, use the left-hand finger that's fretting the adjacent lower-pitched string to mute it by lightly touching it.

Alternate tunings

Modern rock guitar music of the late '80s and '90s makes frequent use of *alternate tunings* — tunings other than the standard EADGBE tuning. By using alternate tunings, you can achieve new, exciting sounds that are impossible to attain in standard tuning. Alternate tunings may also enable you to play licks or chords that are difficult to finger in standard tuning but are easy to finger in alternate tuning. But remember that, after you retune your guitar, all your familiar fingerings are out the window. That's why picking up new licks and riffs in alternate tunings by reading tab can prove especially helpful. Artists as diverse as Joni Mitchell, the Rolling Stones, and Soundgarden make extensive use of alternate tunings.

Drop D (DADGBE)

Drop-D tuning (so called because you detune, or *drop*, the low E string down to D) is the alternate tuning that's closest to standard tuning — you retune only the 6th string. To get into this tuning, lower ("drop") your 6th string until it sounds an octave lower than your 4th string. This tuning enables you to play a D or Dm chord with a low D as a root on the 6th string, giving you a full, rich sound.

Figure 10-16 shows a typical passage in drop-D tuning. It has a bluesy sound. Bend the third-fret note of the 6th string very slightly.

TRACK 64, 0:00

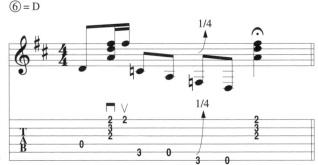

Figure 10-16:
A typical
phrase in
drop-D
tuning.

An advantage of drop-D tuning is that you can play low power chords on the bottom two strings as two-string barres, which enables you to play power chord riffs more easily and faster, as shown in Figure 10-17.

TRACK 64, 0:10

⑥ = D

Figure 10-17:
A low
power-
chord riff in
drop-D
tuning.

Open D (DADF#AD)

In an *open tuning,* the open strings form a major chord. In *open-D tuning,* they form (big surprise) a D chord. In this tuning, most of the chords that you play are nothing but open strings or one finger barring across all six strings. You can, for example, play a G chord simply by barring the entire fifth fret with your index finger. Joni Mitchell has made extensive use of this tuning in songs such as "Big Yellow Taxi."

To get into this tuning, follow these steps:

1. **Drop your 6th string until it sounds an octave lower than the open 4th string.**

2. **Drop your 3rd string so that it matches the note at the fourth fret of the 4th string.**

3. **Drop your 2nd string so that it matches the note at the third fret of the 3rd string.**

4. **Drop your 1st string so that it matches the note at the fifth fret of the 2nd string (and is one octave higher than the open 4th string).**

If you raise all six strings by one whole step (two frets) from open-D tuning, you get open-E tuning (EBEG#BE), which you can consider as essentially the same tuning as open D, because the relationship between the strings remains the same, even though the actual notes differ.

In Figure 10-18 you see a typical phrase using open-D tuning that sounds like something Joni Mitchell may have played on one of her early albums.

Another common alternate tuning that you may run across is open-G (DGDGBD, low-pitched to high), often used by Keith Richards of the Rolling Stones on such songs as "Brown Sugar" and "Start Me Up." (See Chapter 12 for an example that uses open-G tuning.)

TRACK 65

Open D tuning (low to high): D A D F# A D

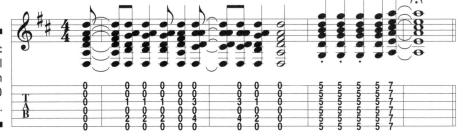

Figure 10-18:
A typical phrase in open-D tuning.

Country-rock and Southern-rock lead

Since the days of the Eagles, the Grateful Dead, and the Allman Brothers Band, country rock and Southern rock have enjoyed mainstream success and appeal. The sound of these styles falls somewhere between that of straight country music and blues, although both are too rock-oriented for straight country and yet not quite hard-edged enough to pass as blues-based rock. The slightly simpler, more major sound of these styles you can attribute to the chords the guitarists typically use and, to a greater extent, the scales that they use in the solo passages. To get a feel for this sound, listen to the music of the Byrds, the Allman Brothers Band, the Marshall Tucker Band, Pure Prairie League, Lynyrd Skynyrd, the Grateful Dead, and the Eagles, as well as that of folk rockers Jackson Browne, J.D. Souther, and Linda Ronstadt.

The Pentatonic major scale

You can define the notes of the pentatonic minor scale in any key as 1, b3, 4, 5, b7, as compared to the parent major scale. You practice the scale as a memorized box, which is just fine. The *pentatonic major scale,* on the other hand, uses the 1, 2, 3, 5, 6 notes of the parent major scale. It's a five-note scale that has no *chromatic alterations* (that is, notes that you alter by raising or lowering a half step), so it sounds just like a major scale with two notes left out. Again, the pentatonic major scale is a very useful scale because it practically makes music itself, and you can't play any "wrong" notes. (See the section "What's behind Box I? The pentatonic minor scale," earlier in this chapter, for more information on scale degrees and the pentatonic minor scale.)

After you master the pentatonic minor scale, the pentatonic major scale is a cinch. Just move the pentatonic minor scale down three frets and *voilà,* you have a pentatonic major scale. Just play the same pattern, and the notes, theory, and all that nonsense take care of themselves.

Say, for example, that you know that you play the A pentatonic minor scale at the fifth fret against a chord progression in the key of A. Well, drop that lead pattern down to the second position (where your left-hand index finger plays the notes on the second fret), and you have an A pentatonic major scale, suitable for more country/Southern-rock-based progressions. (See Chapter 7 for more information on positions.)

Figure 10-19 shows the A pentatonic major scale in second position (Box I) and fifth position (Box II), along with the scale degree and fingering for each note and the good note for bending in each box (circled). Notice that the only real difference from the pentatonic *minor* scale is the starting fret.

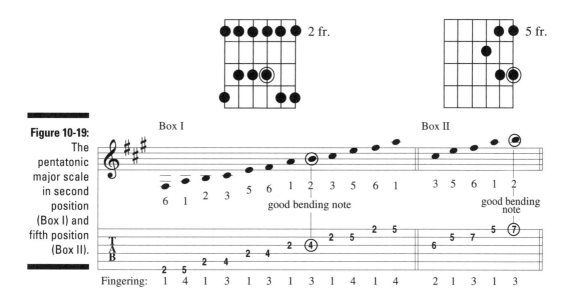

Figure 10-19: The pentatonic major scale in second position (Box I) and fifth position (Box II).

Licks that you base on the pentatonic major scale

The good news is that, as is true of the pentatonic minor scale, the pentatonic major scale has all the right things going for it: Bending notes lie in good places; you use your index finger on each string of Box I for a solid feel; and the scale is especially suitable for the use of hammer-ons, pull-offs, and slides for more expressive possibilities.

The bad news is that, although you're still in A, the fingering is shifted, so you no longer can count on landing on the usual fingers to end your solo. But we don't think that this problem is an especially big one. With just a little reorientation (and your ear), you can find good alternative notes in no time. And here's a tip: Good notes for ending a pentatonic major solo in A are the second fret of the 3rd string (Box I) and the fifth fret of the 1st string (Box I or II).

Figure 10-20 shows a four-bar lick to get you starting down that Southern country road. Notice that this lick features bends in both positions (Boxes I and II) and a slide from Box II back down to Box I to bring you home.

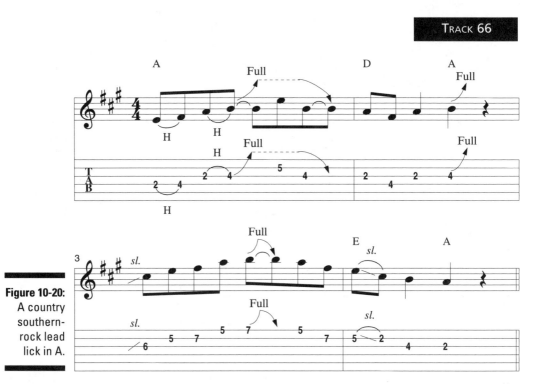

TRACK 66

Figure 10-20:
A country southern-rock lead lick in A.

If you want to play a song in the country- and Southern-rock style, skip to the following section and play "Southern Hospitality."

Playing Songs in the Rock Style

Don your tour jackets and pile into your limousines, because you're going to be rockin' out in style in this part of the chapter.

This section's songs cover two styles: the deliberate-sounding, classic rock 'n' roll of the late '50s and the easy-sounding twang of the country- and Southern-rock movements of the '70s.

About the songs

Here is some special information about the songs to help you along:

♪ **Chuck's Duck.** To play "Chuck's Duck," you need to know how to play licks with the pentatonic minor scale (see the section "What's behind Box I? The pentatonic minor scale," earlier in this chapter); how to play double-stops and double-stop bends (see Chapters 7 and 9); and how to bend down on one knee and hop across a stage without requiring arthroscopic surgery afterward.

Double-stops, the pentatonic minor scale, and continuous eighth notes characterize the classic rock 'n' roll sound. Notice the quick, bursting bends on the 3rd string in bars 6–9.

♪ **Southern Hospitality.** To play "Southern Hospitality," you need to know how to play the pentatonic major scale (see the section "The pentatonic major scale," earlier in this chapter); how to play sus, add, and slash chords (see the section "Modern Rock," earlier in this chapter); and how to grow an overly long beard and not get it caught in your guitar strings.

By taking the pentatonic minor scale and moving it down three frets, you have the pentatonic major scale, which you use to create a true country/Southern-rock sound in the styles of the Eagles, Poco, and Pure Prairie League. After playing the lead part, try the rhythm guitar part, which features sus, add, and slash chords. We've indicated the left-hand chord fingerings for you, but listen to the CD for the right-hand strumming pattern.

Chuck's Duck

(continued)

Chuck's Duck (continued)

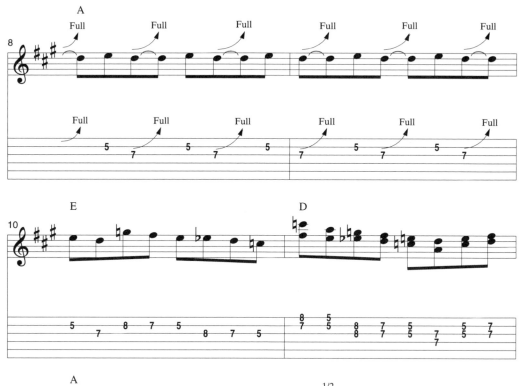

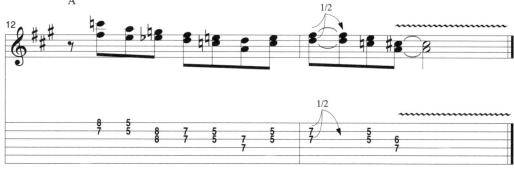

Southern Hospitality

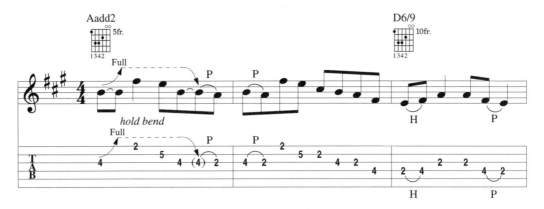

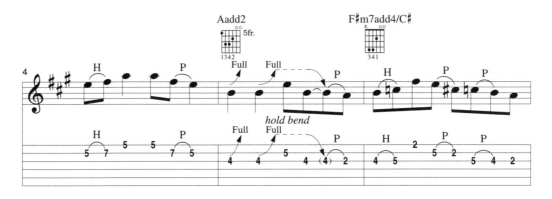

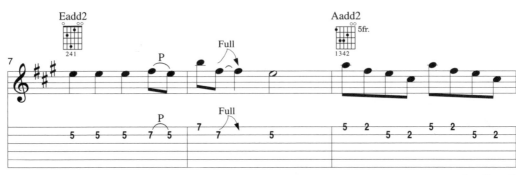

(continued)

Southern Hospitality (continued)

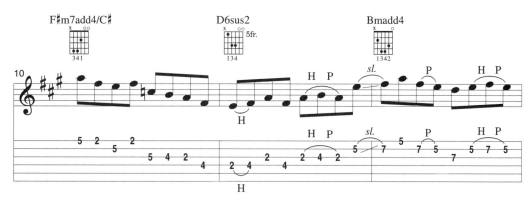

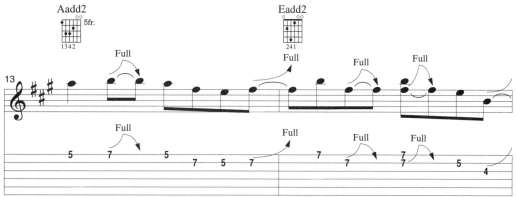

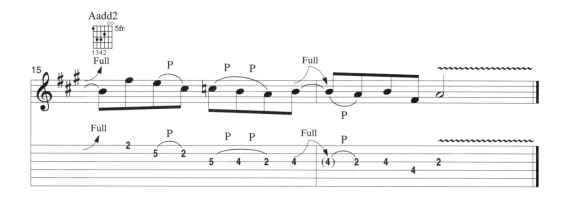

Chapter 11

Blues

· ·

In This Chapter

▶ Playing electric blues

▶ Playing acoustic blues

▶ Playing songs about heartbreak and sorrow and looking good doing it!

· ·

*B*lues is one of the most popular forms of guitar music, both for the listener and the player. And why not? Who could resist the easy rhythms, the expressive melodies, and the soulful lyrics of the blues. Not every form of music can warm your heart as the singer is lamenting his death-row plight for a murder he didn't commit while his baby runs off with his best friend. Ah, the sweet sorrow of the blues.

But before we get too sentimental, we need to explore why the blues just seems born for the guitar. One reason is that it's a relatively easy style to play on the guitar (especially if you compare it to jazz or classical music). Blues accompaniment patterns are accessible and comfortable to the hands. Blues melodies fall particularly well on the guitar's neck because of the scales the style uses and the way you tune the instrument's strings. Blues isn't technically demanding, and you play it best by ear with the heart guiding the way.

Playing great blues — following in the musical footsteps of such blues legends as B.B. King or the late Stevie Ray Vaughan — may be difficult, but playing pretty good blues right away is still fairly easy if you know the form, a couple of scales, and some simple blues moves.

Electric Blues

Electric blues is the kind of blues that all the giants of the genre play: Buddy Guy, B.B. King, Albert King, Albert Collins, Johnny Winter, and Duane Allman, among others. Electric-blues guitar playing breaks down fairly neatly into two categories: rhythm and lead.

Blues rhythm guitar

Rhythm playing is what you do whenever you're not playing lead — such as accompanying a singer or another featured instrument by playing chords, background figures, and repeated low-note riffs. Rhythm generally requires less technical proficiency than playing lead does and relies more on the guitarist's "feel" than on his technique. To put chord playing into some kind of context, you want to begin with the most popular form, or progression, in the style, the *12-bar blues.*

The 12-bar blues form

Blues and rock guitar are similar in that each leans heavily on the 12-bar blues form for song structure (see Chapter 10). Taking the key of A as an example, the 12-bar blues progression consists of four bars of A, two bars of D, two bars of A, one bar of E, one bar of D, and two bars of A. In music notation, the 12-bar blues progression looks like the example shown in Figure 11-1.

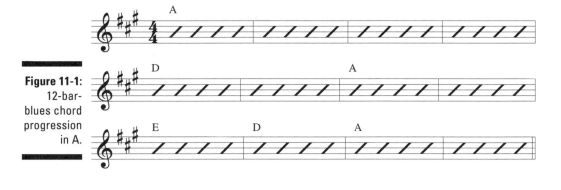

Figure 11-1: 12-bar-blues chord progression in A.

The chords that you use in Figure 11-1 (and in any common progression) are often referred to by Roman numerals. These numerals identify the chords generically rather than by key. In the key of A, for example, the A chord is *I* (Roman numeral one), the D is *IV* (four), and E is *V* (five). (You can count letter names on your fingers, starting from A, to confirm that A is I, D is IV, and E is V.) In the key of G, on the other hand, G is I, C is IV, and D is V. By using such a system, if you decide to switch keys, you can always just say, "Start playing at the IV (four) chord in bar 5." If you know which chords are I, IV, and V in that key, you're ready to play.

If you're playing your blues accompaniment by using barre chords (see Chapter 8 for more information on barre chords), you can remember which chords are which merely by their position on the neck. Say, for example, that you're playing a blues progression in A. If you make an E-based barre chord at the fifth fret (A), you're playing the I chord in A. If you switch to the A-based barre chord form at that same fret, you're now playing the IV chord, or D. Move that same A-based barre two frets higher on the neck — to the seventh fret — and you're playing the V chord, E. See how easy playing the blues can be! Use those same positions anywhere on the neck — an E-based barre chord at any fret, following it with an A-based barre chord at the same fret, and moving that barre up two frets — and you know the I-IV-V progression for whatever key goes with the starting fret.

Two important variations of the 12-bar blues form involve the *quick IV* and the *turnaround*. In the quick IV (still using the key of A as an example), you substitute a D (IV) chord for A (I) in bar 2. Ordinarily, you must wait until bar 5 to play the IV chord, so switching to it in bar 2 feels pretty quick, hence the name. A turnaround is a V chord that you play on the last bar (bar 12) instead of a I chord. This change helps draw the music back to the I chord of the first bar, "turning the progression around" to bar 1. Blues guitarists base many lead licks just on the turnaround at the progression's end.

Blues lyrics and structure

In dealing with the blues, one good way to keep the song's structure straight is to think of the 12-bar progression as three four-bar phrases. You can do so because the lyrics of a typical blues song usually fall in an AAB form (which means that the first two sections of the song are the same and the third one is different), with each of the three sections taking up four bars. A typical blues song, for example, may go something like the following:

First phrase: "I woke up this morning; I was feeling mighty bad." This phrase you sing over the first four bars of the 12-bar progression (I, I, I, I or I, IV, I, I for the quick IV variation).

Second phrase: "I woke up this morning; I was feeling mighty bad." This phrase repeats the same lyrics that you sing in the first phrase, and you sing it over the second four bars of the progression (IV, IV, I, I).

Third phrase: "I can't stop thinking I lost the best gal I ever had." This phrase is different from the first two phrases, and you sing it over the last four bars of the progression (V, IV, I, I — or V, IV, I, V if you're going to repeat).

Usually, you sing each vocal phrase within the first two measures of the four-bar phrase, giving the instrumentalist (maybe even you!) a chance to play some cool blues licks during measures 3 and 4 of each phrase, which gives the song a kind of question-answer feeling. But even if you're not using a vocalist on a particular song, the instrumentalists can still play the tune with this two-bar plus two-bar, question-answer mentality in each four-bar phrase.

Try substituting 7th or 9th chords (A7, D9, or E9, for example) for the basic I-IV-V chords to make the music sound even bluesier (see Chapters 6 and 8).

Triplet feel

Blues relies heavily on a rhythmic feel known as a *triplet feel* (sometimes called a *shuffle feel* or a *swing feel*). In a triplet feel, you divide each beat into three parts (instead of the normal two). You can hear this feel on the CD recording of Figure11-2, but here's a good way to get an understanding of the difference between straight feel and triplet feel. Recite each of the following phrases out loud, snapping your fingers on each capitalized syllable. (Make sure that you snap your fingers — it's important!)

1. **TWIN**-kle **TWIN**-kle **LIT**-tle **STAR**.

That's a straight feel — each finger snap is a beat, and each beat you divide into two parts.

2. **FOL**-low the **YEL**-low brick **ROAD**.

That's a triplet feel — each finger snap is a beat, and each beat you divide into three parts. Because lots of blues uses a triplet feel, you need to know how to play a 12-bar blues accompaniment figure with that feel.

Figure 11-2 shows you an accompaniment figure (here with the "quick IV" variation) consisting of nothing more than strummed chords in a triplet rhythm. Typically, the last bar of a blues song uses a progression in which you approach the final chord from one fret above or below it (see measure 13). See the chord diagrams on the figure for the fingerings of the 9th chords in the song.

If you know how to play a rock boogie-woogie accompaniment figure (in Chuck Berry-style — see Chapter 10), you should have no trouble at all playing Figure 11-3, which is actually the same boogie accompaniment figure (but with the "quick IV" variation), except that you play it in a triplet feel. Again, you approach the last chord from a fret above.

By the way, in the music, the equivalency ($\sqrt{}$ = $\sqrt{}$ $\sqrt{}$) that appears next to the words "Triplet feel" indicates that you should substitute triplet (or shuffle) eighths for straight eighth notes. In triplet eighths, you hold the first note of each beat a little longer than the second.

TRACK 69

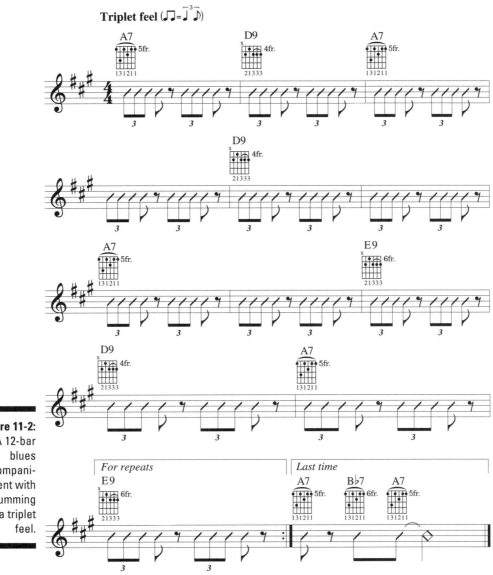

Figure 11-2:
A 12-bar blues accompaniment with strumming in a triplet feel.

TRACK 70

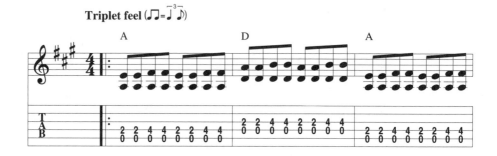

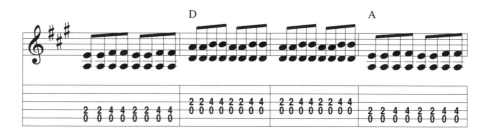

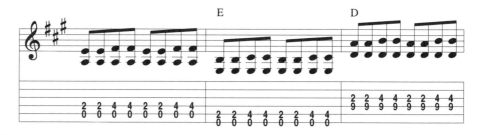

Figure 11-3:
A 12-bar blues accompaniment with a boogie riff in triplet feel.

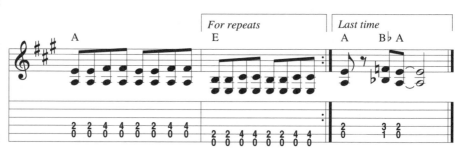

Blues lead guitar

Blues lead is the single-note melodic line, consisting of a mixture of composed lines and improvised phrases. A great lead solo includes both these elements in one seamless, inspired whole.

The boxes

Blues guitarists improvise mostly by using "boxes" — just as rock guitarists do. A *box* is a fingerboard pattern — usually outlining a pentatonic minor scale — that vaguely resembles the shape of a box. (See Chapter 10 for more information on pentatonic minor scales and boxes.) By using notes in the box, you can improvise lead lines that automatically sound good as you play them over a 12-bar blues accompaniment.

You may already know how to use boxes to play rock 'n' roll lead guitar, which employs the same scales and chords as blues. (And we describe these in Chapter 10.) If so, you should have no trouble understanding the example in Figure 11-4, which shows three boxes that you can use for soloing in the key of A; we circle the notes that are good for bending. (For more information on bending, see Chapter 9.)

Figure 11-4:
Grid diagrams for Boxes I, II, and III.

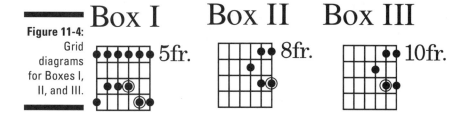

Figure 11-5 shows two new boxes that you can use for blues soloing. The one we're calling "Box IV" (because no standard names or numberings exist for the boxes) is similar to Box III, except that we move it up three frets to the 13th position (for the key of A) and we eliminate the two notes on the 1st string. Again, we circle the good note for bending. Play the notes in this box by using your second finger on the 3rd string and your first and third fingers on the 2nd string.

Figure 11-5:
Grid diagrams for Boxes IV and V.

Box IV 13fr.

Box V 3fr.

Box V is sometimes thought of as a lower extension of Box I. Use your first and third fingers to play the notes on both strings.

You may notice that Box I covers all six strings while the other boxes cover only two or three strings. Actually, what we're showing you in Boxes II through V are *partial boxes*. Full-box versions (using all six strings) exist for these, but in the full versions, you end up with some "bad" or uncomfortable fingerings, such as playing the important notes with fingers 2 and 4 instead of the stronger 1 and 3 or having the good notes for bending end up under a bad finger for bending. That's why most guitarists use just the partial boxes, as shown in these figures.

If you know how to play typical licks by using Boxes I, II, and III (see Chapter 10), the lick in Figure 11-6 that uses Box IV should give you no trouble. Play with a triplet feel, and make sure that you apply vibrato to the last note for a real blues effect. (See Chapter 9 for more information about vibrato.) Notice how the bend falls under the third finger — the favorite finger for bending.

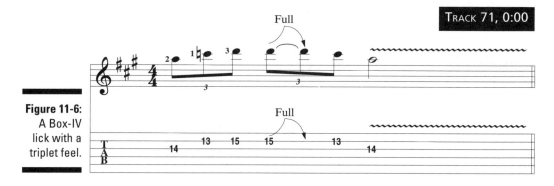

TRACK 71, 0:00

Figure 11-6:
A Box-IV
lick with a
triplet feel.

Figure 11-7 shows a typical lick that uses Box V. A common blues technique is to *slide* on the 5th string (third finger) back and forth between Box V and Box I. (See Chapter 9 for more information about slides.) See how nicely all the notes fall under the first and third fingers, even as you move between the boxes.

Adding the flatted fifth and the major third

The pentatonic minor scale produces good blues notes, but adding two more notes gives you an even richer sonic palette of note choices. The flatted fifth and the major third help give more definition to a line by introducing a *dissonant,* or tension-filled, note (the flatted fifth) and another note (the major third) that reinforces the major quality of the I chord.

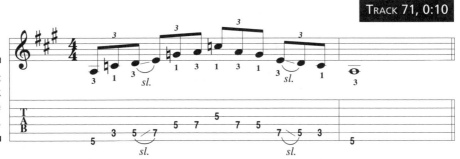

TRACK 71, 0:10

Figure 11-7:
A Box-V lick
with a slide
up to Box I.

A *flatted fifth* is a note that's one half step (or one fret) lower than the regular fifth of a scale. In the A pentatonic minor scale, for example, the E note is the *fifth*. (Count letter names from A to E on your fingers to confirm that E is five notes above A.) The E♭ note is therefore the *flatted fifth*. A *major third* is a note that's one half step (or one fret) higher than the regular (minor) third of a pentatonic minor scale. In the A pentatonic minor scale, for example, the C note is the *minor third*. The C♯ note is the *major third*. (See Appendix A for more information on sharps and flats.)

The flatted fifth and the blues scale

The five-note pentatonic scale works great for basic blues, but for a *really* funky, crying sound, toss in the *flat-five* note (E♭ in the key of A) now and then. Adding the flat-five note to the pentatonic scale creates the six-note *blues scale*. The flat five is particularly dissonant but adds some spice to the more "vanilla-sounding" quality of the straight pentatonic minor scale. But as with any spice, whether salt, fennel, or a flat five, add it sparingly and judiciously.

Boxes I, II, and IV, as shown in Figure 11-8, consist of notes from the pentatonic minor scale. The notes in circles indicate the added E♭ — the ♭5 (flat five) — this time and not the bending notes. Box I shows the complete (two-octave) A blues scale in fifth position, while Boxes II and IV show partial blues scales that are good to use for improvising.

Figure 11-8:
Grid
showing the
addition of
the flat five
(♭5) to
Boxes I, II,
and IV.

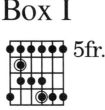

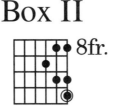

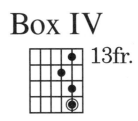

Figure 11-9 shows a typical Box-I blues lick using the blues scale. Notice that you can produce the E♭ in two ways — by playing it at the eighth fret of the 3rd string or by bending the *seventh*-fret note (the typical good note for bending in Box I) up a half step.

Figures 11-10 and 11-11 show a typical blues-scale lick, first using Box II and then (the same lick) using Box IV. Again, you play the ♭5 both straight and as a bent note (with the third finger) in each position.

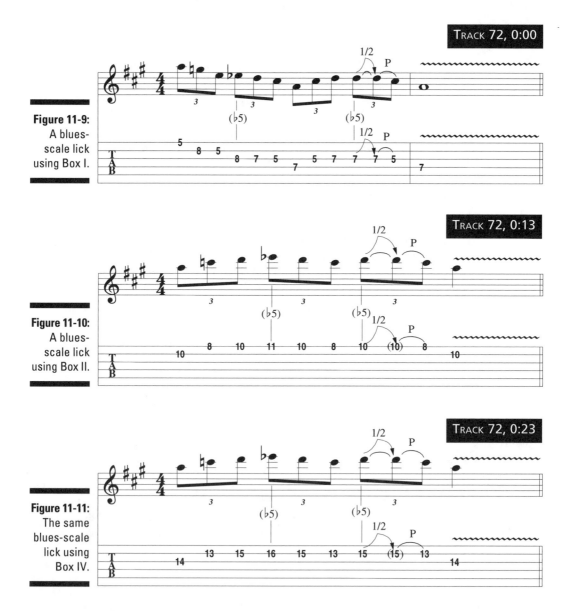

Track 72, 0:00

Figure 11-9: A blues-scale lick using Box I.

Track 72, 0:13

Figure 11-10: A blues-scale lick using Box II.

Track 72, 0:23

Figure 11-11: The same blues-scale lick using Box IV.

The major third

Another note that blues players commonly add to the pentatonic minor or blues scale is the major third. You can think of this note as one that you "borrow" from the pentatonic major scale or from the full major scale. In the key of A, the added major third is C♯, and Figure 11-12 shows where it falls in Box I (the note in the circle). It's the only note that you play with your second finger if you're using Box I (unless you're also using the flat five that we describe in the preceding section).

Figure 11-12:
Grid showing the addition of the major third to Box I.

Box I

5fr.

Very often, you hammer-on the major third from the minor third a fret below it, as shown in Figure 11-13.

TRACK 73, 0:00

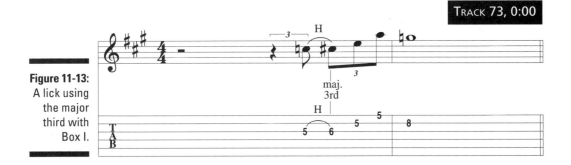

Figure 11-13:
A lick using the major third with Box I.

Even though you use the pentatonic *minor* scale for soloing, the *key* of a typical blues song is *major* (as in A major) because the rhythm guitarist plays *major* background chords (which contain major thirds). In double-stop licks, often heard in the music of Chuck Berry and the Beach Boys, the end of a descending lead lick usually contains a major third to help establish the key as major rather than minor, as shown in Figure 11-14.

TRACK 73, 0:10

Figure 11-14:
A double-stop riff using the major third with Box I.

Phrasing

Although blues soloing uses many of the same techniques, scales, chords, and boxes as rock soloing does, the two styles are probably the most different in the area of *phrasing*. Lots of steady-flowing eighth notes often characterize rock soloing (think of the solo to "Johnny B Goode"). But blues soloing (think B.B. King) more often employs phrases that are shorter and sparser (more separated) than those of rock. (See Appendix A for more information on eighth notes.)

In a typical blues melody, you may hear a very short phrase, some empty space, and then a repetition of the same phrase. Usually, these short phrases have a vocal quality to them in that they're expressive, often conveying pain or sorrow. Sometimes, if the guitarist is also the singer, the vocal phrases and the guitar phrases are practically one and the same.

Figure 11-15 shows you a short passage that demonstrates the short-phrase concept. Notice how the same figure (the pull-off from the eighth fret to the fifth) sounds good but different if you play it against a different chord (first against A7 and then D7). Repeating a figure after the chord changes is a typical blues technique.

TRACK 74

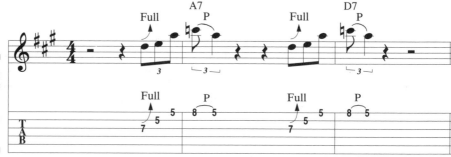

Figure 11-15:
A riff showing typical blues phrasing.

Blues moves

Figure 11-16 shows four typical *blues moves*. A blues move is nothing more than a short, cool-sounding *lick* (that is, a self-contained musical phrase). The CD demonstrates how these moves sound if you play them in the context of a progression.

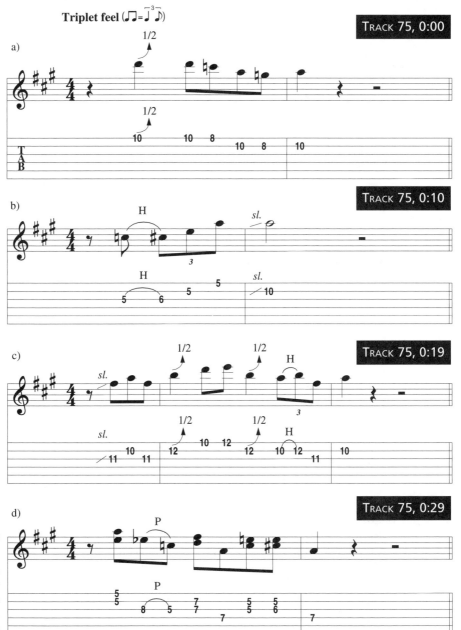

Figure 11-16: Riffs showing four typical blues moves.

Blues moves are easy to create because they're so short. Make up your own and see how they sound as you play them over the 12-bar blues progressions shown in Figures 11-2 and 11-3.

If you want to play an electric blues song right now by using the blues moves of Figure 11-11, skip ahead to "Chicago Shuffle" in the section "Playing Blues Songs," later in this chapter.

Acoustic Blues

Blues guitar today is most often heard on electric guitar. B.B. King, Buddy Guy, Muddy Waters, Johnny Winter, Stevie Ray Vaughan, Albert King, Albert Collins, and Eric Clapton, for example, are all known for their electric guitar playing. But blues started out as an acoustic form, played fingerstyle, and still evokes images of the rural Mississippi Delta, where it originated and flourished.

General concepts

Although you play electric blues in various keys by using movable boxes (see the section "Blues lead guitar," earlier in this chapter), you play acoustic blues (sometimes called *Delta Blues*) in open position (usually playing low on the neck and using a combination of open strings and fretted notes), almost always in the key of E.

Steady bass with open-position pentatonic minor

The basic idea behind acoustic blues is that you're playing a solo that incorporates both the melody (which you often improvise) and the accompaniment at the same time. This method is just opposite that of electric blues, where one guitarist plays the melody (the lead) while another guitarist plays the accompaniment (the rhythm).

The essence of the style is as follows: Your thumb plays the *root* of each chord (the note the chord is named after) in steady quarter notes on the bass strings. (See Appendix A for more information on quarter notes.) Meanwhile, your fingers play melody notes that you take from the E pentatonic minor scale or the E blues scale, in open position. (For more information on the pentatonic minor scale and the blues scale, see Chapter 10 and the section "Blues lead guitar," earlier in this chapter.) You can use either scale or mix them up. Figure 11-17 represents a grid showing the E pentatonic minor/E blues scales in open position. (Without the circled notes, you have the E pentatonic minor scale; with the circled notes — the flat-five (♭5) notes, or B♭ in this key — you have the E blues scale.)

Notice that the scale in Figure 11-17 is actually Box I in open position! For the left-hand fingering, play in first position — that is, use the same finger number as the fret number. Because your thumb is usually steadily plucking away at the low E and A strings, you usually take your melody notes from D, G, B, and high E strings, which are the four highest-pitched strings.

Figure 11-17:
Grid showing the open-position E pentatonic minor and E blues scales.

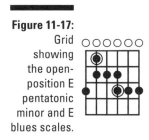

Figure 11-18 shows a simple exercise that demonstrates the basic acoustic blues style by using the E blues scale, first descending and then ascending. Make sure that you play in a triplet feel, as on the CD. You can see how you can play both the melody and accompaniment at the same time — and doing so isn't even difficult. That's because the bass part is so easy to play!

TRACK 76

Figure 11-18:
Combining steady bass notes with treble notes from the E blues scale.

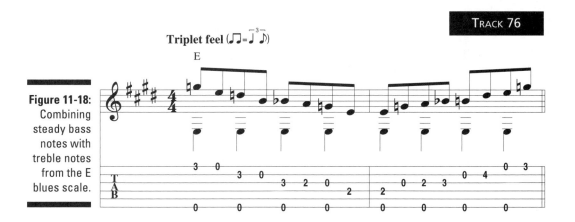

Repetition

An important aspect of acoustic blues (and electric, too) is *repetition*. This idea involves a *motive* (a short musical phrase) that you repeat, sometimes once, sometimes over and over. In acoustic blues, you can achieve this effect in one of the following two ways:

♪ You repeat a phrase *at the same pitch* as the background chord changes. In Figure 11-19, the chord changes from E to A. (The different bass notes that the thumb plays imply the chord change.) The motive, however, repeats at the same pitch. Notice how the same notes sound different if you play them against a different chord (even an implied one). This technique is a blues staple.

♪ You repeat a phrase *at a different pitch* as the background chord changes. If you use this technique, the relationship between the melody and background chord stays the same. This type of repetition is shown in Figure 11-20. Barre the fifth fret to play the A chord in the second measure. (We cover barre chords in Chapter 8.) By the way, notice that, for each chord, you use a hammer-on to move from the minor third to the major third. This technique is common in the acoustic-blues style. (See Chapter 9 for more information about hammer-ons.)

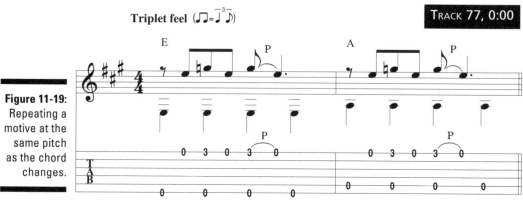

Figure 11-19: Repeating a motive at the same pitch as the chord changes.

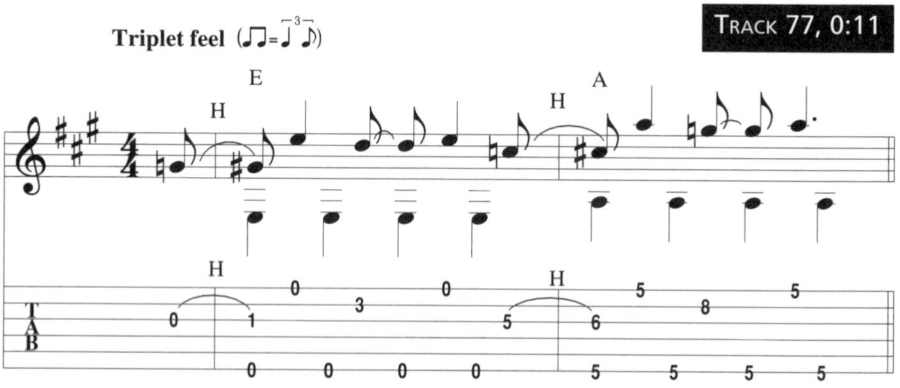

Figure 11-20: Moving a motive to a new pitch as the chord changes.

Specific techniques

You can use two simple techniques to give your blues playing more variety. Alternating the *texture* (that is, combining different musical patterns, such as playing one bar of rhythm and then a bar of lead) creates an unexpected, less homogeneous sound. Combining open strings with fretted ones creates some unusual results by enabling some notes to ring while others move melodically.

Alternation

Alternation refers to the practice of playing the melody and bass parts one at a time, alternating, instead of at the same time. Instead of having the thumb constantly play bass notes while the fingers simultaneously play melody notes, you can sometimes play just melody notes or just bass notes. This technique not only adds variety to the music's texture, but it also enables you (because *all* your fingers are available) to play some cooler-sounding, more-difficult, trickier licks that may otherwise be impossible.

Figure 11-21 shows a phrase that begins with only the melody (which you play in double-stops, a common acoustic blues technique) and ends with only bass (playing a boogie groove). You can see how the bass part — instead of playing merely quarter notes on the low roots — becomes more elaborate if you don't need to worry about melody notes. (See Chapter 7 for more information about double-stops.)

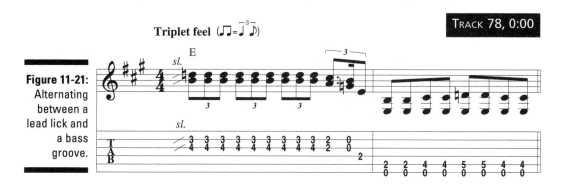

Figure 11-21: Alternating between a lead lick and a bass groove.

An effective and fancy little trick is to play an actual bass lick (that is, a bass *melody* instead of just a boogie figure) in an *alternation* scheme. The example in Figure 11-22 begins like that of Figure 11-21. That's the melody's turn in the alternation scheme. Then, in bar 2, the bass part takes its turn, so you can go to town with an exciting bass lick. Typically, these bass licks use notes of the E pentatonic minor (or E blues) scale with some major thirds (on the fourth fret of the 6th string) and major sixths (on the fourth fret of the 5th string) thrown in.

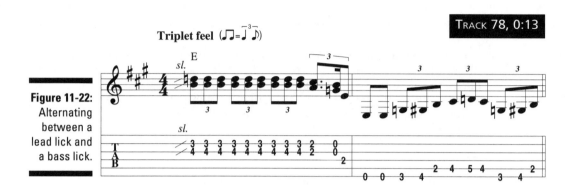

Figure 11-22:
Alternating
between a
lead lick and
a bass lick.

Open-string/fretted-string combinations

Another important acoustic-blues technique is alternating between an open string and a fretted note (on an adjacent string) that's the same pitch or a nearby pitch. You usually play this technique on the treble strings, but you can play it in the bass part as well.

In the example shown in Figure 11-23, you play the first E on the 2nd string (a fretted note); next, you play the E on the 1st string (an open note) and then you play it back on the 2nd string again. The open E then recurs after you play some nearby notes on the 2nd string. Then the same idea occurs with the Bs on the fretted 3rd and open 2nd strings. Measure 2 (with the bass part playing alone) illustrates the same idea in a bass-part setting. On beats 3 and 4, the open D on the 4th string alternates with the 5th-string D and nearby notes.

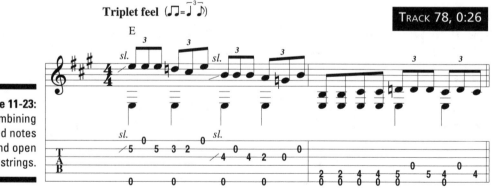

Figure 11-23:
Combining
fretted notes
and open
strings.

Turnarounds

In a typical acoustic blues solo, you play the 12-bar blues progression over and over; otherwise, your entire solo ends up very, very short. Ordinarily, as you get to the end (bars 11 and 12) each time through, you play a fancy little lick known as a *turnaround lick* that's designed to both punctuate the ending and set you up to go back (or turn around) to bar 1 again.

In a broad sense, if you're in the key of E, the turnaround puts you on some kind of B or B7 chord (because that chord best leads back to the E chord — the chord in bar 1 of the next time through). But if you simply play an E7 chord in bar 11 and a B7 in bar 12, you miss out on a world of musical delights, as the following examples demonstrate.

Slide guitar

Slide guitar is an important addition to blues-guitar technique. In playing slide, you don't use your left hand to fret the guitar by pressing the strings to the fretboard, as you normally do. Instead, you hold a metal or glass bar (the *slide*) over the neck and *stop* the strings (shorten their vibrating length) by pressing the slide lightly against the strings at a given fret. To play in tune, you must position the slide directly over the fret wire itself, not behind it as you do in normal fretting.

For the slides themselves, you can use anything from the neck of a wine bottle to a medicine bottle (the cough medicine Corrocidin made the ideal vessel and was a favorite of Duane Allman's), to a small length of brass pipe. The back edge of a knife works in a pinch too. Today, specially made glass and brass slides come in various diameters to accommodate different finger sizes. Most people usually wear the slide on the ring finger or pinkie, which leaves the other fingers free for fretting. The slide material itself determines the weight and tone, and whether you choose a heavier or lighter slide is a subjective matter.

Because the slide lays across the strings in a straight line, playing chords where the notes are on different frets becomes rather difficult. Many guitarists solve this problem by tuning the guitar to an open tuning, such as G or D. (See Chapter 10 for more information on open tunings.) Many slide-blues greats used (or still use) open tunings. Robert Johnson played in open G; Duane Allman played in open D or E; and Bonnie Raitt plays in open A.

The quality of lead guitar becomes sustained, expressive, and vocal-like if you play with a slide. Because the slide rides on top of the strings and doesn't use the frets for its pitches, the response is more like that of a violin or a voice, where the pitch change is smooth and continuous as opposed to the more "detached" sound that results from normal fretting. As you listen to the great slide artists, listen especially to their *phrasing*. That's the best way to appreciate slide guitar's emotional power — in the expressive execution of the melodic line.

Figure 11-24 shows four commonly played acoustic blues turnarounds. Notice that most turnarounds employ some kind of *chromatically moving line* (that is, one that's moving by half steps).

Figure 11-24: Four typical turnarounds in E.

If you feel pretty good about playing the figures in the "Acoustic Blues" section, you are ready to play the song "Mississippi Mud," in the following section. Get down with your bad self!

Playing Blues Songs

B.B. King once said, "I have a right to sing the blues," and if you're ready to try playing a couple of authentic blues songs, so do you! The two songs in this section employ many of the techniques that we present throughout the chapter. As you first attempt to play these pieces, don't try to rush the process. In blues, feel comes before technique, and the best way to develop a feel is to keep the tempo slow and manageable while you work your way up. Focus on your feel and let the technique catch up on its own. It always does — we promise.

About the songs

Here is some special information about the songs to help you along:

♪ **Chicago Shuffle.** To play this song, you need to know how to play single-note blues lines (see the section "Blues lead guitar," earlier in this chapter); how to piece together separate blues moves into a cohesive whole (see the section "Blues moves," earlier in this chapter); and how to boogie like your back ain't got no bone.

The lead guitar in this piece uses several devices common to blues lead playing: short phrases with wide spaces between them, repetition, the blues scale, double-stops, and a turnaround at the end. (For more information on these techniques, see the earlier sections of this chapter.) The rhythm part (not notated here, except by chord names) is the same pattern that you use in Figure 11-3 (also not notated there either, but you can hear it on the CD). Notice that this particular progression includes a "quick IV."

♪ **Mississippi Mud.** To play this song, you need to know how to play an independent bass line with the thumb working against a melody that you play with the fingers (see the section "Steady bass with open-position pentatonic minor," earlier in this chapter); how to alternate textures smoothly (see the section "Alternation," earlier in this chapter); how to play a turnaround; and how to get your mojo workin'.

This song features many of the acoustics blues concepts covered throughout this chapter: E pentatonic minor scale in open position, steady bass notes, alternation (the bass plays alone in measure 2, for example), repetition of a lick at the same pitch even though the background chord changes (measure 5), fretted note/open string combination (measure 9), and a turnaround lick (measures 11–12).

Chicago Shuffle

TRACK 81

Mississippi Mud

Chapter 12

Folk

*I*n terms of a guitar style, "folk" means a lot more today than just playing "Jimmy Crack Corn" around a campfire with a bunch of doleful cowboys and a cook named "Stumpy" wheezing on an out-of-tune harmonica. Although folk guitar did enjoy a humble beginning as a plaintive strumming style to accompany simple songs, it's since evolved as a popular music category all its own and now includes a wide variety of styles and its own brand of virtuosity.

Folk guitar has progressed from cowboy ditties of the 19th century through Appalachian songs and ballads in the '30s and '40s, to the hits of early country artists such as Jimmie Rodgers, Hank Williams, and Johnny Cash, to the rockabilly of the late-'50s. In the '60s, folk music enjoyed a popular revival, beginning with the Kingston Trio and continuing all the way through the heyday of Bob Dylan, Joan Baez, and Peter, Paul, and Mary.

From there, folk guitar crossed over into the mainstream, via the sophisticated pop-folk stylings of John Denver, James Taylor, Joni Mitchell, and Crosby, Stills, and Nash.

Playing Fingerstyle

Folk music favors *fingerstyle* playing (a style in which you pluck the strings with your right-hand fingers instead of a pick). Think of the songs of Peter, Paul, and Mary ("Puff the Magic Dragon"), Bob Dylan ("Don't Think Twice, It's Alright"), and Arlo Guthrie ("Alice's Restaurant"), and you can hear the easy, rolling patterns that the fingers produce in the accompaniment.

But you also hear fingerstyle in rock (the Beatles' "Blackbird," Kansas's "Dust in the Wind," and the intro to Led Zeppelin's "Stairway to Heaven"), country, and blues. And, of course, you play all classical guitar music fingerstyle.

Fingerstyle playing opens a world of musical possibilities that the pick simply can't deliver. You can play two or more lines simultaneously, for example, while fingerpicking: The thumb plays a bass line while the fingers play a melody. Then you can use other fingers to add inner voices (filler or background notes on the middle strings, between the melody and bass) for an even fuller and more complex sound.

Fingerstyle technique

In fingerstyle guitar, you pluck the strings with the individual right-hand fingers instead of striking them with the pick. In most cases, you play the strings one at a time, in some form of repeated pattern, while your left hand holds down a chord. Typically, the thumb, plucking downward, plays the low (bass) strings, and the fingers, plucking upward, play the high strings (one finger per string).

After you strike each note, move your finger away so as not to rest against the adjacent string. This technique enables all the strings to ring out and produce chords instead of merely a succession of individual notes. In this style, you play the guitar much as you would a harp, except that playing this way on a guitar looks so much cooler than it does on a harp.

Right-hand position

As you play with the fingers, you want to rotate your right hand slightly so that the fingers are more or less perpendicular to the strings. Figure 12-1 shows a before-and-after picture of the right hand in the normal, pick-holding position and then in a rotated, perpendicular placement better suited to fingerstyle playing.

By keeping your right hand perpendicular to the strings, you meet them dead-on — as opposed to at an angle if you keep your hand unrotated and in line with the arm. Incidentally, this position represents the same perpendicular approach that you use for playing classical guitar. (See Chapter 13 for more information about right-hand position.)

You can do what many guitarists do and grow your right-hand fingernails a little long so that, as you pluck, you produce a brighter or louder sound. If you want a super-bright sound, use fingerpicks — plastic or metal devices that you actually wear on your thumb and fingers — or adhere acrylic nails to your own natural nails (a common procedure at any nail salon and an emergency measure that many classical guitarists use if they break a nail just before a concert).

Figure 12-1: The photo on the top shows the right hand in pick position; the photo on the bottom shows the right hand in fingerstyle position.

The music notation in this book indicates the right-hand fingers by the letters *p* (thumb), *i* (index), *m* (middle), and *a* (ring). This scheme comes from classical guitar notation. The letters *p, i, m,* and *a* are the first letters of the Spanish words for the fingers (classical guitar being *very* big in Spain): *pulgar* (thumb), *indice* (index), *medio* (middle), and *anular* (ring). Sometimes you see the English equivalents of *t, i, m,* and *r*. You don't ordinarily use the little finger of the right hand in fingerstyle playing.

Using the Capo

A *capo* is a device that clamps down across the fingerboard at a particular fret. Capos can operate by means of elastic, springs, or even threaded bolts, but they all serve the same purpose — they shorten the length of all the strings at the same time, creating, in effect, a new nut. All the "open" strings now play in higher pitches than they do without the capo.

How much higher? One half step for each fret. If you place the capo at the third fret, for example — and that's actually just *before* the third fret (toward the tuning pegs), *not* directly over the third metal fret wire — the open E strings become Gs (three half steps higher in pitch than E). All the strings become correspondingly higher in pitch as well — B becomes D; G becomes B♭; D becomes F; and A becomes C. By the way, you can't play anything below the capo — only above it on the neck.

Figure 12-2 shows a capo set correctly on the guitar at the third fret. See Chapter 15 for more information on different kinds of capos.

Why should you use a capo? A capo enables you to instantly change the key of a song. Say that you know how to play "Farmer in the Dell" in the key of C and only in the key of C. But you want to accompany a singer (maybe yourself) whose vocal range is better suited for singing "Farmer in the Dell" in the key of D.

No problem. Put your capo at the second fret and simply play the song in C as you normally do. The capo causes all the strings to sound two half-steps higher than normal, and the music sounds in D! In fact, you can move the capo to any fret, sliding it up and down the neck, until you find the fret (key) that's perfect for your vocal range.

Of course, if the notes and chords in the song you're playing have no open strings, you can simply change positions on the neck (using movable chords) to find the best key for singing. Use a capo only if the song requires the use of open strings.

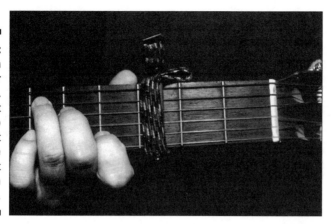

People also use a capo for a reason that has nothing to do with vocal ranges. If you place a capo on the neck (especially high on the neck), the guitar has a brighter sound. It can even sound more like a mandolin (you know, that teardrop-shaped little stringed instrument that you hear gondoliers play in films set in Italy).

Capos can prove especially useful if you have two guitarists playing a song together. One can play the chords without a capo — in the key of C, for example. The other guitarist can play the chords in, say, the key of G with a capo at the fifth fret, sounding in C. The difference in *timbre* (that is, the tone color or the quality of the sound) between the two instruments creates a striking effect.

Some people refer to capos as "cheaters." They think that if you're a beginner who can play only in easy keys (A and D, for example), you need to "cheat" by using a capo if you want to play in B♭. After all, if you're worth your salt as a guitarist, you could play in B♭ without a capo by using barre chords.

But in folk-guitar playing, the combination of open strings and fretted ones is the essence of the style. Sometimes these open-string/fretted-note combinations can become quite intricate.

Think, for example, of the introduction to "Fire and Rain," by James Taylor, which he fingers in the key of A. James plays it, however, by using a capo at the third fret, causing the music to sound three half-steps higher, in C, because that key best fits his vocal range. So why not just play the song in C without a capo? Because the fingering makes that option impossible; the necessary open strings that James plays don't exist in C — only in A!

One more advantage of using a capo: Because the frets get closer together as you go up the neck, playing with a capo requires less stretching in the left hand, making some songs a little easier to play.

Throughout this chapter, as you play the various exercises and songs, experiment with the capo. See how you can use a capo to find the best key for your vocal range. And even on the instrumental selections, experiment by placing the capo at various frets to see how that placement affects the timbre. You're sure to like what you hear.

Sometimes, engaging or disengaging a capo causes the strings to go out of tune. Remember to check your tuning and make any necessary adjustments whenever you attach or remove the capo.

Arpeggio Style

Arpeggio style is also know as *broken-chord* style, because you play the notes of the chord one at a time, in succession, and allow the notes to ring out or sustain. This technique produces a lighter flowing sound to the music than you get by playing all the notes at once, as you do in strumming.

Playing arpeggio style

To play in arpeggio style, put your right-hand fingers on the strings in the following pattern: Rest your thumb *(p)* against the 6th string, your index finger *(i)* against the 3rd string, your middle finger *(m)* against the 2nd string, and your ring finger *(a)* against the 1st string. This pattern is your basic fingerstyle position (with the fingers held perpendicular to the strings).

All the fingers are now ready to pluck. Even without actually fingering a left-hand chord (because all the strings you're plucking are open strings in an Em chord), you can still play an Em arpeggio by plucking first *p,* then *i,* then *m,* and finally *a.* You should hear a pretty Em chord ringing out.

Just so that you know how this pattern looks in notation, see Figure 12-3, which shows you exactly how to play the open strings of an Em chord in arpeggio style.

Now try arpeggiating up (from low-pitched to high-pitched strings) and back down on the open Em chord. Again use only the 6th, 3rd, 2nd, and 1st strings, instead of playing just *p-i-m-a,* as before, play *p-i-m-a-m-i.* Refer to the notation in Figure 12-4 to check that you're playing the correct notes.

TRACK 82 0:00

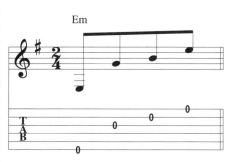

Figure 12-3:
An open-stringed Em arpeggio that you play by using the thumb, index, middle, and ring fingers.

TRACK 82 0:10

Figure 12-4:
An up-and-down Em arpeggio pattern.

Next try fingering various chords and playing *p-i-m-a* or *p-i-m-a-m-i*. But for each new chord, make sure that your thumb hits the correct bass string — the *root* of the chord (the 6th string for all the E and G chords, the 5th string for all the A and C chords, and the 4th string for all the D chords). (The *root* of a chord is simply the note from which the chord takes its name; for example, the root of a C chord is a C note.)

Many arpeggio patterns are possible, because you can pluck the strings in lots of different orders. The *p-i-m-a* and the *p-i-m-a-m-i* patterns are two of the most common.

To play a song right now using the *p-i-m-a-m-i* arpeggio pattern, skip to the section "Playing Folk Songs," later in this chapter, and check out "House of the Rising Sun."

"Lullaby" pattern

Some guitarists refer to the accompaniment pattern shown in Figure 12-5 as the "lullaby" pattern because it's a pretty-sounding pattern suitable for playing accompaniments to lullabies.

This pattern incorporates a double-stop (two notes sounded at once) into an arpeggio pattern. After playing *p* and *i* individually, you play *m* and *a* together (at the same time) on the top two strings. Remember to hold down each chord with the left hand while the notes ring out. Again, use the capo to find your best key for singing.

TRACK 83, 0:00

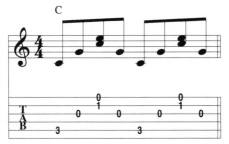

Figure 12-5: The "lullaby" accompaniment pattern.

To play a song right now by using the "lullaby" pattern, skip to the section "Playing Folk Songs," later in this chapter, and check out "The Cruel War Is Raging."

Thumb-Brush Style

The *thumb-brush* style is an accompaniment pattern that has a "boom-chick" sound. Here, the thumb plays normally (plucking a bass string downward), but the fingers strike (brush) the top three or four strings with the backs of the nails in a downward motion (toward the floor).

The fingers actually strum the strings as a pick does but without you moving your arm or your whole hand. Basically, you curl your fingers into your palm and then quickly extend them, changing from a closed-hand position to an open-hand position, striking the strings with the nails in the process.

Simple thumb-brush

Figure 12-6 shows two measures of the thumb-brush pattern on a C chord. Don't worry about hitting *exactly* three strings with the finger brush. Getting a smooth, flowing motion in the right hand is more important.

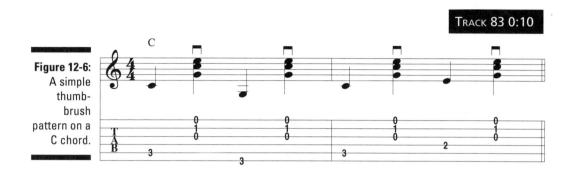

Figure 12-6:
A simple thumb-brush pattern on a C chord.

Thumb-brush-up

A variation of the simple thumb-brush is the *thumb-brush-up* (which yields a "boom-chick-y" sound). After strumming with the backs of the nails of the middle and ring fingers, you use the flesh of your index finger to pluck the 1st string (upward). You invariably perform this technique in an eighth-note rhythm on beats 2 and 4 (one, two-and, three, four-and). (See Appendix A for more information on eighth notes.)

Figure 12-7 shows a two-measure pattern using the thumb-brush-up technique. Keep the down- and upstrokes steady, with no break in the rhythm. (Make sure that you listen to the CD for this one, and don't be discouraged if this pattern takes a little getting used to.)

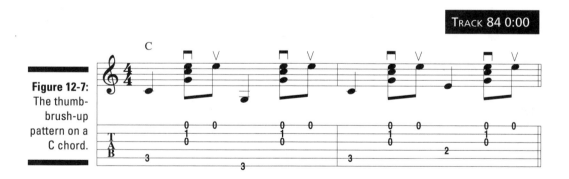

Figure 12-7:
The thumb-brush-up pattern on a C chord.

Don't think of the upstroke with the finger as a fingerpicking move, but as an upward brush with the whole hand. In other words, keep the right hand loose and flowing as you pull it upward to strike the 1st string with your first finger.

You can use the thumb-brush or thumb-brush-up pattern for any song that has a "boom-chick" or "boom-chick-y" sound, such as "Jingle Bells" or "I've Been Working on the Railroad."

Carter Style

In *Carter style,* named after the Carter family (June, "Mother" Maybelle, and "Uncle" A.P.), you play the melody on the low strings with the thumb while the fingers provide an accompaniment in the form of brushes. This style works well for songs with melody notes that fall mostly on beats 1 and 3. (The brushes occur on beats 2 and 4.) But if a melody note falls on beat 2 or 4, you can simply omit the brush on that beat.

You can play this style just as easily by using a pick as you can with the fingers, so try it both ways and see which is more comfortable for you.

Figure 12-8 shows a passage that you can play by using Carter style, where the melody falls entirely on the lower strings. The melody comes from a traditional melody, called "Wildwood Flower," that the Carter family made famous. Woody Guthrie wrote his own lyrics and called it "The Sinking of the Ruben James."

TRACK 84, 0:09

Figure 12-8: Carter style puts the melody in the bass and the accompani-ment in the treble.

To play a song right now in Carter style, skip to the section "Playing Folk Songs," later in this chapter, and check out the tune "Gospel Ship."

Travis Picking

Travis picking, named after country guitarist Merle Travis, is probably the most popular fingerstyle folk technique. Here, the thumb alternates between two (and sometimes three) bass strings in steady quarter notes while the fingers pluck the treble (higher) strings, usually between the quarter notes (on the off-beats). The result is a driving, rhythmic feel that you can use for a variety of settings from ragtime to blues, to the rolling 4/4 accompaniment pattern that you hear in Simon and Garfunkel's "The Boxer" and Kansas's "Dust in the Wind."

This technique is more complex than the ones we discuss in the preceding sections, so we're going to show you how to play it step by step.

Playing the pattern

You can create different Travis figures by varying the timing that you use to hit the treble strings. What remains the same is the steady rhythm that you play with the thumb. One pattern of treble strings is so popular that we're calling it the "basic Travis pattern." You can play it by following these steps:

1. **Start out by fingering a D chord with your left hand and hold the chord down throughout the measure.**

2. **Using only your thumb, alternate between picking the 4th and 3rd strings in steady quarter notes, as shown in Figure 12-9a.**

   The thumb part is the foundation of the pattern. The standard notation marks the thumb part by using *downstems* (descending vertical lines attached to the noteheads). Play this thumb part several times so that it's rock steady.

3. **Now add the 2nd string to the pattern by plucking it with your index finger after beat 2 (between the thumb notes), as shown in Figure 12-9b.**

   Make sure that the 2nd string continues to ring as your thumb hits the 4th string on beat 3. Play this partial pattern several times until it feels natural. Listen to the CD for the rhythm.

4. **Now add the 1st string to the pattern by plucking it with your middle finger after beat 3 (between the thumb notes), as shown in Figure 12-9c.**

   Play this partial pattern several times until it feels comfortable.

5. **Finally, add the 1st string (which you play by using the middle finger) to beat 1, playing the 4th string simultaneously with your thumb, as shown in Figure 12-9d.**

   In Travis picking, playing a treble string and bass string together is known as a *pinch*.

A variation of the basic pattern is sometimes called *the roll*. This pattern uses no pinches, and you pluck every off-beat, as shown in Figure 12-9e. Typically, you play the last off-beat only if you don't change chords as you go to the next measure. If you do change chords, leave out the last off-beat.

You can create other variations of the basic pattern by adding or omitting pinches and off-beats — but *never* omit the thumb notes. You can create these variations as you go, using them to break the monotony of one pattern that you otherwise repeat over and over.

TRACK 85

Figure 12-9:
Travis
picking,
step by
step.

d) Basic Travis Pattern

pinch in-sides out-sides thumb

e) The "Roll"

out-sides in-sides out-sides in-sides

An easy way to remember which strings to hit and in which order to hit them is to think of the group of strings you pluck as a set of *outside strings* and a set of *inside strings*. On the D chord, for example, the 1st and 4th strings are "outside" and the 2nd and 3rd strings are "inside." Look at Figure 12-9d again. Say the following phrase as you play: "Pinch, insides, outsides, thumb." The following steps relate this phrase to the corresponding actions that you take:

1. *Pinch:* **On beat 1, play the outside strings (4th and 1st) as a pinch — the thumb striking the 4th string and the middle finger striking the 1st simultaneously.**

2. *Insides:* **On beat 2, play the inside strings (3rd and 2nd) one at a time — the thumb striking first and then the index finger.**

3. *Outsides:* **On beat 3, play the outside strings (4th and 1st) one at a time — the thumb striking first and then the middle finger.**

4. *Thumb:* **On beat 4, play just the thumb on the bass string of the inside set (the 3rd string).**

Accompaniment style

After you know the basic pattern, you can create an entire accompaniment to a song by simply stringing together a series of chords and applying the appropriate pattern for each chord. You can play the pattern for any chord by memorizing the following information:

♪ Which group of four strings to play for each chord. (See the chart shown in Figure 12-10.)

♪ Which right-hand fingers to use on those strings.

♪ The phrase "pinch, insides, outsides, thumb." By using this phrase, you can play any pattern for any chord.

Figure 12-10 shows which four strings you can use for various chords and identifies the "inside" and "outside" strings for each group. Try the groups indicated for each chord, playing both the basic pattern and the roll.

	higher group	lower group
4th-string root D, Dm, D7, 4-string F	insides [① ② ③ ④] outsides	
5th-string root C, C7, A, Am, A7, B7	insides [① ② ③ ⑤] outsides	insides [② ③ ④ ⑤] outsides
6th-string root E, Em, E7, G, G7	insides [① ② ③ ⑥] outsides	insides [② ③ ④ ⑥] outsides (not good for G7)

Figure 12-10: Inside and outside string pairs for various chords in Travis picking.

To play a song right now by using Travis-style accompaniment, skip to the section "Playing Folk Songs," later in this chapter, and check out "All My Trials."

Solo style

You can use Travis picking to create exciting instrumental solos by placing the song's melody in the treble (as pinches or off-beats) while the bass — along with other, strategically placed off-beats — provides an accompaniment. In this solo style, you don't necessarily play strict four-string groupings — the melody pretty much dictates the groupings, which sometimes expand to five strings.

Figure 12-11 shows how a melody — in this case, "Oh Susanna" — plays in a solo Travis picking style. Notice that beats 1 and 2 in each bar are pinches (the thumb and finger play the strings together), because both the melody and bass fall on these beats. The other melody notes fall on the off-beats, coming in between bass notes.

Figure 12-11:
The first two measures of "Oh Susanna" arranged in solo Travis-picking style.

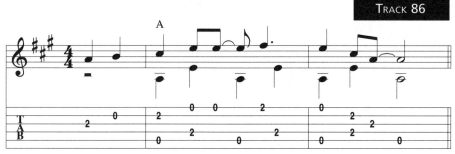

TRACK 86

To play a song right now by using Travis solo style, skip to the section "Playing Folk Songs," later in this chapter, and check out "Freight Train."

Open tuning

You can create some interesting effects if you Travis pick in open tunings. Figure 12-12 is a passage in open-G tuning (D-G-D-G-B-D, low pitched to high) that sounds like something Joni Mitchell may have played on one of her early albums. The only unusual thing here is that you tune the guitar differently. Nothing in the right hand changes from a normal Travis pick.

Notice that you use only one string set (5th, 4th, 3rd, and 2nd). The 5th and 3rd strings are open till the very end, when you play the barred 12th-fret *harmonics* (see the following paragraph for information about producing harmonics). Think "pinch, insides, outsides, thumb" throughout this example.

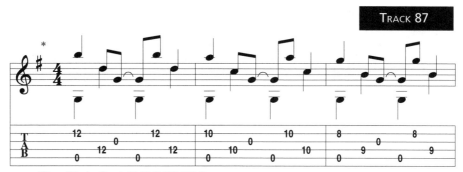

TRACK 87

*Open G tuning (low to high): D G D G B D

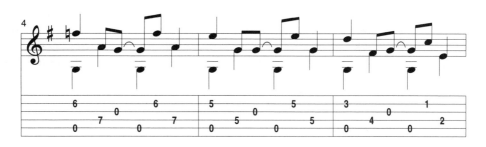

Harm.⌐

Harm.⌐

Figure 12-12:
Travis
picking in
open-G
tuning.

A harmonic is a pretty, high-pitched, bell-like tone that you produce by lightly touching a string (with the fleshy part of a left-hand finger) at a certain fret (usually the twelfth, seventh, or fifth) directly over the metal fret wire rather than in front of it and then striking the string.

Playing Folk Songs

The range of songs that we present here runs the gamut from a simple accompaniment pattern that you repeat over and over to a solo-style treatment of a tune, with independent bass, superimposed melody on top, and a couple of tricks thrown in. In these five songs, you find just about every fingerpicking approach possible that's appropriate for songs in the folk vein. Don't let the simple nature of the songs themselves deceive you, however; the guitar parts here make them sound full and complete. After you get these arrangements down, all you need is the requisite flannel shirt and hiking boots and you're on your way to a career in hoboing, labor organizing, and political protest.

About the songs

Here is some special information about the songs to help you along. Some of the songs employ a technique known as a *bass run*. This technique is a single-note line — played by the thumb — that leads to the next chord and serves to break up the monotony of a repeated pattern.

♪ **House of the Rising Sun.** To play "House of the Rising Sun," you need to know how to play an up-and-down arpeggio pattern (see the section "Arpeggio Style," earlier in this chapter); how to finger basic major and minor chords (see Chapter 4); and how to make a song about a wasted life in a house of ill repute sound light and frothy.

The up-and-down arpeggio pattern *(p-i-m-a-m-i)* makes a nice accompaniment for "House of the Rising Sun" and other songs like it. Your left hand should hold down each chord for the entire measure. Think *broken chords* (where the notes ring out) and not *individual notes* (where the notes stop short). Notice that the fingers play only the top three strings for every chord in the song, even though the thumb changes strings from chord to chord.

♪ **The Cruel War Is Raging.** To play "The Cruel War Is Raging," you need to know how to play the "lullaby" pattern (see the section "Arpeggio Style," earlier in this chapter); how to finger basic major and minor chords (see Chapter 4); and how to coo a baby to sleep with a song about annihilation and destruction.

Remember to hold down each chord with the left hand while the notes ring out. Use a capo to find your best key for singing.

♪ **Gospel Ship.** To play "Gospel Ship," you need to know how to play a Carter-style solo (see the section "Carter Style," earlier in this chapter); how to play hammer-ons and pull-offs (see Chapter 9); and whether any person on the planet actually knows the lyrics to this song.

Hammer-ons, pull-offs, and bass runs are an important part of Carter style, as you see in this arrangement, loosely based on the traditional song "Gospel Ship." (See Chapter 9 for more information on hammer-ons and pull-offs.) The standard notation helps you determine which notes you play with the thumb (downstems) and which you play by using the fingers (upstems). This song works equally well, however, if you use a pick and play all downstrokes. Try it both ways.

♪ **All My Trials.** To play "All My Trials," you need to know how to play a Travis-style accompaniment (see the section "Travis Picking," earlier in this chapter); how to play hammer-ons (see Chapter 9); and how to convincingly sing a song about toil and hardship without sounding pretentious because you've lead a life of relative ease and privilege.

Measure 1 uses the lower string group for the G chord, because if you use the higher set, you end up with an incomplete chord. Because measure 2 has only two beats, you play only half the pattern in that measure. Measure 5 begins as if you're using the higher string set (to smoothly resolve the high note of the previous bar), but then on beat 2, it switches to the lower string set, again to avoid an incomplete chord. Measure 9 incorporates a little bass line into the pattern on the way from G to Em. In measure 12, a pinched hammer-on adds an extra-folky flavor.

♪ **Freight Train.** To play "Freight Train," you need to know how to play a Travis-style solo (see the section "Travis Picking," earlier in this chapter); how to play hammer-ons (see Chapter 9); and how to sound like a simple hobo while playing a sophisticated fingerpicking arrangement with four new techniques.

A bass run breaks up the monotony in measures 4 and 8. In measure 9, you're fingering an E chord, and you can use your first finger, flattened into a barre, to play the 1st string, first fret. Use your left thumb, wrapped around the neck, to finger the 6th string in bars 11 and 12. Measure 14 features a fancy little trick — you hammer a treble note at the same time that you strike a bass note. In measure 15, the bass alternates between three notes, not two.

House of the Rising Sun

(continued)

House of the Rising Sun (continued)

TRACK 89

The Cruel War Is Raging

TRACK 90

Gospel Ship

All My Trials

(continued)

All My Trials (continued)

TRACK 92

Freight Train

Chapter 13

Classical

· ·

In This Chapter

▶ Sitting correctly

▶ Positioning the right and left hand

▶ Cutting and filing your nails

▶ Free strokes and rest strokes

▶ Playing arpeggios

▶ Playing counterpoint

▶ Playing classical pieces

· ·

Classical guitar not only suggests a certain musical style, but also implies an entire approach to the instrument that's uniquely different from that of any other style, whether folk, jazz, rock, or blues. Classical guitar encompasses a long tradition of techniques and practices that composers and performers have observed throughout the ages and to which they still adhere, even with the advent of more modern and avant-garde musical compositions.

To play the great music of Bach, Mozart, and Beethoven — and to have it sound authentic — you must play it in the classical style. Even if you have no intention of becoming a serious classical guitarist, you can glean much about tone, technique, and phrasing by practicing classical techniques.

Don't get the impression that, because it adheres to certain disciplines, classical music is all rigid rules and regulations. Many guitarists with careers in both the pop and classical fields feel that some aspects of classical guitar are more liberating, and these rugged individualists have actually tried to infuse classical techniques into pop and rock playing. Steve Howe of Yes, the late Michael Hedges, and Chet Atkins have each appropriated classical techniques into their own inimitable styles. Still, we can't quite picture the heavy-metal rock band Metallica having the same headbanging effect if they were to perch on straight-backed chairs with left legs raised and wrists folded at right angles.

Getting Ready to Play Classical Guitar

You always play classical guitar on a nylon-string guitar, in a sitting position. Beyond that, you must employ certain right-hand *strokes* (methods of plucking the strings) to get the expected sound.

How to sit

Real classical guitarists (that is, *most* real classical guitarists) sit differently from other guitarists in that they hold the guitar on the *left* leg — which they elevate about six inches by means of a foot stool — instead of on their right. If you perform this balancing act, you accomplish the following two goals:

♪ You rest the guitar's treble side (the side closer to the higher-pitched strings) on the left leg, with the back of the instrument resting against your abdomen. The weight of your right arm on the bass side holds the instrument in place (balanced, so to speak). Your hands are thus completely free to play — and only play. You don't need to use your hands to keep the guitar from falling to the floor (unless you jump up suddenly to answer the phone).

♪ You position the guitar so that the left hand can play any fret at the correct (perpendicular) angle. The higher frets (the 12th and up) are especially easier to play than they are in steel-string acoustic sitting position.

The truth is, however, that a lot of people who attempt classical guitar simply don't even bother with all this stuff about how to hold the instrument. Why? Because it's too much trouble. Where would you even get a foot stool? (Okay, you can get one at your local music store — maybe.) If you just want to try out a few classical-guitar pieces for the fun of it, hold the guitar as you normally do. The music police aren't likely to arrest you, and you can still hear the beautiful arrangement of the notes, even if you're not playing strictly "by the rules."

But if you're really serious about playing classical guitar, buy a foot stool and refer to Figure 13-1, which shows the correct sitting position for classical guitar. You can also use a special gizmo that pushes the guitar up from your leg, enabling you to keep both feet flat on the floor. These devices are gaining popularity because they don't create the uneven pull on your leg and back muscles that often results from elevating one leg and keeping the other flat. Oh, and if you want to pursue classical guitar, learn to read music (if you can't already), because lots of printed classical guitar music comes without tab. (Check out Appendix A to get started in music reading.)

Figure 13-1:
Sitting
position for
classical
guitar.

Whichever method you employ, make sure that you sit upright and at the edge of the chair, elevating your left leg (or the guitar) and holding the instrument in the center of your body. Keep the head of the guitar (where the tuning pegs connect) at about the same height as your shoulder, as shown in the photo.

The right hand

Other than posture, your right-hand approach is the most critical consideration for achieving a true classical guitar sound. You must play with your right hand in the correct position and execute the correct finger strokes.

Right-hand position

The most important concept about right-hand position is that you hold your fingers — index, middle, and ring — perpendicular to the strings as they strike. (You normally don't use the little finger in classical guitar.)

This positioning is no easy feat. Why? Because your hand, which is an extension of your arm, naturally falls at about a 60-degree angle to the strings. Try it. (See?) But if you hold your fingers at an angle, you can't get maximum vibration from the strings. For that, you need to strike the strings at a 90-degree angle — perpendicular.

You must rotate your right hand at the wrist so that the fingers fall perpendicular to the strings and your thumb stays about an inch and a half to the left (from your vantage point) of your index finger, as shown in Figure 13-2. Rest your right-hand fingers on the 6th, 3rd, 2nd, and 1st strings, as shown in the figure. This setup is the basic classical-guitar position for the right hand. Are your fingers perpendicular to the strings?

Figure 13-2:
Correct
right-hand
position.

If you're serious about perfecting classical right-hand technique (which you can also use in fingerstyle folk guitar), here's a tip to force your fingers into the correct position: Place all four fingers (thumb, index, middle, and ring) on the *same string* (the 3rd, say), lining them up in a row. By positioning your fingers this way, your thumb can't rest to the right of your index finger. Then, without turning your hand, move each finger to its normal place: thumb to the 6th string, index staying on the 3rd, middle to the 2nd, and ring to the 1st. Refer to Figure 13-2 to make sure that your thumb is in the correct position with respect to the fingers (to the side and not behind them).

The fingernails

Your right-hand fingernails affect the tone of your playing. Some guitarists own a special fingernail-care kit that contains scissors or clippers, nail files, emery boards, and fine abrasive cloths to enable them to keep their nails at a desired length, shape, and smoothness.

If your nails are very short, only the flesh of your finger hits the string, and the resulting tone is rather mellow and soft. Conversely, if your nails are very long, only the nail hits the string, and the tone is sharper and more metallic. Most classical guitarists grow their nails somewhat long so that both the flesh and the nail hit the string at the same time, giving a pleasing, well-rounded tone.

If you're serious about playing classical guitar, grow your nails a bit long and cut them so that they're rounded, following the same contour as your fingertips. Then file or buff them with a nail file or emery board. Grow only the right-hand nails. You must keep the left-hand nails short so that they don't hit the fretboard as you press down the strings, preventing the notes from sounding out correctly. But if you're playing classical guitar casually, for fun or just to try it out, don't bother worrying about the length of your right-hand nails. Lots of people play classical guitar with short nails (and with the guitar set on their right leg, too!).

Changing tone color

You can alter the tone color of the strings by placing your right-hand at different points along the string — closer to the bridge or closer to the fretboard or directly over the sound hole. If you play directly over the sound hole, the tone is full and rich. As you move toward the bridge, the tone becomes brighter and more metallic; and as you move toward the fretboard, the tone becomes more rounded and mellow.

Why do you need to change *timbre* (tone color)? Mostly for the sake of variety. If you're playing a piece with a section that repeats, you may play over the sound hole for the first pass and then on the repeat play closer to the bridge. Or maybe you're approaching the climax in a piece and you want to heighten the effect by playing with a brighter, more metallic sound. You can then play closer to the bridge. Printed classical guitar music often indicates these positions, and you can clearly hear the changes in recordings of classical guitar pieces.

Left-hand position

As you're fingering frets in the classical style, try to think of your left hand as a piece of machinery that you lock into one position — a position that you can characterize by right angles and perpendicularity (to achieve ease of playing and optimal sound). As you move up and down the neck or across the strings, the little machine never changes its appearance. You simply move it along the two directions of a grid — as you would an Etch-a-Sketch. Here's how the machine works:

♪ Keep your fingers rounded and arched so that the tips come down to the fingerboard at a 90-degree angle and place them perpendicular to the strings.

♪ Straighten your thumb and keep it pretty much opposite the index finger as you lightly press it against the back of the guitar neck. As you move to higher frets, bring your thumb along, always keeping it opposite the index finger. You can move it across the neck as your fingers do, but don't ever have it creeping above the fingerboard.

♪ Move your arm with your hand so that your hand stays perpendicular to the strings. As you play the lower frets, keep your elbow out, away from your body. At the higher frets, bring your elbow in, closer to your body.

Theoretically, no matter what string or fret you play, your left hand position looks the same — as shown in Figure 13-3. Of course, special requirements of the music *could* force you to abandon the basic left-hand position from time to time. So think of the preceding guidelines as just that — guidelines.

Figure 13-3:
Correct
left-hand
position.

If you've been playing other guitar styles (such as rock or blues) for a while, you probably often see your left thumb tip coming all the way around the neck, sticking out above the 6th string. This creeping-thumb habit is a no-no in classical guitar, however, where the thumb *always* stays behind the neck. Here's a sure way to cure you of old habits (although you must be willing to suffer a little pain). Have a friend hold a sharp object (such as a pencil) while watching you play. Every time your thumb peeks out from behind the neck, have your friend lightly poke your thumb with the sharp object! (Ouch!) This training method may hurt a bit, but after a few pokes, your thumb stays tucked away behind the neck, where it belongs. This method is how children in Charles Dickens' time learned correct left-hand technique.

Free Strokes and Rest Strokes

If you had a golf or bowling coach, he'd probably lecture you on the importance of a good follow-through. Well, believe it or not, the same thing's true in plucking a guitar string. Your finger can follow through after plucking a string in one of two ways, giving you two kinds of strokes. One is the *free stroke,* which you use for arpeggios and fast scale passages. The other, the *rest stroke,* you use for accentuating melody notes. The following sections describe both strokes.

The free stroke

If you pluck a string at a slightly upward angle, your finger comes to rest in the air, above the next adjacent string. (Of course, it doesn't stay there for long, as you must return it to its normal starting position to pluck again.) This type of stroke, where your finger dangles *freely* in the air, is called a *free stroke.* Figure 13-4, with its before and after pictures, shows you how to play a free stroke.

Figure 13-4:
The free stroke. Notice that, after striking a string, the right-hand finger dangles in the air.

Playing free strokes

In classical guitar, you use *free strokes* for playing nonmelodic material, such as arpeggios (chords played one note at a time instead of all at once); you also normally use these strokes in playing fingerstyle folk guitar (see Chapter 12). The thumb pretty much always plays free strokes. Try arpeggiating the open strings (thumb on the 6th string, index finger on the 3rd, middle on the 2nd, and ring on the 1st), using all free strokes.

Figure 13-5 is an excerpt from a Spanish piece, "Malagueña," that just about every guitar player picks up at some time or other. You play the melody with the thumb while the middle finger plays free strokes on the open high-E string. Classical guitar notation indicates the right-hand fingers by the letters *p, i, m,* and *a,* which stand for the first letters of the Spanish names for the fingers: The thumb is *p (pulgar),* the index is *i (indice),* the middle is *m (media),* and the ring is *a (anular).*

TRACK 93

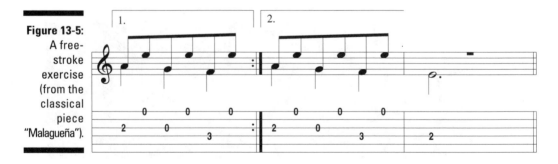

Figure 13-5:
A free-stroke exercise (from the classical piece "Malagueña").

The rest stroke

The *rest stroke* uses a different kind of follow-through from the free stroke. Instead of striking the string at a slightly upward angle, pluck straight across (not upward) so that your finger lands, or *rests,* against the adjacent lower-pitched string. By coming straight across the string (instead of coming across at an upward angle), you get the maximum sound out of the string. That's why rest strokes are good for melody notes; the melody notes are the prominent ones — the ones that you want to accentuate.

Figure 13-6, with its before and after pictures, shows how to play a rest stroke.

Figure 13-6: The rest stroke. Notice that, after striking a string, the right-hand finger rests against the next string.

Playing rest strokes

Use rest strokes to accentuate melody notes in a classical piece — especially in pieces that have a combination of melody notes, inner voices, (played with free strokes), and bass notes.

Play the two-octave C major scale shown in Figure 13-7 *slowly,* using all rest strokes. Change from second to fifth position at the end of measure 1 by smoothly gliding your first finger along the 3rd string, up to the fifth fret. (See Chapter 7 for more information on playing in position.) On the way down, shift back to second position by smoothly gliding your third finger along the 3rd string, down to the fourth fret. Alternate between *i* (index finger) and *m* (middle finger) as you go. For the sake of speed and accuracy, alternating between two right-hand fingers (usually *i* and *m*) is customary for playing classical-guitar melodies.

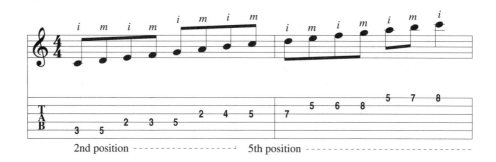

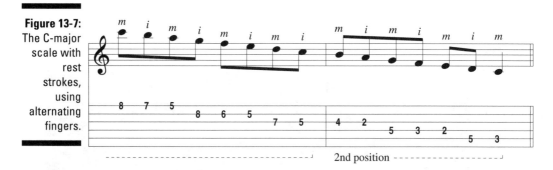

Figure 13-7:
The C-major
scale with
rest
strokes,
using
alternating
fingers.

Arpeggio Style and Contrapuntal Style

You play most classical guitar pieces in either an *arpeggio* style or a *contrapuntal* style. In arpeggio style, you hold chords with the left hand while plucking the strings in succession with your right hand (so that each string rings out and sustains). Usually, you simultaneously play a melody on the top strings (using rest strokes) over the arpeggios.

Contrapuntal classical guitar music usually has two parts — a bass part, all of which you play with the thumb, and a treble part (the melody) that you play (usually by using free strokes) with alternating fingers (for example, *i* and *m*). The word *contrapuntal* refers to the *counterpoint* style, where you play two or more melodies (usually with different or contrasting rhythms) simultaneously — sort of like what you get if two people with opposing ideas talk at the same time. In music, however, the separate lines support rather than negate each other. Imagine if political debates had that effect.

Combining free strokes and rest strokes in arpeggios

Figure 13-8 shows an exercise in arpeggio style. You play the first note of each measure and the notes with stems that point downward in the standard notation with the thumb; the other notes you play with the fingers (*i* on the 3rd string, *m* on the 2nd, and *a* on the 1st). The notes that you play on the 1st string have an accent mark (>) over them. The *sim.* means to keep playing the same fingering pattern throughout the exercise.

Accent marks tell you to accentuate (or stress) certain notes by playing them louder to bring them to the fore. In other words, use the more powerful rest stroke for accented notes and free strokes for all other notes. Remember to hold down all the notes of each measure simultaneously with the left hand, for the duration of the measure.

Before combining rest strokes and free strokes, play Figure 13-8 using all free strokes to get the feel of the piece. After you're comfortable with it, add the rest strokes to the notes on the 1st string.

Point/counterpoint

Figure 13-9 is an excerpt from a composition by an unknown composer of the Baroque era — an era during which contrapuntal music was very popular. Play the downstem notes (in the standard notation) by using the thumb. Use alternating fingers (free strokes) to play the melody.

The piece doesn't indicate any particular right-hand fingering. As long as you apply the concept of alternating fingers (even loosely) to attain speed and accuracy, you can use whatever fingering feels most comfortable to you. No single way is really right or wrong.

We do indicate the left-hand fingering, however, because this particular fingering is the only one that's feasible for this piece. The slanted line in front of the *2* on the second beat of measure 3 and the third beat of measure 5 indicates that you're using the same finger you used to play the previous note.

Practice by playing only the top part with the (alternating) fingers a few times. Then play the bass line alone with the thumb a few times. Then play both parts simultaneously. Listen to the CD to help you with the rhythm.

TRACK 94

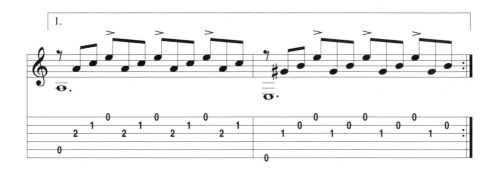

Figure 13-8: An arpeggio exercise combining free strokes and rest strokes.

TRACK 95

Figure 13-9:
A
contrapuntal
exercise.

Playing Classical Pieces

Playing classical guitar pieces is never a hassle because you don't need to sing and you don't need an amplifier. You can do it any time, any place (as long as you have a nylon-string guitar).

Standard classical guitar notation uses some special symbols for indicating barre chords. The symbol *C* with a Roman numeral after it indicates a barre across all six strings. (The Roman numeral tells you which fret to barre.) A *C* with a line (|) through it indicates a partial barre (fewer than six strings). And a dotted horizontal line to the right of the *C* tells you how long to hold down the barre.

About the songs

The songs that you play in this chapter are ones that all classical players meet at one time or another. They're great if you want a life full of Romanza that's always exciting and never Bourrée.

♪ **Romanza.** To play "Romanza," you need to know how to play free strokes and rest strokes (see the section "Free Strokes and Rest Strokes," earlier in this chapter); how to barre chords (check out Chapter 8); and how to roll your *R*s while saying "Romanza" to sound truly continental.

"Romanza" is a simple arpeggiated piece that gives you an opportunity to accentuate the melody notes with rest strokes (all of which you play on the 1st string with the *a* finger). For practice, you can play the piece by using all free stokes, adding the rest strokes later. Use the thumb to play all the bass notes (downstems in the standard notation). Use the right-hand fingering that we give you in the first measure throughout the piece. We indicate left-hand fingering in only a few spots (measures 7–10 in the standard notation). In measures 9–10, make sure that you keep your first finger barred at the seventh fret with your second finger pressing down at the eighth fret (3rd string) *the whole time*. Stretch your little finger up to the 11th fret for the first beat of measure 10.

♪ **Bourrée in E minor.** To play "Bourrée in E minor," you need to know how to play a melody by using alternating fingers while playing a bass line with the thumb (see the section "Point/counterpoint," earlier in this chapter); how to barre chords (see Chapter 8); and how to pronounce and spell *bourrée*.

A bourrée is a dance people did a couple hundred years ago (just slightly before the advent of the "funky chicken"). This contrapuntal piece is an excerpt that's loads of fun to play because it sounds beautiful and intricate, but it's actually rather simple to play. Leo Kottke plays a fingerstyle version of it, and Jethro Tull did a jazz arrangement of it. Play all the bass notes (downstems in the standard notation) by using the thumb. Alternate fingers (for example, *m-i-m-i* and so on) with the right hand. The alternation doesn't need to be strict. Use what feels the most comfortable to you. We indicate some left-hand fingerings at the very beginning to get you going. After that, use whatever fingering feels natural. For inspiration, listen to recordings of this piece by classical guitarist John Williams, as well as the folk version by Kottke and the swing-jazz version by Jethro Tull. Heavy-metal guitarist Yngwie (pronounce *ING-vay*) Malmsteen even does a version with ear-splitting stun-gun distortion. Although J.S. Bach never imagined all these wacky settings for his unprepossessing little dance suite segment, they all sound great.

TRACK 96

Romanza

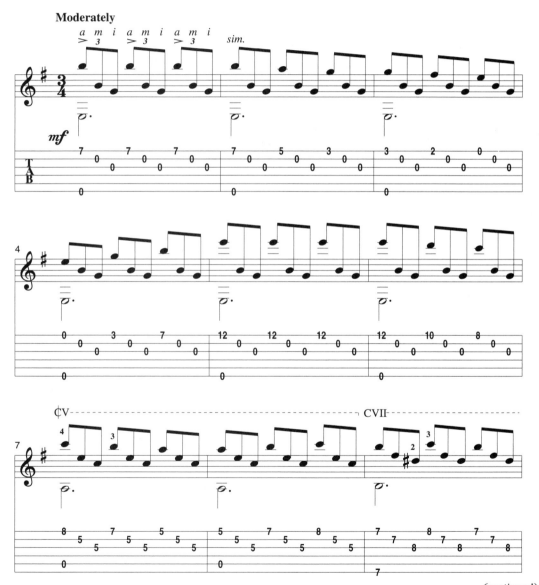

(continued)

Romanza (continued)

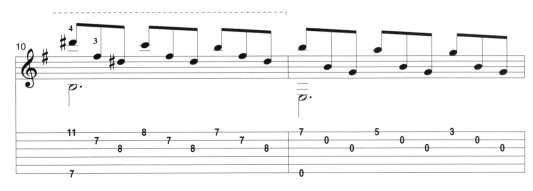

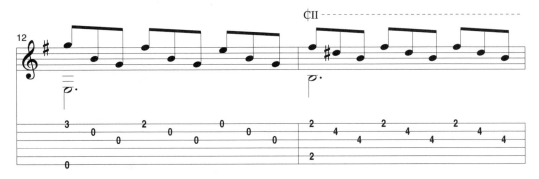

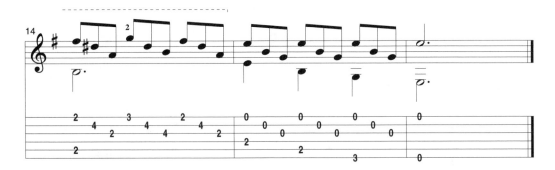

TRACK 97

Bourrée in E minor

Moderately

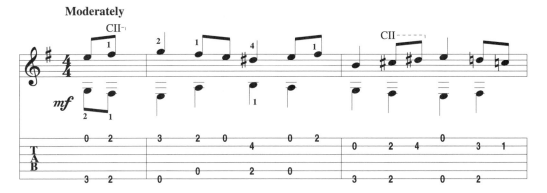

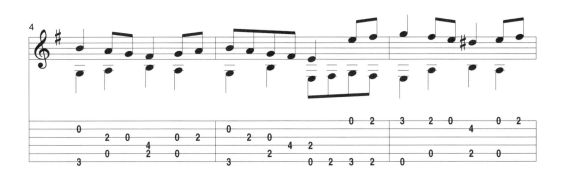

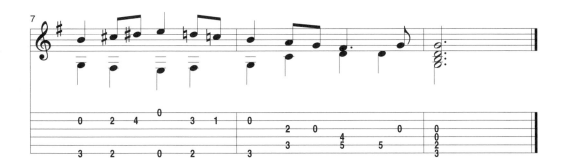

Part V
Gearing Up: A Buyer's Guide

The 5th Wave   By Rich Tennant

©RICHTENNANT

"Gee thanks, but I don't think a gingham neck cozy and peg board bonnet really go with the rest of my guitar."

In this part . . .

Whether you want to figure out how to buy your first practice guitar, your second electric guitar, or your first amp to take on tour, you can find what you need in this part. Chapter 14 shows you what to look for in a guitar that matches your playing level, style, and budget, and Chapter 15 tells you about the extras that you either desperately need or desperately want.

Chapter 14

Perfectly Good Guitars

. . . .

In This Chapter

▶ Developing a buying strategy

▶ Knowing what you want in a guitar

▶ Understanding quality

▶ Matching music styles to guitar models

▶ Graduating to your second guitar (and third and beyond. . . .)

. . . .

*B*uying a new guitar is an exciting proposition. You go to the music store and immediately face a world of possibilities, a supermarket of tantalizing choices. Every guitar on the wall seems to scream, "Pick me! Pick me!" Should you resist, exercise restraint, and avoid the models you know you can't afford?

Heck, no. Be bold and just try any model that strikes your fancy. After all, you're not asking to test drive the Ferrari appearing in the showroom window; you're simply asking the salesperson to see how different guitars feel and sound. And you're not being frivolous either. Playing a range of guitars helps you understand the differences between high-quality, expensive guitars and acceptable but affordable guitars.

So indulge yourself. Even if you don't have enough experience to recognize the subtle differences between a good guitar and a great guitar, at least expose yourself to them. And don't wait until the day that you decide to buy an instrument to pick one up for the first time. Make several visits to the music store before you're ready to buy and then take the time to absorb your experiences. You pick up far more knowledge about what makes a good, playable guitar than you may think just by handling several different instruments.

Buying a guitar can be like what happens after you think that you have the basics of a foreign language down pat and then visit the country where it's spoken: You practice your best Berlitz for weeks, but the first time that a native starts speaking to you, you're completely flustered. But don't rush it; hang in there. You're just buying a guitar; you're not in a strange land trying to find the closest restroom facilities. You're eventually gonna sort it all out.

Before Breaking Out Your Wallet

Before you walk into your local music store ready to plop down your hard-earned dough on a new guitar, you need to take stock of what you're doing. You need to ask yourself some tough questions about your pending purchase — and you need to do so *now*. Don't simply wait until you get to the store to develop a buying strategy (which, by that time, usually translates into no strategy at all). Keep in mind that the two most important factors in making any purchasing decision — especially concerning a guitar, where passions tend to run high — are to develop a plan and to gather all the information you need to make the best choice.

Start developing your purchasing plan by answering some specific questions about exactly what you want in a guitar — and how much you can spend to attain it. Narrowing your scope doesn't mean that you can't change your mind after you get to the store and see all the nifty instruments available or that you can't let on-the-spot inspiration and whim play a significant part in your final decision. ("I just *can't* decide between these two guitars . . . oh, what the heck! Just give me *both* of them!") But you *do* need a point from which to depart.

In focusing in on the instrument of your (practical) dreams, ask yourself the following questions:

♪ **What's my level of commitment?** Regardless of your current ability, do you realistically envision yourself practicing every day for the next five years, pursuing a dedicated program of guitar excellence? Or do you first want to see whether this whole "guitar thing" is going to stick? Just because you can *afford* a $1,000 guitar doesn't mean that you should necessarily buy it. Before plunking down any cash, honestly determine the importance of the guitar in your life and then act responsibly according to that priority. (Or completely ignore this advice and go crazy, you guitar-playing rebel, you!)

♪ **What's my spending limit?** The answer to this question is critical because, often, the more expensive the guitar, the greater its appeal. So you need to balance your level of commitment and your available resources. You don't want to have to give up food for six months and live in a cardboard box just because you got carried away in a moment of buying fever at the music store. You can very easily overextend yourself — especially in these days of generous credit limits. If you don't set a limit on how much you can spend, you can't know whether you exceed that limit . . . or by how much.

♪ **Do I buy retail or mail order?** If you know exactly what you want — down to the color and options — you may consider buying a guitar through mail order or online; you often get the best deal available on your chosen instrument by going either route and may even avoid paying sales tax on your purchase (if the music company is out of state). Buying sight unseen is common with many products, such as automobiles and computers. But if you can't cotton to buying something as personal as a guitar without falling in love with it first — and you want to "date" your guitar before "marrying" it — you definitely want to stick with retail. A retail outlet usually comes with an official service agreement and unofficial, friendly cooperation from the staff that's worth its weight in gold. Music stores know they're competing with online and mail-order services, and they make up for it in spades with service.

♪ **Am I a "new-guitar person" or a "used-guitar person"?** You're going to have a much easier time comparing attributes among new guitars. And all the retail and discount prices of new instruments are pretty much standardized — which is not, however, to say that all the prices are the same; stores usually discount at different rates. Expect to pay between 10 and 35 percent off the "list" price (manufacturer's suggested retail price) at a music store and a slightly higher discount if you're going online or mail order. Big chains offer better discounts than smaller mom-and-pop stores, because they buy in quantity and get a better price from the manufacturer.

Retail and mail-order operations also offer a warranty against any manufacturer defects on new instruments. You don't find any comparable protection if you're buying a guitar from a newspaper ad (although music stores also sell used instruments, usually with warranties). But on the other hand, you *can* sometimes get a really good deal on a used instrument . . . *if you know what to look for*. And, of course, if you want a vintage instrument, you're looking at a used guitar by definition.

As a rule, most asking prices in newspaper ads are too high. Be ready to dicker to get a better price for such a guitar — even if it's exactly what you're looking for.

After you feel that you have satisfactory answers to the preceding questions, proceed to the second prong of your guitar-purchasing attack plan: *gathering information*. Being an informed buyer is the best defense against making a bad deal in the retail arena.

Beginner Guitars

If you're just starting out as a novice guitarist, you may ask the musical question, "What's the minimum I need to spend to avoid winding up with a piece of junk?" That's a good question, because modern manufacturing practices now enable *luthiers* (the fancy term for guitar makers) to turn out some pretty good stuff for around $200 — and even less sometimes.

If you're an adult (that is, someone older than 14), and you're looking to grow with an instrument, plan to spend between $200 and $250 for an acoustic guitar and a little less for an electric. (Electric guitars are a little easier to build than acoustics are, so they usually cost a bit less than comparable acoustics.) Not bad for something that can provide a lifetime of entertainment and help you develop musical skills, is it?

In trying to decide on a prospective guitar, consider the following criteria:

♪ **Appearance.** You must like the way a particular guitar looks, or you're never really happy with it. So use your eye and your sense of taste (and we're referring here to your sense of aesthetics, so please, don't lick the guitar with your tongue) to select possible candidates. A red guitar isn't inherently better or worse than a green one, but you're perfectly free to base your decision to buy simply on whether you like the look of the guitar.

♪ **Playability.** Just because a guitar is relatively inexpensive doesn't necessarily mean that it's difficult to play (although this correlation was often the case in the past). You should be able to press the strings down to the fretboard with relative ease. And you shouldn't find the up-the-neck frets unduly difficult either, although they're sometimes harder to play than the lower frets are.

Here's a way to get some perspective on playability. Go back to that Ferrari — er, more expensive guitar — at the other end of the rack and see how a high-quality guitar plays. Then return to the more affordable instrument you're considering. Is the playability wildly different? It shouldn't be. If your prospective instrument doesn't feel comfortable to you, move on.

♪ **Intonation.** Besides being relatively easy to play, a guitar must play in tune. Test the intonation by playing a 12th fret harmonic (see Chapter 12 for information on how to produce a harmonic) and match that to the fretted note at the 12th fret. Although the notes are of a different tonal quality, the pitch should be exactly the same. Apply this test to all six strings. Listen especially to the 3rd and the 6th strings. On a guitar that's not set up correctly, these strings are likely to go out of tune first. If you don't trust your ears to tell the difference, enlist the aid of an experienced guitarist on this issue; it's *crucial*.

♪ **Solid construction.** Rap gently on the top of the instrument (like your doctor does to check your ribs and chest) to make sure that it's rattle free. Peer inside the hole, looking for gobs of glue and other evidence of sloppy workmanship. (Rough-sanded braces are a big tip-off to a hastily constructed instrument.) On an electric, test that the metal hardware is all tightly secured and rattle free. Without plugging into an amp, strum the open strings hard and listen for any rattling. Running your hand along the edge of the neck to check that the frets are smooth and filed correctly is another good test. If you're not sure what you should be feeling, consult an experienced guitarist on this "fret check."

Models for a Particular Style

Can you imagine walking into a music store and saying, "I'm a folk player. Do you have a folk bassoon? No, not a rock bassoon or a jazz bassoon — and *please,* not that country bassoon. How about that nice folk bassoon over in the corner?"

But you're a guitarist, so asking for a type of guitar by musical style is completely legitimate. Ask for a heavy-metal guitar, for example, and the salesperson nods knowingly and leads you to the corner of the store with all the scary-looking stuff. If you request a jazz guitar, you and the salesperson trundle off in a different direction (down toward the guys wearing berets and black turtlenecks sporting "Bird lives!" buttons).

Figure 14-1 shows a collection of some popular models. Notice the diversity in shape and style.

Figure 14-1:
Different downstrokes for different folks.

Now some musical styles do share guitar models. You can play both blues and rock, for example, with equal success on a Fender Stratocaster. And a Gibson Les Paul is just as capable of playing a wailing lead as a Strat. (As a rule, however, the tone of a Les Paul is going to be fatter and less jangly than that of a Strat.) Making your own kind of music on the guitar of your choice is part of the fun.

Following are some popular music styles and classic guitars that most people associate with those styles. This list is by no means exhaustive but does include recognized standard bearers of the respective genres:

- ♪ **Acoustic Blues:** National Steel, Gibson J-200.

- ♪ **Bluegrass:** Martin Dreadnought, Taylor Dreadnought, Collings Dreadnought, Santa Cruz Dreadnought, Gallagher Dreadnought.

- ♪ **Classical:** Ramirez, Hopf, Khono, Humphrey, Hernandez, Alvarez.

- ♪ **Country:** Fender Telecaster, Gretsch 6120, Fender Stratocaster.

- ♪ **Electric Blues:** Gibson ES-355, Fender Telecaster, Fender Stratocaster, Gibson Les Paul.

- ♪ **Folk:** Dreadnoughts and Grand Concerts by Martin, Taylor, Collings, Larrivée, Lowden, and Guild; Gibson J-200; Ovation Adamas.

- ♪ **Heavy Metal:** Gibson Explorer, Flying V, and SG; Fender Stratocaster; Dean; Ibanez Iceman; Jackson Soloist.

- ♪ **Jazz:** Gibson ES-175, Super 400 L-5, and Johnny Smith; archtops by D'Angelico, D'Aquisto, and Benedetto; Epiphone Emperor Regent; Ibanez signature models.

- ♪ **New Age, New Acoustic:** Taylor Grand Concert, Ovation Balladeer, Takamine nylon-electric.

- ♪ **R&B:** Fender Stratocaster, Gibson ES-335.

- ♪ **Rock:** Fender Stratocaster, Gibson Les Paul and SG, Ibanez RG and signature series, Paul Reed Smith, Tom Anderson.

Although the preceding list contains guitars that people generally associate with given styles, don't let that limit your creativity. Play the music you want to play on the guitar you want to play it on, no matter what some chart tells you. In other words, after you study this list, take it with a grain of salt and go pick out the guitar you want, play the music you want, and never mind what some chart tells you.

The Second (And Third . . .) Guitars

Your toughest decisions in buying a guitar may come not with your first instrument at all but with your second. Admit it — your first time out was probably a blur, but now that you know a little bit about guitar playing and what's available out there, you face perhaps an even more daunting prospect than before: What should you choose as your *next* guitar?

If you haven't already developed gear-lust for a certain model but are hankering for a new toy just the same, consider the following three common approaches to choosing another guitar:

♪ **The contrasting and complementary approach.** If you own an acoustic, you may want to consider getting an electric (or vice versa), as having an array of different guitars in your arsenal is always nice. Diversity is very healthy for a person seeking to bolster a collection.

♪ **The clone approach.** Some people just want to acquire as many, say, Les Pauls as they can in a lifetime: old ones, new ones, red ones, blue ones . . . hey — it's *your* money. Buy as many as you want (and can afford).

♪ **The upgrade approach.** If all you ever want to do is master the Stratocaster, just get a better version of what you had before. That way, you can use the new guitar for important occasions, such as recording and performing, and the old ax for going to the beach.

How much should you spend on your second (or later) instrument? One guideline is to go into the next spending bracket from your old guitar. This way, you don't end up with many similar guitars. Plan on spending about $200 more than the current value (not what you paid) of the guitar you own. By doing so, you ensure that, even if you stick with a certain model line, you're getting a guitar that's categorically different from your initial instrument.

When should you stop buying guitars? Why, as soon as the money runs out, of course. Actually, no hard-and-fast rules dictate how many guitars are "enough." These days, however, a reasonably well-appointed guitar arsenal includes a single-coil electric (such as a Fender Strat), a humbucker electric (such as a Gibson Les Paul), a semihollow-body electric, a hollow-body jazz (electric), an acoustic steel-string, an acoustic 12-string, and a nylon-string classical. Then maybe you can add one or two more guitars in a given specialty, such as a guitar set up especially for playing slide, a 12-string electric, or an electric bass.

Then, of course, you can start collecting nonguitar fretted instruments, such as mandolins, banjos, *Dobros* (fretted and played with a slide) . . . but that's another story.

Quality time

In upgrading to a second guitar, the issue again becomes one of quality. But this time, instead of just making sure that you have an instrument that plays in tune, frets easily, and doesn't collapse like a house of cards if you breathe on it, you also need to *make informed decisions*. Don't worry — that's not as grave as it sounds.

At a certain point, the difference between a $600 and a $400 acoustic is that the more expensive guitar has a *solid top*. You may be thinking, "Does that mean that, if I *don't* get a solid top, I'm going to have a guitar that looks like Swiss cheese?"

Not quite. But you can sort out the solid-top issue and more in the following sections. Consider for the moment, however, the following four pillars for judging quality in an instrument:

♪ **Construction:** How the guitar is designed and put together

♪ **Materials:** The woods, metals (used in hardware, pickups, electronics), and other substances used

♪ **Workmanship:** The quality of the building

♪ **Appointments:** The aesthetic additions and other doo-dads

Not sure just what all those terms mean in determining the quality of a guitar? The following sections clue you in.

Construction

How a guitar is built defines what type of guitar it is and (generally) what type of music it's used for. A solid-body guitar has no holes in the body (which adds to its sustain when electrified) and is used for rock. An acoustic archtop is used for traditional jazz, because it has a carved, contoured top, which produces the mellow tones most associated with that style. Here are three of the most important issues regarding guitar construction:

♪ Solid-wood versus laminated-wood construction

♪ Whether the guitar has a body cap

♪ The neck-attachment method

Solid wood versus laminated wood

A solid-wood acoustic guitar is more desirable than a *laminated* acoustic guitar (where, instead of using a solid, thicker piece of top-wood, the guitar maker uses several layers of inexpensive wood pressed together and covered with a veneer). Guitars made completely out of solid wood are very expensive — costing more than $1,000. A good compromise is a solid-top guitar with laminated back and sides. The guitar's top is the most critical element in sound production; the back and sides primarily reflect the sound back through the top.

Another very popular configuration, just a step higher in quality than the solid-top/laminate-back-and-sides combo, is a guitar with a solid top, a solid back, and laminated sides. You can find a wide variety of acoustics constructed this way at around the $1,000 mark and even slightly less. Because the sides have a negligible effect on the sound (even less so than the back does) and because laminates are structurally stronger than solid woods, this setup equates to a win-win situation for both manufacturer and buyer. Some people argue, therefore, that the cheaper manufacturing process (using laminated sides) is also the superior one (because the laminates are stronger than the solid-wood construction).

Body caps

In the electric realm, one big determinant of price is whether the top has a *cap*. A cap is a layer of fine wood — usually a variety of *figured* maple (one having a naturally occurring decorative grain pattern) — that sits on top of the body. Popular cap woods include flame maple and quilted maple. Figured-wood tops usually come with clear, or see-through, finishes to show off the wood's attractive grain pattern.

Neck construction

Neck construction is another area that can affect the price of a guitar. The following list describes the three most common types of neck construction, from the least expensive to the most expensive:

♪ **Bolt-on.** The neck attaches to the back of the guitar at the heel with four or five bolts (although a heel plate sometimes covers the bolt holes). Fender Stratocasters and Telecasters have bolt-on necks.

♪ **Set in (or glued in).** The neck joins the body with an unbroken surface covering the connection, creating a seamless effect from neck to body. The joint is then glued. The Gibson Les Paul and the Paul Reed Smith have set-in necks.

♪ **Neck through body.** A high-end construction where the neck is one long unit (although usually consisting of several pieces of wood glued together) that doesn't stop at the body but continues all the way through to the tail of the guitar. This type of neck is great for getting maximum sustain. A Jackson Soloist is an example of a guitar with a neck-through-body design.

Just because a construction technique is more advanced or expensive doesn't mean that it's necessarily better than other techniques. Could you "improve" the sound of Jimi Hendrix's Strat by modifying its neck to a glued-in configuration? *Sacrilege!*

Materials

A guitar isn't limited by what it's made of any more than a sculpture is. Michelangelo's *David* and your Aunt Agnes' candy dish are both made of marble, but which one would you travel to Paris to see? (*Hint:* Assume that you don't have an overly developed sweet tooth.) So don't judge a guitar only by its materials, but consider that a guitar with better materials (abalone inlays as opposed to plastic ones) has commensurately better workmanship — and therefore is a better guitar — than a model that uses inexpensive materials.

Woods

As you may expect, the more expensive or rare a wood, the more expensive the guitar you construct from that wood. Guitar makers break woods down into categories, and each category has a bearing on the guitar's overall expense. Following are the three criteria used for classifying wood:

♪ **Type.** This category simply determines whether a piece of wood is mahogany, maple, or rosewood. Rosewood tends to be the most expensive wood used in the construction of acoustic-guitar bodies, followed by maple, and then mahogany.

♪ **Style.** You can classify woods further by looking at the wood's region or grain style. Brazilian rosewood is redder and wavier than East Indian rosewood and is also more expensive. The figured maples, such as quilted and flame, are more expensive than rock or bird's-eye maples.

♪ **Grade.** Guitar makers use a grading system, from A to AAA (the highest), to evaluate woods based on grain, color, and consistency. High-quality guitars get the highest-grade wood.

Hardware: Tuners and bridge assemblies

In more expensive instruments, you see upgrades on all components, including the *hardware,* or the metal parts of the guitar. Chrome-plated hardware is usually the cheapest, so if you begin looking at more expensive guitars, you start to see gold-plated and black-matte-finished knobs, switches, and tuning machines in place of chrome.

The actual hardware the manufacturer uses — not just the finishes on it — changes, too, on more expensive instruments. High-quality, name-brand hardware often replaces the guitar maker's less prestigious, generic brand of hardware on high-end axes. For example, manufacturers may use a higher-grade of product for the tuning machines on an upscale guitar — such as *locking Spurzels* (a popular third-party tuner type and brand), which lock the string in place as opposed to forcing the user to tie the string off at the post.

The bridge is an important upgrade area as well. The so-called *floating bridge* (so designated because you can move it up and down by means of the whammy bar) is a complicated affair of springs, fine-tuning knobs, and anchors. The better floating assemblies, such as the Floyd Rose system or systems manufactured under a Floyd Rose license, operate much more smoothly and reliably than do the simple three-spring varieties found on low-cost guitars. (The strings spring right back to pitch on a Floyd Rose system, even after the most torturous whammy bar abuse.)

Pickups and electronics (electrics only)

Unless a guitar manufacturer is also known for making great pickups, you see more and more use of third-party pickups as you go up the quality ladder. In the electric arena, Seymour Duncan, DiMarzio, Bartolini, Bill

Lawrence, Lace, and EMG are examples of high-quality pickup brands that guitar makers piggy-back onto their models. Fishman and L.R. Baggs are two popular acoustic pickup systems found on many well-known guitars.

Although they're not known by name brands, the electronics in guitars also improve along with the other components as you venture into more expensive territory. You can see a greater variety, for example, in pickup manipulation. Manufacturers can *tap* double-coil, or humbucker, pickups, turning them into single coils to emulate the behavior of Stratlike pickups. Having one guitar that can imitate the pickup behavior of other guitar types provides you with a tonally versatile instrument. You also see more manipulation in wiring schemes. For example, guitar makers may reverse the *polarity* of a pickup — the direction the signal flows — to make the guitar sound softer and more swirly. You may also encounter improved *calibration,* or, more correctly for guitar applications, *taper,* on the volume and tone knobs.

Taper is the gradualness or abruptness of change (also called *response*) of a signal's characteristics (in this case, volume and tone) as you turn a knob from its minimum value to its maximum. A knob exhibiting a smoother taper is evidence of a higher grade of electronics. Really cheap guitars give you no sound at all until turned up to 3; then you get a swell of sound from about 4 to about 7 and no change at all between 7 and the knob's maximum value, 10 — or, on those really rare, loud guitars, 11. (And if you don't get that last joke, go out and rent the hilarious rockumentary spoof *This Is Spinal Tap*. It's required viewing for all guitarists.)

Workmanship

For more expensive guitars, you can really bring out the white glove and get fussy. We've seen prospective buyers bring in a dentist's mirror to inspect the interior of an acoustic guitar.

For acoustic guitars more expensive than the $600 range, you should expect to find *gapless joints* — solid wood-to-wood connections between components, especially where the neck meets the body. You should also expect clean and glob-free gluing (in the top and back bracing), a smooth and even finish application, and a good setup: the strings at the right height with no buzzing, the neck warp- and twist-free, and the intonation true. (See Chapter 17 for more information on intonation.)

You can glean all this information by simply playing the guitar and noting your impressions. Like traveling in a Rolls-Royce or Bentley, playing a quality guitar should be one smooth ride.

Appointments (cosmetics)

Appointments are the fancy stuff that have no acoustic or structural effect on the guitar. They exist solely as decorative elements. Some people find fancy appointments showy or pretentious, but remember that a great guitar is a work of art to behold with the eye as well as the ear.

Typical appointments include intricate neck inlays (such as abalone figures countersunk into the fretboard), a fancy headstock design, gold-plated hardware, and, on an acoustic guitar, lining around the edges of the body and the sound hole.

One subtle aspect about appointments: You may think that the only difference between two guitars is in the appointments — for example, a fancy inlay job may seem to be the only thing that distinguishes between a certain company's Grand Deluxe and Deluxe models. But the truth is that the more expensive guitar — although nominally the same in materials and construction — often gets the choicest materials and enjoys higher quality-control standards.

This situation is just a Darwinian reality. If 12 pieces of wood, all destined to become guitar tops, come into the factory, slated for six Grand Deluxes and six Deluxes (fictitious titles, by the way, bearing no resemblance to actual guitar models, living or deceased), the six best pieces of wood go to the Grand Deluxes and the six next-best pieces to the Deluxe models. They all share identical grading, but humans with subjective powers decide which models get which tops.

The best materials, however, don't always equate to the best sound. Remember the adage about wine: The best soil isn't what produces good wine but the poor soil. You need to "stress" guitars (you know, make 'em work!), as you do grapes (and humans!), to produce their best work.

Buying an Ax to Grind

Buying a guitar is no more different than buying a car or house (okay, it's a *little* less monumental than buying a house) in that it's an exciting endeavor and lots of fun, but you must exercise caution and be a savvy customer, too. Only *you* know the right guitar for you, what the right price is for your budget and commitment level, and whether a deal feels right or not. Don't deny your natural instincts as a shopper, even if you're new to guitar shopping. Look, listen, consider, go have lunch before the big buy, and talk it over with your sweetie.

Bringing along an expert

A certain saying goes, "An expert is someone who knows more than you do." If you have such a friend — whose knowledge and experience in guitars exceeds your own — bring the friend along, by all means. This friend not only knows about guitars, but also knows *you*. A salesperson doesn't know you, nor does he necessarily have your best interests in mind. But a friend does. And another opinion never hurts, if only to help you articulate your own.

Enlist your guitar teacher (if you have one) to help you navigate through the guitar buyer's jungle, especially if he's been with you awhile and knows your tastes and playing style. Your teacher may know things about you that you may not even realize about yourself — for example, that you've gotten sidetracked in the steel-string section although your principal interests lie in nylon-string guitar music. A good teacher asks questions, listens to your answers, and gently guides you to where *you* want to go.

Another saying, however, goes, "Moe was the smartest of the Three Stooges." If you have a friend who's like Moe — smarter than you in matters of the guitar but otherwise one string short of a set — leave him at home. You don't need a wise guy goofing around (and tweaking the salesperson's nose with a pair of pliers) while you're trying to concentrate.

Meeting the salesperson

Dealing with a salesperson doesn't need to become a stressful, adversarial affair, but some people get pretty anxious about the entire situation. If you establish your priorities before you enter the store, you don't come off as vague and unprepared as he begins his salvo of questions.

A typical first question from a salesperson may be "How much do you want to spend?" In essence, the question means "What price range are you looking at so that I know to which end of the store to take you?" It's a fair question, and if you can answer directly, you end up saving a lot of time. He may also ask about your playing ability and your style preferences, so be ready to answer those questions, too.

Be prepared to answer the salesperson's questions succinctly — for example, "I prefer Strat-style guitars, although not necessarily by Fender, and I'm an intermediate blues player — not a shredder — and I'd like to keep costs at less than $600." Answers such as these make you sound decisive and thoughtful. The salesperson should have plenty to go on from that kind of information. But if you instead say, "Oh, for the right guitar, price is no object; I like the one that what's-his-name plays on MTV," you're not going to be taken seriously — nor are you likely to end up with the instrument you need.

As the salesperson speaks, listen carefully and ask questions. You're there to observe and absorb, not impress. If you decide you're not ready to buy at this point, tell him that. Thank him for his time and get his card. You're certainly free to go elsewhere and investigate another store. To do so not only is your option — it's your duty!

Remember that you're *shopping*. And the whole shopping experience is no different with guitars than it is with any other commodity. Do your research and get differing opinions *before* you buy. And trust your instincts.

The art of the deal

You can find out the *retail* or *list price* of an instrument before you walk into the store. The manufacturer presets these numbers, and they're public knowledge. Look at the ads in guitar magazines for the company's contact info and call the company or visit its Web site to determine the manufacturer's suggested retail price on a particular product or to receive literature. As of this writing, a Gibson Les Paul Standard *lists* for $2,399, and a Fender American Standard Stratocaster *lists* for $979.99. Figure 14-2 shows these two industry stalwarts.

Gibson Les Paul

Fender Stratocaster

Figure 14-2:
Two
standards
by which
players
judge
most of
the electric
guitars on
the market.

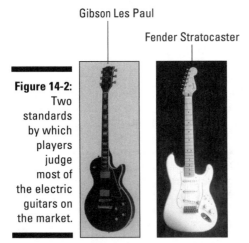

Again, the preceding numbers are *list* prices. Music stores offer discounts, and the range can vary greatly. Big, urban-based stores that buy mass quantities of instruments can usually offer greater discounts than can smaller (mom-and-pop) stores in outlying or remote areas. Mail-order outlets can match and sometimes beat big-store prices, because they don't have the overhead of maintaining a retail facility.

In deciding where to buy, don't neglect the value of service. Retail stores — unlike mail-order houses — are in a better position to devote close, personal service to a new guitar customer. Perhaps as a result of facing stiff competition from the booming mail-order biz, many stores are upping their service incentives. Service includes anything from fixing minor problems and making adjustments to providing periodic *setups* (sort of like a tune-up and oil change for your guitar).

Remember, however, that list prices are public knowledge, and salespeople from all types of vendors must tell you their selling price *with no strings attached* (uh, by that we mean *unconditionally*). The vendor can rightfully charge up to list price; you must wrangle the maximum discount yourself. How you do that is as old as bargaining itself, but a reasonable haggling range is somewhere between the cut-rate quote of a nationally advertising mail-order house and 10-percent-off list.

Chapter 15

Guitar Accessories

● ●

In This Chapter

▶ Cranking up the wattage with amps

▶ Completing your arsenal

▶ Understanding the importance of the little things

● ●

*A*fter you get your guitar squared away, you need to think about all the little (and not-so-little) items that make life so much easier — if you're a guitarist, that is. Some of the products that we describe in this chapter are essential — for example, cases and strings (and amps if you're playing electric) — while you can think of others merely as accessories. But all these items are useful and have some musical or practical application. You find no plugs for bumper stickers and mugs that read "Guitarists are *strum-thing special*" in these pages — just the short list of stuff that's really useful.

Amps

Strictly speaking, you can play an electric guitar without any amplification, but playing that way's not much fun. Without an amp, you hear the notes buzzing like little musical mosquitoes, but you don't achieve any expression or tone. And you can't possibly rattle the windows and shake the floorboards with your newly learned "Smoke on the Water" riff unless you're wired up and have decibels to burn.

We recommend that you save your most critical purchasing decision for the guitar. But after you break the bank to get that guitar that's just beyond your means, you may as well go right out and exercise some more financial irresponsibility and get a good amp. You can't start to develop a fully mature and individual tone until you have both a quality guitar and a decent amp to run it through. But if you *must* skimp somewhere, we suggest that you skimp on the amp side — at first.

The biggest differences between practice amps and performance amps boil down to size, wattage, and cost. Figure 15-1 shows a practice amp and a performance amp.

Figure 15-1:
Performance amps (such as the one on the left) are bigger and more powerful than the practice amp at the right.

Getting started with a practice amp

If you have limited funds, start out with what's known as a *practice amp* — one with a decent feature set (tone controls, reverb, and two or more volume controls so that you can sculpt your distorted sound) and that delivers a good sound but at low volumes (6 to 12 watts is typical on practice amps). This type of starter amp accustoms you to hearing the electric guitar as it's designed to be heard — through a guitar amp. Practice amps also help prepare you for the next step up: *performance amps.*

Practice amps can run as little as $175 and boast features that appear on their higher-priced performance counterparts. In amplifiers, power — not features — is what drives up the price.

Power is expensive to build, requiring heavy-duty transformers, speakers, and cabinetry. For home and casual use — such as jamming with a couple of friends in a garage or basement — 15 or 20 watts is often plenty loud enough, and 6 to 12 watts is sufficient for solo practicing and playing along with your stereo.

Features, on the other hand, such as tone controls and effects (reverb, tremolo), are easier to implement because the manufacturers can stamp them onto a chip and install it on a circuit board. Following are some useful things to look for in a practice amp:

♪ Multiple-gain stages (two or more volume controls)

♪ Three-band EQ (*equalization,* or tone controls for bass, mid, and high)

♪ Built-in reverb

♪ Channel switching via footswitch

♪ Headphone jack

Amplification without an amp

You can get away without buying an amp by plugging your electric guitar into the *auxiliary inputs* of your home stereo, but you do need to buy a special adapter. You can readily purchase these devices at Radio Shack or at a music store for about $2. (Just tell the salesperson what you want to do, and he can supply you with the right unit.) The adapter is just a metal or plastic-coated plug that has a mono, female, quarter-inch jack on one end and a male, RCA (sometimes called *phono*) plug on the other.

Warning! Before you go plugging anything in to a stereo or boom box, make sure that the volume control on the receiver is turned *all the way down*. This precaution prevents any sudden pop or surge in the system, which is potentially damaging to the speakers.

Because you plug into, say, the left input of your receiver, you hear music only out of the left speaker. Some higher-end receivers enable you to set the *output mode* (the stereo configuration) of the source signal. If you see a bunch of settings such as L, R, L+R, and so on, set that knob to L (meaning left channel out of both speakers). It's not stereo, but it sounds fuller and more widely dispersed than if it's coming out of only one speaker.

The figure below shows the procedure for plugging into the back of your receiver. Plug one end of the guitar cord into your guitar and the other end into the adapter. Plug the adapter into the left auxiliary input in the back of your receiver. On the receiver's front panel, select Aux 1 or whatever is the corresponding name of the input into which you plugged your guitar. (It may be Tape 1 or some other name — check the input itself or your owner's manual if in doubt.) Turn your guitar's volume up full. Then, slowly, turn up the receiver's volume knob until you hear sound.

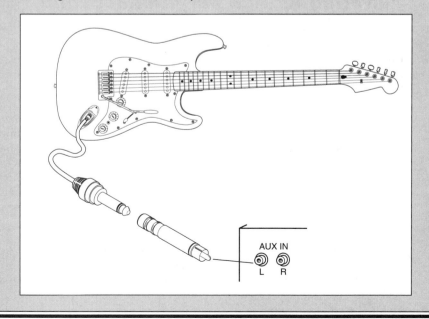

AUX IN
L   R

Some practice amps include *channel switching* (which enables you to access different sets of volume and tone control); others don't. Decide whether that feature's important enough to pay for in a practice amp. You can always get your distorted sound through an external effect, such as a stomp box, but that's a little bit more of a hassle. (See the section "Effect Pedals and Devices," later in this chapter for more information on distortion and other effects.)

A headphone jack is a very handy thing in a practice amp as it enables you to get a fully amp-treated sound without going through the speaker. Great for late-night practice sessions!

Because of the miniaturization of all things electronic, you can now get full-sounding, authentic guitar sounds from a unit the size of a disposable camera — as long as you listen to it through headphones (meaning that it has no speaker or amplifier of its own). These strap-on wonders come with belt clips and are battery powered for untethered practicing (great for walking into the bathroom and standing in front of the mirror). And they offer distortion, EQ, reverb, and other effects; numerous *presets* (sounds programmed or set up by the manufacturer); and stereo sound. These units are great for playing in a moving vehicle and can even output a signal to tape or disk, suitable for recording. They cost about $200 (the Korg Pandora, Scholz Rockman, and Zoom 9000 series are just some makes and models) but are worth the price if portability, privacy, and authentic tone are important to you.

Powering up to a performance amp

Where practice amps start to pale is if you try to turn them up to performance levels. *Performance,* in this case, means anything from cutting through three friends in a garage jam to making yourself heard over the antics of the overly zealous drummer and bass player at Slippery Sam's Saturday Night Blues Bash.

After you decide to take the plunge into higher-quality amps, you have a galaxy of makes and models from which to choose. Talk to other guitarists and music salespeople, read guitar magazines, and listen to CDs to find out what amps the artists you like are using. Remember that your choice of amp is just as personal and individual as that of your guitar. The amp must not only sound good, but also look good and *feel* as if it's just the right amp for you. The pursuit of the perfect amp is as elusive as the quest for the perfect guitar. Well, almost.

Performance amps are more powerful than practice amps. More power doesn't just mean a louder amp. Increased power also delivers a cleaner, purer signal at higher volumes. In other words, if two amps of different power are producing the same overall loudness, the more powerful amp yields the cleaner signal.

Buying a recording amp is one case where power is not a significant indicator of price. Many manufacturers make high-quality amps that deliver only low power, and these amps are especially popular for recording because they don't shake the foundations of your house to make music. For many people who record at home, an amp that's *running hot* (one at full or near-full volume) gives the best performance, and yet they don't need the overall loudness (what you actually hear) hovering at high levels, because the only thing you need to impress is the microphone in front of your speaker.

A 50-watt amp is usually more than sufficient for home and normal performing circumstances, such as playing in a five-piece band at a local pub. If you play larger venues or play in a genre that requires unusually loud levels — such as heavy metal — go with 100 watts. Some players who desire a squeaky-clean sound and who run in stereo (requiring double the power) may opt for 100 watts regardless, because they can stay cleaner at louder levels.

Many amps can operate at either 100 or 50 watts by enabling you to select the power via a switch. Why would you want to operate at 50 watts if you paid for a 100-watt amp? For precisely the same strategy toward cleanness of the signal. A 50-watt amp breaks up or distorts sooner than a 100-watt one does, and for many types of music (blues, rock, metal), this distortion is desirable.

Once upon a time, all electronic circuits were powered by vacuum tubes — those glass cylinders that glow red in the back of old radios. As technology has developed, solid-state electronics (which consists of transistors and, later, microchips) has replaced tubes, except in guitar amps. Tube technology produces the "best" tone for guitars because, although they're not as efficient or even as accurate in faithfully reproducing the original signal, the tube amps actually deliver the most musical results. All your favorite guitarists record and play exclusively with tube amps, from the 100-watt Marshall to the Fender Twin, to the Vox AC30 and the MESA/Boogie Dual Rectifier.

As a beginner, you may not appreciate (or care about) the differences between tube and solid-state tone. You can get good-sounding distortion out of a solid-state amp anyway, and these are usually cheaper, so you should probably go with a solid-state amp and ignore the whole tone debate. Besides, you may prefer to get your distortion sound from a pedal, and then the whole issue is moot. Look instead for features such as built-in effects (reverb, chorus, and so on) and a headphone jack. Above all, listen to the sound and turn the knobs. If you like what you hear and you feel comfortable dialing in the different sounds, that's the amp for you.

A Case for Cases

A guitar case is so important to your guitar that many manufacturers include the case in the price of the guitar. Many manufacturers make cases specially designed for particular models and ship the guitars inside these cases to the retailer. This practice makes buying the guitar without the case difficult — and rightly so. To buy a serious instrument and then try to carry it away from the store without the appropriate, quality protection is a foolish way to save a few bucks. The most important gesture of respect that you can show your instrument is to give it a safe place to sleep.

Cases come in three basic types: the hard or hard-shell type; the soft variety; and the gig bag. Each has its advantages, and the protection factor is proportional to cost: The more expensive the case, the better the protection that it offers your instrument.

Hard cases

The *hard case* is the most expensive ($80–$120 and more) but offers the best insurance against damage to your guitar. It's composed of leather- or nylon-covered wood and can even survive the rigors of airline baggage handlers, providing crush-proof protection to your instrument. They can drop heavy objects on the case and stack it safely under other luggage items without any damage accruing to the precious guitar inside.

The safest thing to do is to go with a hard case, unless you have some really compelling reason not to. If you don't already have a case for your guitar and are thinking of buying one, try to think of any situation where a hard case may *not* be appropriate. If you can't produce a quick and ready response, spring for the hard case and be done with it.

Soft cases

The *soft case* is not completely soft, being in fact more stiff than truly soft. It usually consists of some pressed-particle material, such as cardboard, and can provide some protection for your instrument — for example, if someone drops a coffee mug on it (an empty coffee mug, that is). But that's about it. You can pick up these cases for about $30.

The soft case is the inexpensive alternative to the hard case because it enables you to transport your instrument without exposing it to the elements and at least prevents an outside intruder from scratching it. But these cases easily buckle if put to any real stress (such as getting caught in an airport conveyer belt) and cave in, fold, and puncture much more easily than a hard case does. In most cases, however, a soft case provides protection against the daily bumps and grinds that would otherwise scratch an unprotected guitar.

Gig bags

The *gig bag* provides almost no protection against shock because it's a form-fitting nylon, leather, or other fabric enclosure — you know, a bag. Gig bags zip shut and are about the consistency of any other soft luggage carrier. They cost anywhere from $25 to $150.

The advantage of gig bags is that they're light, they fit on your shoulder, and they take up no more room than the guitar itself — making them the ideal case if you're trying to fit your electric guitar into the overhead bin of an airplane.

People who live in big cities and take public transportation favor gig bags. With the gig bag over their shoulder and a luggage cart toting an amp in one hand, they still have a hand free to feed a token into a subway turnstile and hold the poles on a train car. But a gig bag is not nearly as protective as a soft case, and you can't stack anything on top of a bagged guitar.

Capos

A *capo* (pronounced KAY-po) is a spring-loaded, adjustable-tension (or elastic) clamp that wraps around the neck of a guitar and covers all the strings, forcing them all down to the fretboard at a given fret. This device effectively raises the pitch of all the strings by a given number of frets (or half steps). In some cases, you may want to tune your guitar with the capo on, but most of the time, you tune up without it and then place it on the desired fret. Capos enable you to transpose the music you play on your guitar to another key, while you still play the chord fingerings in the original key. (See Chapter 12 for more information on capos.) Figure 15-2 shows a few different capo types you can find at most music stores.

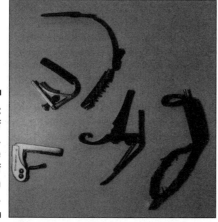

Figure 15-2:
A variety of capos. Capos raise the pitch of the open strings.

Capos cost between $5 and $25, with the elastic-band type being the cheapest. The higher-priced clamp and screw-on types are more popular with serious capo users because you can put them on with one hand, and these types of capos generally hold the strings down better than the elastic kind does. The screw-on type, such as the one made by Shubb is a particular favorite because you can vary the size and tension of the capo's grip, which enables you to customize the capo size for different parts of the neck. (The lower frets of the neck, toward the headstock, require a smaller capo opening than do the higher frets.)

Effect Pedals and Devices

Electric guitarists seldom just plug into an amp and start playing. Well, they may start out that way, but if you listen to the radio — or any recorded guitar music, for that matter — you quickly notice a lot more going on than just a "straight" guitar sound. At the very least, you hear some ambient treatment in the form of artificially created echo, or *reverb,* as the effect is known in guitar lingo. You may hear some (intended) distortion, especially in rock and blues music, and you may hear additional effects, such as wah-wah, vibrato, and other electronic manipulations.

Welcome to the wonderful, wacky world of *effects*. Effects are devices that plug in between your guitar and amplifier and enable you to alter your signal in all sorts of creative and unusual ways. Scores and scores of these little devices are available from all different manufacturers and in all price ranges. You can buy them as individual units or as an all-in-one box, called a *multi-effects processor*. But whether you go for the package deal or à la carte, effects can spice up the basic sound of your guitar in all sorts of exciting ways.

Most effects come in the form of foot-accessed pedals, also known as *stomp boxes* because they reside on the floor and you activate them by stepping on a footswitch. This setup enables you to selectively turn effects on and off while playing the guitar without interruption. Figure 15-3 shows a typical effects setup with a reasonable number of pedals in the *signal chain* (that is, the path from guitar to amp).

If you plug, say, a reverb device *inline* (that is, between the amp and guitar), you can make your guitar sound as if you're playing in a cathedral. A distortion unit can make your tones sound like those of Jimi Hendrix, even at low volumes and with your amp set to a clean sound. An EQ device is a fancy tone control that gives you increased flexibility over the bass, midrange, and treble makeup of your sound.

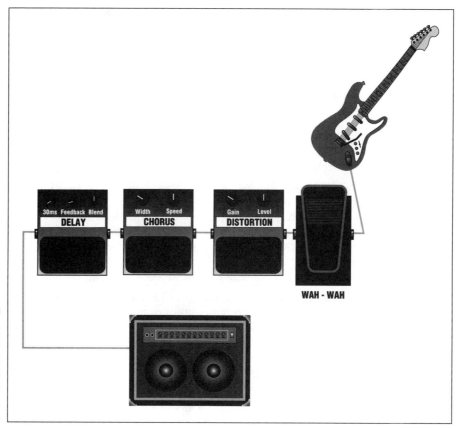

Figure 15-3:
A typical setup for a guitarist using effects.

Dozens of different types of effects are available — more than you could possibly own, not to mention use all at once. The price of these individual units varies, too, with distortion boxes as cheap as $45 and digital reverbs and delays as much as $175 (or more). To help you sort through the myriad of flavors and types, following is a list of some of the most popular effects:

♪ **Distortion.** This effect simulates the sound of a guitar signal driven too hard for the amplifier; the device overdrives the signal to the point that it breaks up — but in a musically pleasing way. Distortion, to a guitarist, can mean anything from a slightly fat, warm quality to a fuzzy sustain, to screaming chain-saw fuzz, as used by metal and grunge bands.

♪ **Chorus.** This effect simulates the sound of many guitars playing at once, making the overall sound fatter. Tuning up the speed yields a warbling or tremolo-like effect.

♪ **Flanger/phase shifter.** These two devices produce similar effects that create a whooshy, swirly, underwater sound, kind of like that of the revolving Leslie speaker cabinets popular for Hammond organs in the '60s and '70s.

♪ **Pitch shifter.** This device (also known as a *harmonizer*) enables you to play in harmony with yourself by splitting your signal into two paths, the original and a user-defined musical interval, such as a major third (four half steps away); it also provides choruslike effects. A popular fixed-interval pitch shifter is the *octave pedal,* used to great effect by Jimi Hendrix, which produces a pitch one or two (or both) octaves (12 half steps) lower than the original.

♪ **Digital delay.** This device produces a discrete repetition of your sound, good for echoes, spacious effects, and creating rhythmically timed repeats of your notes. The analog version was a tape-echo device that actually recorded the sound on magnetic tape and played it back moments later. Tape echoes still enjoy some popularity because of their unique, vintage-sounding, tonal quality (which is inferior to the digital version in terms of exact replication of the original signal).

♪ **Wah-wah pedal.** This effects pedal is a type of frequency filter (which varies the bass and treble content of a signal) that imbues the guitar with expressive, vocal-like characteristics (it actually sounds as if it's saying "wah"). You control the sound by raising and lowering a foot pedal. This device was made popular by Jimi Hendrix and was a staple of the disco-guitar sound. Eric Clapton also gave the wah a workout on "White Room" during his Cream days.

♪ **Reverb.** This effect reproduces the natural echo sound produced in environments such as a large room, gymnasium, cathedral, and so on. It's usually included on amps in a limited version (often having only one control), but having it as a separate effect gives you a lot more variety and control.

♪ **Tremolo.** Like reverb, tremolo was included on many amps from the '50s and '60s (such as the Fender Twin Reverb) and is now available in a pedal. Tremolo is the rapid wavering of the volume (not pitch, like vibrato) that makes your guitar sound as if you're playing it through a slowly moving electric fan.

♪ **Multi-effects units.** Individual pedals are a great convenience because they enable you to buy effects one at a time and use them in a *modular* fashion — you can choose to include them in your chain or not, and you can rearrange their order to create different effects. But many guitarists opt for a multi-effects unit, which puts all the individual effects into one housing. Multi-effects units are *programmable,* meaning that you can store different settings in your individual effects and recall these with the tap of a foot. Multi-effects units can also offer modularity, although they accomplish it electronically rather than physically.

Generally, a multi-effects unit can do anything that individual pedals do, so most guitarists who use a lot of effects eventually buy one. You can still use your individual pedals, too, by hooking them up with the multi-effects unit. Most guitarists still keep their individual pedals even after acquiring a multi-effects unit, because the individual pedals are small and convenient, and a guitarist may not want to lug the larger, more cumbersome multi-effects unit to a casual jam session. The price range for guitar multi-effects units is $140 to $1,500.

Picks

You're sure, in your musical career, to lose, break, toss to adoring fans as souvenirs, and otherwise part company with hundreds of picks, so don't get attached (in a sentimental sense) to them. Treat them as the inexpensive, expendable commodity they are. Stock up by the gross with your favorite color and gauge (thickness) and always carry spares in your wallet, the car, the flaps of your penny loafers, and any other . . . er, convenient place. After you get used to a certain gauge, shape, and make of pick, you don't change around much, even going from electric to acoustic or vice versa.

Strings

You always need to keep extra strings on hand for the simple reason that, if you break one, you need to replace it immediately. To do so requires that you carry at least an extra full set to prepare for any one of your six strings breaking. (Unlike with a car, where one spare fits all, guitars use six individually gauged strings, which means that you must always carry a full set as a spare. And woe to the guitarists who keep breaking the same string over and over — they're going to have an awful lot of partial sets around.)

Fortunately, string sets are cheap — about $7 if you buy them in single sets and cheaper still if you buy in boxes of 12 sets. In a pinch, you can substitute an adjacent string (a B string for a G, for example). Remember to *always* keep at least *one full set* in your case at all times.

The higher, unwound strings tend to break more easily than do the lower wound ones, so try to carry three spares each of the high E, B, and G strings (on an electric and nylon, the G is unwound). You can buy single strings for about $1.50 apiece.

Straps

Straps come in all kinds of styles and materials, from nylon to woven fabric to leather. The first rule in choosing a strap is that you get the most comfortable one that you can afford. Wearing a guitar on your shoulder for long periods of time can cause discomfort, and the better the strap is, the more it protects your muscles against strain and fatigue.

Appearance is a close second to comfort as a factor in deciding what strap to buy. You must like the look of your strap, as its function isn't just utilitarian but aesthetic as well. Because it drapes over your shoulder, a strap functions almost like an article of clothing. So try to match the look of your strap to your own look as well as to the look of your guitar.

You can get custom-made straps with your initials embroidered in them, if that's your thing (a must-have if you plan on being a country music matinee idol). Or you can get them in all sorts of motifs, from Southwest patterns to lighting bolts and pentagrams. But if you're looking at strictly the price, a simple, no-frills nylon strap costs as little as $5 and holds your guitar as securely as a $200 one with your name embossed in leather.

If you own more than one guitar, you're best off with a strap for each type of guitar, electric and acoustic. That way, you don't need to keep adjusting it as you switch from electric to acoustic and back again.

Electronic Tuners

Although you can tune a guitar to itself, keeping the guitar up to *concert pitch* — the absolute tuning reference of A-440 — is best, especially if you plan to play with other instruments. A guitar is also structurally and acoustically happiest at that tuning. (See Chapter 2 for more information on tuning your guitar.) The best way to keep your guitar at this tuning is to secure a battery-powered electronic tuner and keep it in your guitar case. You can either plug your electric guitar right into the tuner or use the turner's built-in microphone to tune your acoustic.

Obviously, if you're using an electric guitar, you should plug into the tuner first; then, from the tuner's output jack, plug into your amp. That way, your tuner stays inline the entire time you play. Turn off the tuner, however, after you're done tuning to preserve the life of its battery. The signal passes through the dormant tuner unaffected.

If you have an acoustic, you can use the tuner's built-in microphone for tuning. You don't need to go to great pains to get the microphone to pick up the guitar. Placing the tuner an arm's length away on a table top is fine;

balancing it on your knee works well, too. If the surrounding atmosphere is quiet enough, you can even keep your tuner on the floor. (But excessive room noise can confuse a tuner.)

Virtually all electronic tuners sold these days are the auto-sensing, chromatic type. *Auto-sensing* means that the tuner listens to your note and tells you what its nearest pitch is (with indicator lights). A meter with a moving needle or array of indicator lights then tells you if you're flat or sharp of that note. As you tune the guitar, you see the meter change in the direction of your tuning motions. The word *chromatic* just means that the tuner shows you all the notes in the musical scale (flats and sharps, too), not just the notes of the open strings of the guitar. Having all notes available on your tuner is important should you ever decide to tune the guitar differently. (See Chapter 10 for more information on alternate tunings.) The prices of electronic tuners range from $20 to $300.

Some Other Helpful (But Nonessential) Goodies

You can treat yourself to a number of other little doo-dads and contraptions that make guitar playing a lot more painless and convenient. In no particular order, consider some of these gizmos, which are often worth their weight in thumbpicks. Figure 15-4 shows these items, which we define in the following list:

- ♪ **Batteries.** Tuners, effects pedals, and even some guitars (those with *active electronics*) run on batteries. Stock up on a couple of nine-volts and a few AAs and store them in a sealed plastic bag.

- ♪ **Bridge pins.** These little plastic pieces wedge your strings into the bridge of your acoustic. The problem is that, if you lose one (because it goes flying off a dock or into the grass after you yank it out), you can't find anything to substitute for it. Match sticks are the closest thing, but who carries those things around these days? The next time you're at the music store buying strings, make sure that you also pick up a couple of extra bridge pins.

- ♪ **Cords and cables.** A crackling cable is no fun for either you or your audience. That nasty sound means that your connections are worn and bad — it happens. Keep extra cables on hand of both the long variety (for connecting your guitar to an effect or an amp) and the short (for interpedal connections).

- ♪ **Cassette recorder.** Don't miss capturing a once-in-a-lifetime musical moment because you don't have a tape recorder on hand. You never know when inspiration may strike. If you play with other people —

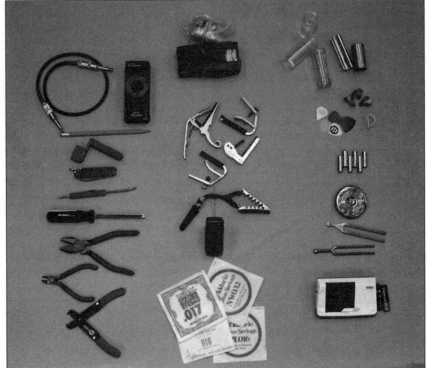

Figure 15-4:
Some helpful accessories designed to make guitar life just a little easier.

especially those who can teach you something — keep the recorder handy so that you can preserve licks, riffs, and other cool moves for later study. Microcassette recorders are great because they fit right into your guitar case. After you get good at recording your ideas, you may even consider taking along a four-track recorder (one that enables you to *overdub*, or add parts to, existing tracks). You can create multipart arrangements with a four-track instead of being limited to only the simple ideas that you can capture on a normal cassette recorder. You can get a four-track for as little as $200.

♪ **Cloth.** You should always wipe down your guitar after playing to remove body oils that can corrode strings and muck up the finish. Cotton is good, and chamois is better. At least give your fingerboard a wipe before you put it in the case, and if you're playing with short sleeves, give the top a rubdown, too.

♪ **Ear plugs.** If you play electric guitar and find yourself in a lot of im-promptu jam sessions, you should carry ear plugs. Your ears are your most precious musical commodity — more important than even your fingers. Don't damage them by exposing them to loud noises in close rehearsal quarters. Buy the kind of ear plugs made especially for music listening; they *attenuate* (reduce) frequencies at equal rates across the spectrum. So it's like hearing the original music . . . only softer. Many guitarists are advocates of ear plugs, including the Who's Pete Townshend, who claims to have suffered significant hearing loss resulting from long-term exposure to loud music.

♪ **Pencil and paper.** Always carry something that you can write with and on. That way, you can jot down lyrics, a cool chord that someone shows you, a cheat sheet so that you can pick up a chord progression in a jiffy, or even a surreptitious note to another musician. ("Please tell your bass player to turn it down — I've lost three fillings already!")

♪ **Reversible screwdriver.** You can fix everything from a rattling pickup to a loose set screw in a tuning key with such a handy screwdriver. Get one that has both a Phillips and straight-blade tip.

♪ **Peg winder.** This inexpensive ($2) crank turns your tuning keys at about 10 times the rate that you can turn them by hand. At no extra charge, these devices include a notched groove that's perfect for removing stuck bridge pins in your acoustic.

♪ **Wire cutters/needle-nose pliers.** Strings are, after all, wires. They can bind up, and they need to be cut. Pack a pair of clips for snipping away the excess and for digging out a stubborn remnant from a tuning post.

Other doo-dads you may want to consider throwing in your back pack, gym bag, or all-leather monogrammed accessories case include the following:

♪ **Tuning fork/Pitch pipe.** Having one of these low-tech tuning devices as a spare never hurts, in case the battery on your electronic tuner fails or the tuner itself gets stepped on by the gravitationally challenged drummer. Both of these devices are like rowboats in a speedboat and sailboat world: After the gas is gone and the wind stops blowing, you can still function using your own power.

♪ **Penlight.** You don't need to wait until night to use a flashlight. Shadows and small sizes pose as much a problem for diagnosing, say, a simple electrical problem as does the complete absence of light. You can hold a penlight between your teeth as you reach into the back of your amp to fix a broken speaker lead.

♪ **Cable tester and volt/ohm meter.** These items cost about $12 and $20, respectively, and earn their keep the first time they diagnose a bad or reverse-wired cable. Learn how to use the volt-ohm meter with respect to your equipment — that is, know what power supplies you have and what the appropriate settings are on the meter. You can impress your friends with your "gearhead-geek" aptitude.

♪ **Fuses.** Any new environment can have unpredictable wiring schemes that could cause havoc with your gear — and especially your amp. Your amp's first line of defense is its fuse. If the house current is weird, the fuse blows, and you must have a replacement to get the amp working again.

♪ **Duct tape.** This stuff is the musician's baking soda — an all-purpose utility product that cures a multitude of maladies. You can use duct tape to fix everything from a rattling tailpiece to a broken microphone clip. Even the roll itself is handy: You can use it to tilt your amp up for better monitoring. Use duct tape to fix your car's upholstery or even patch the holes of your jeans, onstage or off. In some circles, it's even considered fashionable.

Part VI
Care and Feeding

The 5th Wave   By Rich Tennant

You still sound a little flat.

In this part . . .

As you practice on your guitar more and more, you're likely to find that it's not unlike a favorite pet. You become very attached to it, but you also have to take care of it and baby it. Okay, you probably won't find yourself dropping it table scraps, but you do have to know how to do some everyday maintenance. Chapter 16 outlines the procedure for dealing with broken strings, and Chapter 17 tells you about the daily maintenance that every guitarist should be able to perform.

Chapter 16

Getting Strung Along: Changing Strings

. . . .

In This Chapter

▶ Restringing a steel-string acoustic guitar

▶ Restringing a nylon-string guitar

▶ Restringing an electric guitar

. . . .

Many people consider their guitars to be delicate, precious, and fragile instruments: They seem reluctant to tune their strings, let alone change them. Although you should be careful not to drop or scratch your guitar (and setting guitars afire à la Jimi Hendrix generally causes *significant* damage), you needn't worry about causing damage by changing, tuning, or overtightening guitar strings. The fact is that guitars are incredibly rugged and can deal with hundreds of pounds of string tension while enduring the playing styles of even the most heavy-handed guitarists.

Changing strings isn't something you should be shy about: You can jump into it with both feet. The task's sort of like giving your dog a bath: It's good for the dog, you're be glad you did it, and it gives you an opportunity to get closer to man's best friend. Similarly, changing your guitar strings has little downside: It improves the sound of the guitar, helps to prevent broken strings at inopportune moments, and aids you in identifying other mainte-nance problems. During periodic string changing, for example, you may discover a gouged bridge slot or a loose or rattling tuning post. (We cover these maladies more fully in Chapter 17.)

Restringing Strategies

Old guitars improve with age, but old strings just get worse. The first time you play new strings is the best they ever sound. Strings gradually become worse until they either break or you can't take the dreary sounds they produce. Old strings sound dull and lifeless, and they lose their *tensility* (their capability to hold tension), becoming brittle. This condition makes the strings feel stiffer and harder to fret, and because the strings no longer stretch to reach the fret, they get tighter, causing your notes to go sharp, particularly up the neck.

Unless you break a string and must replace it in an emergency, you should replace all the strings at once. The strings tend to wear at the same rate, so if you replace all the old strings with new ones simultaneously, the strings start the race against time on an equal footing.

The following list contains the conditions under which you should probably replace your strings:

♪ They exhibit visible signs of corrosion or caked-on dirt or grime.

♪ They don't play in tune, usually fretting sharp, especially in the upper register.

♪ You can't remember the last time you changed them and you have an important gig (and don't want to chance any breakage).

Removing Old Strings

Obviously, to put on a new string, you have to remove the old one. Unless you're really in a hurry (such as in the middle of the first verse, trying to get your new string on and tuned up by the guitar solo), you can take off any string by turning the tuning peg to loosen the string so much that you can grab the string from the center and pull it off the post. You don't need to wind it completely off the post by using the peg.

A quicker method is to simply snip off the old string with wire cutters. It seems weird and brutal to snip off a string, but neither the sudden release of tension nor the cutting itself hurts the guitar. It does a number on the old string, but you don't need to concern yourself with that. (We have it on good authority that guitar strings have no pain receptors.)

The only reason *not* to cut the string is to save it as a spare, in case the new one breaks while putting it on (rare, but it happens). An old B string is better than no B string.

A common misconception is that you should maintain constant string tension on the guitar neck at all times. You may hear that you should replace the strings one at a time because removing all the strings is bad for the guitar, but this simply isn't true. Replacing strings one at a time is *convenient* for tuning but is no healthier for the guitar. Guitars are made of tougher stuff than that.

However you remove the old string, after it's off, you're ready to put on a new one. The methods for stringing a guitar diverge slightly, depending on whether you're stringing a steel-string acoustic, classical, or electric guitar.

Stringing a Steel-String Acoustic Guitar

You string virtually all steel-string acoustic guitars the same way (unlike, say, classical guitars and electric guitars). The strings attach to the guitar in two places, and you use the same methods on all steel-string acoustic guitars, both at the bridge and the headstock.

Changing strings step by step

Following are step-by-step instructions on restringing your guitar. You have two places to attach your new string: the bridge and the neck. Start by attaching the string to the bridge, which is a pretty straightforward task.

Step 1: Attaching the string to the bridge

Acoustic guitars have a bridge with six holes leading to the inside of the guitar. To attach a new string to the bridge, follow these steps:

1. **Remove the old string (see the section "Removing Old Strings") and pop out the bridge pin.**

   Bridge pins sometimes stick, so you may need to use a table knife to pry it out, but be careful not to ding the wood. A better alternative is the notched edge in a peg winder or needle-nose pliers. (See Chapter 15 for more information on peg winders.)

2. **Place the end of the new string that has a little brass ring (called a *ball*) inside the hole that held the bridge pin.**

   Just stuff it down the hole a couple of inches. (How far isn't critical, because you're going to pull it up soon.)

3. **Wedge the bridge pin firmly back in the hole with the slot facing forward (toward the nut).**

   The slot provides a channel for the string to get out. Figure 16-1 shows the correct disposition for the new string and the bridge pin.

4. **Pull gently on the string until the ball rests against the bottom of the pin.**

   Be careful not to kink the string as you pull it.

Figure 16-1:
How to
place the
new string
in the
bridge and
position the
bridge pin.

5. **Test the string by gently tugging on it.**

   If you don't feel the string shift, the ball is snug against the bridge pin, and you're ready to secure the string to the tuning post, which is the focus of the following section.

Step 2: Securing the string to the tuning post

After securely attaching the string to the bridge pin, you can focus your attention on the headstock. The steps are slightly different for the treble strings and the bass strings. You wind treble strings clockwise and bass strings counterclockwise.

To attach a treble string to the tuning post, follow these steps:

1. **Pass the string through the hole in the post.**

   Leave enough slack (about 4 inches is enough) between the bridge pin and the tuning post to enable you to wind the string around the post several times.

2. **Kink (or crease) the metal wire toward the inside of the guitar.**

   Figure 16-2 shows how to kink the string to prepare it for winding and about how much slack to leave for those windings.

Figure 16-2:
String kinked to the inside of the headstock, with slack for winding.

3. **While keeping the string tight against the post with one hand, wind the tuning peg clockwise with the other hand.**

   This step is a bit tricky and requires some manual dexterity (but so does playing the guitar). Keep your eye on the post to ensure that the string winds *down* the post. Figure 16-3 shows how the string wraps around the post on the treble, or right, side of the guitar, as it appears as you face the headstock. Don't get discouraged if you can't get your windings to look exactly like the strings shown in Figure 16-3. Getting everything to go smoothly takes a bit of practice.

   Winding the string downward on the post increases what's called the *breaking angle.* The breaking angle is the angle between the post and the nut. A sharper angle brings more tension down onto the nut and creates better *sustain,* the length of time the note continues. To get the maximum angle, wind the string so that it sits as low as possible on the post. (This fact is true for all guitars, not just acoustics.)

4. **Repeat Steps 1–3 for the bottom three (bass) strings, but wind the tuning pegs counterclockwise.**

   You follow the same steps *except* that you wind the strings counterclockwise in Step 3 so that the string goes up the middle and goes over the post to the left (as you face the headstock).

Figure 16-3:
The treble
strings
wrap
around the
posts in a
clockwise
direction.

If you find that you've left too much slack, unwind the string and start again, kinking the string farther down. If you don't leave enough slack, your winding doesn't go all the way down the post, which may result in slipping if the string doesn't have enough length to grab firmly around the post.

Neither situation is tragic. You simply undo what you've done and try again. As may happen in trying to get the two ends of a necktie the same length, you may need a couple tries to get it right.

Tuning up

After you secure the string around the post, you can begin to hear the string come up to pitch. As the string draws tight, place it in its correct nut slot. If you're changing strings one at a time, you can just tune the new one to the old ones, which, presumably, are relatively in tune. Check out Chapter 2 for the nuts and bolts (or was that nuts and posts?) of tuning your guitar.

After you get the string to the correct pitch, pull on it in various places up and down its length to stretch it out a bit. Doing so can cause the string to go flat — sometimes drastically if you left any loose windings on the post — so tune it back up to pitch by winding the peg. Repeat the tune-stretch process two or three times to help the new strings hold their pitch.

Using a *peg winder* to quickly turn the tuning pegs reduces your string-winding time considerably. A peg winder also features a notch in one side of the sleeve that can help you pop a stuck bridge pin. Just make sure that you don't lose the pin when it comes flying out! Chapter 15 has more information on peg winders.

After the string is up to pitch and stretched out, you're ready to remove the excess string that sticks out from the post. You can snip this excess off with wire cutters (if you have them) or bend the string back and forth over the same crease until it breaks off.

Whatever you do, don't leave the straight string length protruding. It could poke you or someone standing next to you (such as the bass player) in the eye or give you a sharp jab in your fingertip.

Stringing Nylon-String Guitars

Stringing a nylon-string guitar is different from stringing a steel-string acoustic because both the bridge and the posts are different. Among nylon-string guitars themselves are several varieties of bridges, requiring a different approaches to attaching the string. All nylon-string headstocks, however, are identical in terms of the stringing process.

Changing strings step by step

In one sense, nylon strings are easier to deal with than steel strings are because nylon isn't as springy as steel. Attaching the string to the tuning post, however, can be a bit trickier. As you do with the steel-string acoustic, begin by securing the bridge end of the string first and then turn your attentions to the headstock.

Step 1: Securing the string to the bridge

Whereas steel-string acoustic strings have a ball at one end, nylon strings have no such ball: Both ends are loose. (Well, you *can* buy ball-ended nylon-string sets, but they're not what you normally use.) You can, therefore, choose whichever end of the guitar string that you want to secure to the bridge. Just follow these steps:

1. **Remove the old string, as we describe in the section "Removing Old Strings," earlier in this chapter.**

2. **Pass one end of the new string through the hole in the the top of the bridge, leaving about an inch and a half sticking out the rear of the hole.**

   If the ends look different, use the one that looks like the middle of the string, not the one that has the loosely coiled appearance.

3. **Tie off the end by looping the short end back up and wrapping it over and under itself on the top of the bridge, as shown in Figure 16-4.**

   You may need a couple tries to get the end at just the right length, where not too much excess is dangling off the top of the bridge. (You can always cut the excess away, too.)

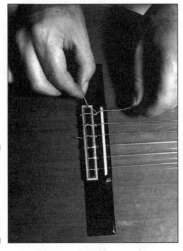

Figure 16-4:
Tying off
the bridge
end of the
string.

4. **Pull on the long end of the string with one hand and move the knot with the other to remove excess slack and cause the knot to lie flat against the bridge.**

If your guitar is the 12-hole variety, you have a separate hole to thread the string through for securing it to the bridge. Pass the string through the hole as you did in Step 2, but bring the string back over the top of the bridge and pass it through the adjacent hole. Then tuck the loose end (now sticking out of the rear of the bridge) under the loop that you just created between the rear first hole and the forward second hole. After that you pull the string taut, the loop clamps down on the tucked string end, locking it in place. Many guitarists feel that the 12-hole system for attaching the string at the bridge is superior to the 6-hole system, because the 12-hole approach removes the tied end of the string from the taut part, which increases the breaking angle of the string over the *saddle* (the strip of hard plastic that the strings sit on). If you steepen the breaking angle, you create more downward force on the bridge, which increases sustain.

Step 2: Securing the string to the tuning post

On a nylon-string guitar, the tuning posts (called *rollers*) pass through the headstock sideways instead of going through perpendicularly as on a steel-string acoustic or electric guitar. This configuration is known as a *slotted headstock*.

To attach the string to the tuning post in a slotted headstock, follow these steps:

1. **Pass the string through the hole in the tuning post. Bring the end of the string back over the roller toward you; then pass the string under itself in front of the hole. Pull up on the string end so that the long part of the string (the part sitting on the bridge) sits in the U-shaped loop you just formed.**

Make your loop come from the outside (that is, approaching from the left on the lower three bass strings, and from the right on the upper three treble strings). Leave enough slack in the string length for five or six wraps. Doing so should hold the loose end firmly in place and prevent slippage in the string length (the section of the string between the tuning roller and the bridge) itself.

2. **Wind the peg so that the string wraps on top of the loop you just formed, forcing it down against the post.**

3. **Pull the string length taut with one hand and turn the tuning peg with the other hand.**

Wrap the windings to the outside of the hole, away from the center of the guitar.

Tuning up

As you continue turning the tuning peg, the string slowly comes nearer to pitch. Nylon strings, as do steel strings, require quite a bit of stretching out, so after you get the string initially up to pitch, grab it at various places around its length, pull on it, and then tune it up again. Repeat this process two or three times to keep the guitar in tune longer.

Snip away the excess after you're done with all six strings. Nylon strings aren't as dangerous as steel strings if their excess protrudes, but the extra string hanging out is unsightly, and besides, classical guitarists are a little fussier about how their instruments look than acoustic guitarists are.

Stringing an Electric Guitar

Generally, electric guitarists need to change their strings more often than do steel-string acoustic or classical guitarists. Because changing strings is so common on electric guitars, builders take a more progressive approach to the hardware, often making changing strings very quick and easy. Of the three types of guitars — steel-string acoustic, classical, and electric — you can change the strings on electric guitars most easily by far.

Changing strings step by step

As you would on steel-string acoustic and nylon-string guitars, begin stringing an electric guitar by first securing the string to the bridge and then attaching the string to the headstock. Electric strings are similar to steel-string acoustic strings in that they have ball ends and are made of metal, but electric strings are usually composed of a lighter-gauge wire than steel-string acoustic strings, and the 3rd string is unwound, or plain, whereas a steel-string acoustic guitar's is wound. (A nylon-string's 3rd string also is unwound but is a thicker, nylon string.)

Step 1: Securing the string to the bridge

Most electric guitars use a simple method for securing the string to the bridge. You pass the string through a hole in the bridge (sometimes reinforced with a collar, or *grommet*) that's smaller than the ball at the end of the string — so the ball holds the string just as the knot at the end of a piece of thread holds a stitch in fabric. On some guitars (such as the Fender Telecaster), the collars anchor right into the body, and the strings pass through the back of the instrument, through a hole in the bridge assembly, and out the top.

Figure 16-5 shows two methods of attaching a string to an electric: from the top of the guitar and through the back.

In any case, on all but a few guitars (such as those fitted with a Floyd Rose mechanism which we discuss at the end of the chapter), you anchor the string at the bridge by passing the string through the hole until the ball stops the movement. Then you can move up to the headstock area.

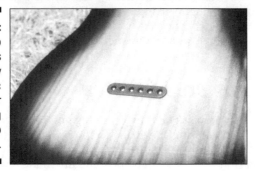

Figure 16-5: Two methods used by electric guitars for securing strings to the bridge.

Step 2: Securing the string to the tuning post

In most cases, the posts on an electric resemble those of a steel-string acoustic. A post protrudes through the headstock, and you pass your string through the post's hole, kink the string to the outside (away from the center of the headstock), and begin winding while holding the string length with one hand for control. (See "Step 2: Securing the string to the tuning post" in the section "Stringing a Steel-String Acoustic Guitar," earlier in this chapter.)

Some electric guitars, notably Fender Stratocasters and Telecasters, feature *string retainers,* which are little rollers or channels screwed into the top of the headstock that pull the top two or four strings down low onto the headstock, sort of like a tent stake. If your guitar has string retainers, make sure that you pass the strings under them.

Some tuners feature a *locking mechanism,* so that you don't need to worry about winding, slack, and all that bother. Inside the post hole is a viselike device that clamps down on the string as it passes through. A *knurled* (ridge-covered) dial underneath the headstock loosens and tightens the vise. Perhaps the best-known company to make this locking device is Spurzel.

Some guitars make tuners with slotted posts instead of a hole. These devices also enable quick string changes, because you simply lay the string in the slot — aligned with the string length — kink it and begin winding. You don't even need to leave any slack for winding.

The special case of the Floyd Rose bridge

Rock music in the '80s made extensive use of the whammy bar and *floating bridge* (where the bridge isn't fixed, but floats on a spring assembly). Standard floating bridges weren't meant for the kind of abuse that creative guitarists such as Steve Vai and Joe Satriani cook up, however, so manufacturers developed better ways to make sure that bridges return to their original position and the strings remain in tune.

Floyd Rose invented the most successful of these assemblies. Rose used his own patented design to ensure a highly accurate, movable bridge system and *locking nut* (a clamplike device that replaces the standard nut).

The bridge takes the strings in a top-mounted approach, instead of a pass-through one but with one notable difference: Guitarists must snip the ball end off before attaching the string so that the end can fit in the tiny viselike mechanism that holds the string in place. If you own a Floyd, you must carry a set of spare strings with the balls snipped off or at least have wire cutters always at the ready.

Because the Floyd Rose also features a locking nut, winding the string on the post isn't so critical. After you lock the nut (by using a small Allen wrench), what you do with the tuning pegs doesn't matter. You then do all tuning by using ridge-covered knobs on the bridge. These knobs are known as "fine tuners" because their movements are much smaller and more precise than are those on the headstock.

Stringing up an electric guitar fitted with a Floyd Rose system takes a little longer than it does on a regular electric, but if you plan to do a lot of whammy bar work, a Floyd Rose is well worth the effort.

Chapter 17

Staying Fit: Basic Maintenance and Repairs

Guitars are surprisingly hardy creatures. You can subject them to a rigorous performing schedule, keep them up all night, bang on them relentlessly, and they don't even mind a bit.

Generally speaking, guitars never wear out, although you may need to replace some parts and perform some tweaks along the way. But unlike with your car or body, you don't need to do anything much to a guitar to keep it in excellent health.

If you don't abuse it or subject it to extreme conditions, a guitar not only stays structurally sound for decades, but it also plays in tune and remains comfortable in your hands. In fact, guitars actually *improve* with age and use. We should all be so lucky.

Even so, preventing a guitar from sustaining some injury or needing a few repairs along the way is virtually impossible. You can and should practice good guitar maintenance, and if your guitar does go out of whack, you can perform the repairs yourself in most cases. If you're at all in doubt about your technical abilities, however — or if you're just a plain klutz — you want to consult a qualified repair person.

Before starting on individual maintenance and repair issues, it may be helpful to consult this quick guide to diagnose a guitar-related problem that you may already have. Take a look at Table 17-1 to see whether your guitar suffers from any of these musical maladies.

Table 17-1	Guitar Problems and Solutions	
Symptom	**Solution**	**Refer to Section**
Strings have lost luster, are difficult to play, or fret sharp	Replace strings (see Chapter 16) and wipe down new strings after every use to prolong their life	Removing dirt and grime: The strings
Dull or dirty wood surface	Wipe with cotton or chamois cloth, apply guitar polish	Removing dirt and grime: The wood
Dull or greasy-looking hardware	Wipe with cloth, apply jewelers' polish	Removing dirt and grime: The hardware
Guitar absorbs too much humidity, causing it to swell and crack; or guitar dries up because of insufficient humidity, causing it to shrink and crack	Place in a humidity-controlled environment of 45–55 percent at room temperature (65–75° F)	Providing a Healthy Guitar Environment: Humidity
Rattling or buzzing from hardware as you play	Tighten loose hardware connection with screwdriver or wrench	Do-It-Yourself Repairs: Tightening loose connections
Neck bows outward (away from strings) between seventh and twelfth frets, causing strings to be too high and difficult to fret	Tighten truss rod to make neck arch upward slightly	Adjusting the neck and bridge: Tightening and loosening the truss rod
Neck bows inward (into strings) between seventh and twelfth frets, causing strings to be too low and making strings buzz	Loosen truss rod to make neck sag slightly	Adjusting the neck and bridge: Tightening and loosening the truss rod
Strings too high, making fretting difficult, although neck is straight; or strings too low, causing string buzz, although neck is straight	Lower or raise the string saddles at the bridge	Adjusting the neck and bridge: Action
Strings fret sharp; or strings fret flat	Adjust intonation by moving saddles toward bridge; or adjust intonation by moving saddles toward nut	Adjusting the neck and bridge: Intonation

Symptom	Solution	Refer to Section
Tuning machine breaks or gears strip	Purchase and install replacement, making sure that mounting holes align exactly with holes already in headstock	Replacing worn or old parts: Tuning machines
Strap pin screw comes loose and doesn't hold tight in hole	Apply plastic wood or white glue and replace, allowing substance to dry completely	Replacing worn or old parts: Strap pins
Movable bridge has too much play or feels too loose; or bridge feels stiff and doesn't respond well to whammy bar manipulations	Replace, tighten, or add springs to the tailpiece in the rear cavity; or remove springs or loosen plate	Replacing worn or old parts: Bridge springs
Crackling volume or tone knob or pickup selector switch	Vigorously turn the knob or switch back and forth to work out the dirt or corrosion	Replacing worn or old parts: Crackling controls
Crackling pickup jack	Solder loose or broken wire back to appropriate lug	Replacing worn or old parts: Loose jacks
Pickups break, wear out, or no longer give you desired sound	Purchase compatible replacement set, follow included directions, neatly solder all connections	Replacing worn or old parts: Replacement pickups

Cleaning Your Guitar

The simplest type of maintenance is cleaning. You should clean your guitars regularly or, intuitively enough, every time they get dirty. If a guitar gets dirty, it doesn't exactly come home with mud on its shirt and grass stains on its pants, but it does collect a laundry list of its own washday terrors.

Removing dirt and grime

Unless you live in a bubble, dust and dirt are part of your environment. Certain objects just seem to attract dust (for example, the top of a TV set), and guitars seem to attract their fair share. If dust collects under the strings on your headstock and bridge, you can dust them off by using a cloth or a feather duster. Feather dusters may seem silly things that only uniformed maids in old movies use, but they serve a purpose: They knock the dust off an object without applying pressure (which can scratch a delicate finish). So even if you don't use a feather duster — or if your maid's outfit is at the cleaners — follow the example of old Alice from *The Brady Bunch* and dust lightly.

As dust mixes with the natural moisture content of your hands and fingers (and forearm, if you play in short sleeves, shirtless, or in the raw), that dust becomes grime. Grime can stick to all surfaces, but it's especially noticeable on your strings.

The strings

The natural oils from your fingertips coat the strings every time you play. You can't see this oily coating, but it's there, and over time, these oils corrode the string material and create a grimy buildup (which is not only icky, but also impedes play and can actually injure the wood over time). String grime makes the strings go dead sooner and wear out faster than they normally do; if you let the condition go too long, the string grime can even seep into the pores of the fingerboard. Yuck!

The best way to combat the grimy-buildup menace is to wipe down the strings after every playing session, just before you put the guitar back in the case. (Notice that we're assuming that you put the guitar back in the case — another "case" of good preventative maintenance.) *Chamois* (pronounced "shammy") is a great material to use to wipe the strings because it doubles as a polishing cloth; a (clean) cotton diaper, however, works well, too (but *no* disposable diapers, please). Bandannas may give you that Willie Nelson/ Janis Joplin persona, but they're not made of good absorptive material, so don't wipe your guitar with a bandanna.

Give the strings a general wipe down and then pinch each string between your thumb and index finger, with the cloth in between, and run your hand up and down the string length. This dries the string all the way around its circumference and shucks off any grunge. That's all you need to do to maintain clean strings and increase their useful life many times over. (And while you're at it, wipe the back of the guitar neck, too.)

The wood

A guitar is mostly wood, and wood likes a good rubdown. (Hey, who doesn't?) If you have a really dusty guitar — for example, one that's been sitting open in a musty attic for a while — blow the excess dust off before you start dusting with a cloth (or feather duster). This simple act could prevent a possible scratch or abrasion in the finish.

Gently rub the various places on the guitar until it's dust-free. You may need to frequently shake out your dust cloth, so do so outside, or you're going to be wiping sneezes off your guitar as well as the dust. Unless your guitar is *really* dirty — maybe displaying some caked-on gunk that you don't even want to *know* the origin of — dusting is all you need to do to the wood.

If dullness persists or a film is clearly present over the finish, you can rub your guitar down with furniture polish or, better yet, *guitar polish*. Guitar polish is made specifically for the finishes that the manufacturers use on guitars, whereas some furniture polish may contain abrasives. If you're at all in doubt, use the guitar goop that music stores sell. And follow the directions on the bottle.

Although the guitar-goop companies write this information on the label, it bears repeating here: *Never* put any liquid or spray polish directly onto the guitar surface. Doing so could soak and stain the wood permanently. Pour or spray the substance onto your dust cloth and work it in a bit before putting the cloth to wood.

To dust between the strings in hard-to-reach places such as the headstock, bridge, and pickup areas, use a small camel's hair paintbrush. Keep the brush in your case.

The hardware

Grimy buildup doesn't really *hurt* hardware (tuners, bridges, and so on) the way that it can more porous wood, but it sure looks bad — and you don't want to appear on MTV with hardware that's duller than your drummer. (Just kidding, fellow percussionists!)

Rubbing with a dust cloth is all you really need to do for your guitar's hardware, but you can certainly use a mild jewelry or chrome polish if you want — as long as it's not abrasive. Polish not only removes really greasy residue (which a simple wipe won't do), but also brings the hardware to a luster — very important for TV lights.

Many inexpensive hardware components are *dipped,* meaning that they have a thin coating of shiny metal over an otherwise ugly and mottled-looking surface. So you don't want to rub through the coating (which could happen with repeated polishing). And you *certainly* (we hope) don't want to get any liquid polish in the moving parts of a tuning machine.

Don't *ever* touch the pickups of an electric guitar with anything other than a dry cloth or your dusting brush. Pickups are magnetic and abhor liquid as much as the Wicked Witch of the West did. You don't want to risk upsetting a pickup's sensitive magnetic fields with liquid, my pretty.

Caring for the finish

Acoustic guitars have a finish of lacquer or another synthetic coating to protect the wood's surface and give it a shiny appearance. Whether your instrument has a high-gloss finish or the satin variety (more subdued and natural-looking), the plan is the same: Keep the finish dust-free so that it stays shiny and transparent for years. Don't subject your guitar to direct sunlight for long periods of time and avoid drastic humidity and temperature changes. Following these simple guidelines helps keep the finish from *checking* (cracking) as it swells and shrinks along with the wood.

If your finish ever cracks because of a *ding* (a small inadvertent gouge, such as occurs if you bang your guitar into the corner of the table), take it to a repair person quickly to prevent the crack from spreading like a spider pattern on a windshield.

Protecting Your Guitar

If you play guitar, you certainly don't want to keep it a secret. Well, in the beginning maybe, but after you can play a little bit, you want to bring your music to the people. Unless you plan on doing a lot of entertaining — as in having people come over to your place — you need to take your guitar out into the world. And that requires protection. *Never* leave the house without putting the guitar in some kind of protective case.

On the road

Most people don't even think about the guitar's health as they toss their favorite acoustic into the woody and head for the beach. But they should. Using a bit of common sense can keep your guitar looking like a guitar instead of a surfboard.

If you're traveling in a car, keep the guitar in the passenger compartment where you can exercise control over the environment. A guitar in a trunk or untreated luggage compartment gets either too hot or too cold in comparison to what the humans are experiencing up front. (Guitars like to listen to the radio, too, as long as it's not playing disco or Milli Vanilli.)

If you must put the guitar in with the spare tire, push it all the way forward so that it can benefit from some "environmental osmosis" (meaning that it's not going to get quite as cold or hot next to the climate-controlled passenger cabin as it is at the rear of the car). This practice also helps if, heaven forbid, you're ever rear-ended. You can pay a couple of bucks to have Freddie's Fender Fix-it repair your car, but all the king's horses and all the king's men can't restore the splinters of your priceless acoustic should it absorb the brunt of a bumptious Buick.

A hardshell case is a better form of protection for a guitar than either a nylon gig bag or a cardboardlike soft case. With a hardshell case, you can stack things on top, whereas other cases require the guitar to be at the top of the heap, which may or may not please an obsessive trunk-packer. (You know, like your old man used to pack before the big family vacation.) See Chapter 15 for more information on cases.

Nylon gig bags are lightweight and offer almost no protection from a blow, but they do fend off dings. If you know the guitar is never going to leave your shoulder, you can use a gig bag. Gig bags also enable an electric guitar to fit in the overhead compartments of most aircraft. Savvy travelers know what kinds of crafts can accommodate a gig bag and stand in line early to secure a berth for their precious cargo.

In storage

Whether you're going on a long vacation or doing three-to-five, you may, at some point, need to store your guitar for a long period of time. Keep the guitar in its case and put the case in a closet or under a bed. Try to keep the guitar in a climate controlled environment rather than a damp basement or uninsulated attic.

If you store the guitar, you can lay it flat or on edge. The exact position makes no difference to the guitar. You don't need to loosen the strings significantly, but dropping them down a half step or so ensures against excess tension on the neck, should it swell or shrink slightly.

Providing a Healthy Guitar Environment

Guitars are made under specific temperature and humidity conditions. To keep the guitar playing and sounding as the builder intended, you must maintain an environment within the same approximate range of the original. Fortunately, that means an environment that's very comfortable for humans.

Temperature settings

A guitar can exist comfortably in a range of temperatures that's also ideal for humans — 65–80° F. For a guitar, heat is worse than cold, so keep the guitar out of the sun and avoid leaving a guitar to sit in a hot car trunk all day.

If your guitar's been cold for several hours because it was riding in the back of the truck that you drove from North Dakota to Minnesota in December, give the guitar time to warm up gradually after you bring it indoors. A good practice is to leave the guitar in its case until the case warms up to room temperature. Avoid exposing the guitar to radical temperature shifts if at all possible to prevent *finish checking,* the cracking of your finish that results because it can't expand and contract well enough with the wood beneath it.

Humidity

Guitars, whether they're made in Hawaii or Arizona, are all built under humidity-controlled conditions, which stay at about 50 percent. So to enable your guitar to maintain the lifestyle that its maker intended for it, you must also maintain that humidity control to about 45–55 percent. If you live in a dry or wet climate and compensate with a humidifier or dehumidifier, you should aim for those settings as a healthy human anyway. Guitars that get too dry crack; guitars that absorb too much moisture swell and buckle.

If you can't afford either a humidifier or dehumidifier, you can achieve good results with the following inexpensive solutions:

♪ **Guitar humidifier:** This item is simply a rubber-enclosed sponge that you saturate with water, squeeze the excess out of, and then clip onto the inside of the soundhole or keep inside the case to raise the humidity level.

♪ **Desiccant:** A desiccant is a powder or crystal substance that usually comes in small packets and draws humidity out of the air, lowering the local relative humidity level. Silicagel is a common brand, and packets often come in the cases of new guitars.

♪ **Hygrometer:** You can buy this inexpensive device at any hardware store; it tells you the relative humidity of a room with a good degree of accuracy (close enough to maintain a healthy guitar anyway). Get the portable kind (as opposed to the wall-hanging variety) so that you can transport it if you need to or even keep it inside the guitar case.

A general rule is as follows: If a human is comfortable, a guitar is comfortable. Keep the environment near room temperature (about 72° F) and the relative humidity at about 50 percent, and you're never going to hear your guitar complain (if you have a talking guitar, that is).

Don't go too far with this rule about guitars and humans being comfortable under the same conditions, however. You shouldn't put your guitar in a hot tub even if you offer it a margarita, no matter how comfortable that makes you.

Do-It-Yourself Repairs

If you turn on the light in your house and the bulb blows, do you call a handyman? Of course not. You look at the dead bulb to note its wattage, go to the closet, get the right replacement bulb, and in a jiffy, you're bathed in 60-watt luminescence. You suffer no anxiety about performing that "repair," right?

If you can develop this same intuitive approach toward your guitar, you can perform simple adjustments, tweaks, and repairs. Nothing magical goes on in a guitar mechanically. The magic comes in the way that it produces that glorious sound, not in how the tuning machines work or the way the strings attach to the bridge.

Some examples of repairs that you can perform yourself include eliminating rattles, raising and lowering the strings at the bridge, removing dirt and grime, replacing some worn or broken parts, and changing strings. Actually, we devote all of Chapter 16 to changing strings, so turn to that chapter if you just want to replace a broken or worn string.

Tightening loose connections

A guitar is a system of moving parts, many of which are mechanical, and as anyone who's ever owned a car can attest, moving things come loose. In guitars, the hardware connections are what typically work themselves loose, such as the nuts on the bridge post or the screws that hold down the pickup covers.

If you hear a rattle, try strumming with one hand to re-create the rattle while touching the various suspects with your other hand. As you touch the offending culprit, the rattle usually stops. Then you can take appropriate measures to tighten up whatever's come loose. (A screw in a tuning machine, pickup cover, or jack plate are the most common.) Usually that involves using ordinary tools — screwdrivers, wrenches, chain saws (just kidding about the last one) — but designed for the appropriated-sized screws, nuts, and so on. Take an inventory of the sizes and shapes of the screws, nuts, and bolts on your guitar and create a miniature tool kit just for fixing your instrument.

Adjusting the neck and bridge

Guitars do change over time (such as in going from one season to another) and especially if your environment experiences temperature and humidity swings. If the temperature and humidity change frequently, the guitar naturally absorbs or loses humidity, which causes the wood to swell or shrink. This condition is normal and doesn't hurt the guitar.

The problem with this expansion and contraction lies in the fact that the playing and setup tolerances are fairly critical, so a slight bow in the neck results in a guitar that plays buzzy or is suddenly much harder to fret. If this situation occurs, you can often correct the problem through a simple adjustment of the neck and/or bridge.

Tightening and loosening the truss rod

The neck of most guitars has what's known as a *truss rod,* which is a one- or two-piece adjustable metal rod that goes down the inside of the center of the neck. All truss rods are adjustable by a nut at one end. Different manufacturers put them in different places, but they're usually at the headstock, under a cap just behind the nut, or where the neck joins the body, just under the fingerboard. Some older models don't have truss rods or, in the case of old Martin guitars, have truss rods that you can't adjust without taking off the fingerboard. But all guitars these days have accessible truss rods.

If your neck bows *outward* between the seventh and twelfth frets, creating a large gap that makes pressing down the strings difficult, tighten the truss rod by turning the nut clockwise (as you face the nut straight on). Tighten the nut a quarter turn at a time, giving the neck a few minutes to adjust after each turn. (You can play during the adjustment time.) All guitars come with their particular truss-rod wrench, so if you don't have a truss rod wrench for your guitar, try to find a replacement immediately. (Try your local guitar store first and, failing that, get in touch with the manufacturer itself.)

If your neck bows *inward* between the seventh and twelfth frets, causing the strings to buzz and *fret out* (that is, come in contact with frets they're not supposed to as you press down the strings), loosen the truss rod with the truss-rod wrench. Turn the nut a quarter turn at a time, enabling the neck to adjust after each turn.

If you can't correct the problem in a few full turns, stop. You may need a qualified repair person to investigate. Overtightening or overloosening a truss rod can damage the neck and/or body.

Action

Action is how a guitar plays, specifically the distance of the strings to the fingerboard. Because of the narrow range of *tolerances* (allowable measurements), your action can get out of whack very easily. Usually, you can compensate for the changes in action by adjusting various components on the bridge, such as the height of the *saddle* (the part just in front of the bridge that holds the strings off the top).

To adjust the action, you need to adjust the up and down components that affect string height. You can't adjust the nut unless you cut the grooves deeper (not recommended), but you can adjust the bridge without permanently altering the instrument. On a Fender Telecaster, for example, you can move the individual saddle up or down as well back and forth (by turning tiny hex screws). Move the saddle up or down to raise and lower the string height, back and forth to adjust the intonation. (Now where's my tiny hex wrench?)

Intonation

Intonation refers to the accuracy of the tuning. If you find that a particular string is "fretting" sharp or flat (that is, the guitar's fretted notes are out of tune to what its true pitch should be) and you have an adjustable bridge, you can correct the intonation by moving the saddle toward the nut if the guitar plays flat and away from the nut if the guitar plays sharp. Different bridges have different methods for this, but it's pretty obvious after you look at the bridge assembly carefully. In one type of mechanism (used on Fender Stratocasters and Telecasters), screws at the back of the bridge determine the saddle front-to-back position. Turning the screw clockwise (with a simple Phillips or straight-blade screwdriver — being careful not to ding the top with the handle as you turn the screw) pulls the saddle back toward the bridge, which corrects a string that plays sharp. Tuning the screw counter-clockwise moves the saddle toward the nut, which corrects a string that plays flat. Keep in mind that adjusting the saddle for a string corrects only that string. You must perform intonation adjustments for each string. So don't invite me to that 38-string guitar's intonation adjustment!

Put on brand-new strings before you adjust the intonation. Old strings often fret sharp and don't give you a true reading of your intonation. For more information on replacing strings, see Chapter 16.

Replacing worn or old parts

The following sections list all the parts on your guitar that, statistically, are most likely to wear out or break and need replacing. All these fixes you can perform yourself and not do any damage to the guitar — even if you screw up.

Tuning machines

Tuning machines consist of a system of gears and shafts, and as the clutch on your car usually does eventually (or the automatic transmission if you never got that whole stick thing), tuners can wear out. Tuning machines deal with a lot of stress and tension, and we don't mean the kind that you endure at your job.

Tuning machines simply screw into the guitar's headstock with wood screws (after you push the post through the hole and fasten the hex nut on top), so if you have a worn or stripped gear, consider replacing the entire machine. If more than one tuner is giving you trouble, consider replacing the entire set. Check that the replacement machine has its screws in the same positions as the original, because you don't want to drill new holes in your headstock. If you're having trouble matching the holes of your new machines with the existing ones already drilled in your headstock, take the guitar to a repair person.

Strap pins

Strap pins are the little "buttons" that you put through your strap holes to attach the strap to your instrument. The strap pins usually attach to the guitar with ordinary wood screws, and they can sometimes work themselves loose. If simply tightening the wood screw with a screwdriver doesn't do the trick, try applying a little plastic wood or white glue on the screw and put it back in. If it's still loose, take the guitar to a repair person.

Bridge springs

You can find the springs that anchor a Strat-type bridge in the back cavity of the body. Some people like a loose bridge (which is more responsive but goes out of tune more easily) and some like a tight bridge. The more springs, the tighter the bridge. If one of the springs wears out, you get uneven play in your bridge if you hit the whammy bar. Change the springs as a set so that they wear evenly. You can consider switching from a two-spring setup to a three-spring setup (or vice versa) at this time, too. The springs just hook onto little hooks, and with a little tugging and the aid of pliers, you can pop them off and on in no time. You can even tighten the screws on the plate (called the *claw*) where the hooks attach, increasing the spring tension. Don't worry — these springs aren't like strings; they don't go *sproingggg* and hit you in the eye or go flying off across the room.

If you like a stiff bridge that stays in tune (and who doesn't!) and you only occasionally hit the whammy bar, go for a stiff bridge setup. If you're willing to trade a little tuning trouble for having a bridge with great freedom of movement and a lot of play, consider a looser bridge. Guitarists who like to create *ambient* music (atmospheric music without a defined melody) prefer flexible bridges, because they do a lot of dips and pulls on the bar.

Crackling controls

Dust and rust (oxidation) pose a potential threat to any electronic connection, and your guitar is no exception. If your volume and tone knobs start to "crackle" (make popping noises through your speaker whenever you're plugged in) or the signal is weak, inconsistent, or cuts out all together in certain positions on your controls, some foreign matter (however minute) has probably lodged itself in your controls. Vigorously turn the knobs back and forth around the trouble spot to work out the dust or rub off the little bit of corrosion that may be causing the problem. You may need to perform this action several times on each knob, in different places in the knob's travel. If turning the knobs doesn't do the trick, you may need a repair person to give your *pots* (short for *potentiometer,* the variable resistors on your volume and tone controls) a thorough cleaning.

Loose jacks

On electric guitars, you do a lot of plugging and unplugging, and these actions can eventually loosen a jack, causing it to crackle through the speaker. This crackle indicates a loose ground wire. Take off the jack plate or pick guard and see whether you can spot the loose wire causing the problem. If you're handy with a soldering iron, attach the broken ground wire or lead wire back to its appropriate lug, and you're done. You may even feel like a real electrician. If you're not handy, have a friend who is do the job or take the instrument in to the shop.

Replacement pickups

Replacing your pickups can seem like a daunting task, but it's really a very simple one. Often, the best way to change your sound (assuming that you like the way your guitar plays and looks) is to substitute replacement pickups for the originals — especially if the originals weren't too good to begin with.

Make sure that you purchase pickups of the same size and type as the originals so that they fit into the existing holes and hook up the same way electrically. Beyond that, the job's a snap. Clear directions come with the new pickups, and all you need to do is connect and solder two or three wires and then seat the pickups in the cavities. You're not dealing with high-voltage electricity either, so you can't hurt yourself or the electronics if you wire something backward. Again, however, if you don't feel comfortable doing the job yourself, enlist the aid of a handy friend or take your guitar to a repair person.

Changing your pickups is like changing your car's oil. You can do the job yourself and save money, but you may choose not to because of the hassle.

Having the Right Tools

Look at your guitar to determine what kind of tools you may need should something come loose. A quick inspection of the kinds of screws on an electric guitar reveals different-sized Phillips-head and slotted varieties in several places: the strap pins, the pickup cover, the pickguard, the tuning-machine mounts, the *set screws* (the screws that hold the tuning button to the shaft), the *string retainers* (the metal devices on the headstock — between the tuning posts and the nut — that hold down the strings on Strats and Teles), the volume and tone controls, and the on-the-neck back plates.

You can also find several places for bolts: the output jack and the tuning-post *collars* (hex-shaped nuts on top of the headstock that keep the posts from wobbling). A miniature ratchet set gives you better leverage and a better angle than does a small crescent wrench. Make sure that you know whether your guitar is metric or not.

The truss rod takes its own tool, usually a hex wrench, which usually comes with the guitar if you buy it new. If your guitar doesn't have one (because you bought it used or you've lost it since buying it new), get the right one for your guitar and keep it in the case at all times.

Floating bridge systems, including those by Floyd Rose, require hex or Allen wrenches to adjust the saddles and other elements of the assembly. Keep these wrenches on hand in case you break a string.

Assemble a permanent tool kit containing all the tools that you need for your guitar. Don't "cannibalize" this set if you're doing other household fixes. Buy two sets of screwdrivers, wire cutters, and wrenches — one for general use and one that never leaves your guitar case or gig bag.

Ten Things That You Can't Do Yourself

Some repairs *always* require a qualified repair person to fix (assuming that anyone can repair them at all). Among such repairs are the following:

- ♪ Fixing finish cracks.
- ♪ Repairing dings and scratches (if they're severe and go through the finish to the wood).
- ♪ Filing worn frets. (If frets start to develop grooves or crevices, they need a pro to file or replace them.)
- ♪ Fixing pickup failure or *weakening*. (One pickup is seriously out of balance with another, you have possible magnetic damage to the pickup itself, or one of the electronic components in a pickup fails.)
- ♪ Fixing dirty volume and tone knobs (if vigorous turning back and forth no longer eliminates the crackle such dirt causes).
- ♪ Solving grounding problems. (You check the cavity and no wires are loose, but you still have inordinate noise problems.)
- ♪ Fixing severe neck distortion (twisting or severe bowing).
- ♪ Healing certain injuries and breakage (such as the nut, fingerboard, or headstock).
- ♪ Refinishing or restoring your guitar's wood. (Don't even get *near* your guitar's finish with a sander or wood chemicals.)
- ♪ Rewiring your electronics. (You decide, say, to replace your five-way with on/off switches, install a coil-tap and phase-reversal switch if any two adjacent pickups are active, plus insert a presence-boost knob in place of the second volume control . . . .)

Huh?! If you understand that last one, you may be beyond *Guitar For Dummies!*

If you have *any* anxiety about performing any repair or maintenance routine, *take the guitar to a repair person.* A repair person can tell you whether it's something you can do yourself and maybe even show you how to do it correctly the next time the problem occurs. You're much better off being safe (and out a couple of bucks) than taking a chance of damaging your guitar.

Part VII
The Part of Tens

The 5th Wave   By Rich Tennant

On July 9th, 1983, Andres Segovia inexplicably began duck walking through the adagio section of Bach's Suite for Guitar.

In this part . . .

What ...*For Dummies* book would be complete without a Part of Tens? Certainly not *Guitar For Dummies.* In this part you'll find a couple of cool top ten lists: one on ten great guitarists and the other on ten guitars that will have your mouth watering.

Chapter 18
10 Guitarists You Should Know

· ·

· ·

Regardless of style, certain guitarists have made their mark on the world of guitar so that any guitarist who comes along after them has a hard time escaping their legacy. We present here in chronological order ten who mattered and why they mattered.

Andrés Segovia (1893–1987)

Not only was Segovia the most famous classical guitarist of all time, but he also literally invented the genre. Before his arrival, the guitar was a lowly instrument of the peasant classes. Segovia began performing Bach pieces and other serious classical music on the guitar (writing many of his own transcriptions), eventually elevating this "parlor" activity to a world-class style. His incredible performing career lasted more than 70 years. Signature pieces: Bach's "Chaconne," Albeniz's "Granada."

Charlie Christian (1916–42)

In a word, Charlie Christian invented the art of electric jazz guitar. His fluid solos with Benny Goodman's big band and smaller combos were sophisticated, scintillating, and years ahead of their time. After hours, he used to jam with fellow jazz rebels at Minton's in New York, where his adventurous improvisations helped create the genre known as *bebop*. Christian played the guitar like a horn, incorporating intervallic (non-stepwise) motion into his lines. Signature tunes: "I Found a New Baby," "I Got Rhythm."

Chet Atkins (1924–)

Known as "Mr. Guitar," Atkins is perhaps the definitive country guitarist. Building on Merle Travis' fast fingerpicking technique, Atkins refined the style, adding jazz, classical, and pop nuances to create a truly sophisticated country-guitar approach. He's played with Elvis Presley, the Everly Brothers, and countless country stars over the decades. Signature tunes: "Stars and Stripes Forever," "Yankee Doodle Dixie."

Wes Montgomery (1925–68)

A legendary jazz player, Wes' brand of cool jazz was based on the fact that he used his thumb to sound notes, instead of a traditional guitar pick. Another of his innovations was the use of octaves (that is, two identical notes in different ranges) to create fat, moving, unison lines. He died young, but his proponents still call him one of the all-time jazz greats. Signature tunes: "Four on Six," "Polka Dots and Moonbeams."

B.B. King (1925–)

Although he wasn't the first electric bluesman, B.B. King is easily the most popular: His swinging, high-voltage guitar style complements charismatic stagemanship and a huge, gospel-fueled voice. Along with his trademark ES-355 guitar, nicknamed "Lucille," King's minimalist soloing technique and massive finger vibrato has cemented his place in the annals of electric blues history. Signature tunes: "Every Day I Have the Blues," "The Thrill Is Gone."

Chuck Berry (1926–)

Perhaps rock's first real guitar hero, Berry used fast, rhythmic double-stops to create his signature guitar style. Although some regard him equally for his songwriting and lyric-writing skills, his fire-breathing breaks made his signature tunes "Johnny B. Goode," "Rockin' in the U.S.A.," and "Maybelline," bona fide guitar classics.

Jimi Hendrix (1942–70)

Considered the greatest rock guitarist of all time, Hendrix fused R&B, blues, rock, and psychedelia into a mesmerizing sonic soup. His 1967 breakthrough at the Monterey Pop Festival instantly rewrote the rock guitar textbook, especially after he whipped off his Stratocaster and lit it on fire. His licks are religiously copied by young guitarists to this day. Hendrix was known for his fiery abandon (even when his guitar wasn't actually on fire) and innovative work with feedback and the whammy bar. Signature tunes: "Purple Haze," "Little Wing."

Jimmy Page (1944–)

Page succeeded Eric Clapton and Jeff Beck in the Yardbirds, but he didn't really find his niche until forming Led Zeppelin, one of the great '70s rock bands. Page's forte was the art of recording guitars, layering track upon track to construct thundering avalanches of electrified tone. Yet he could also play sublime acoustic, regularly employing unusual tunings and global influences. In rock circles, his six-string creativity in the studio is un-matched. Signature tunes: "Stairway to Heaven," "Whole Lotta Love."

Eric Clapton (1945–)

In many ways, Clapton is the father of contemporary rock guitar. Before Hendrix, Beck, and Page showed up, the Yardbirds-era Clapton was already fusing electric Chicago blues with the fury of rock 'n' roll. He later ex-pounded upon this style in Cream, Blind Faith, and the legendary Derek and the Dominoes. Clapton eventually went solo, turning into one of the most popular recording artists of the last 20 years. A true living legend. Signature tunes: "Crossroads," "Layla."

Eddie Van Halen (1955–)

Rock guitar's equivalent to Jackson Pollock, Eddie Van Halen's splatter-note approach to metal guitar completely reinvented the style starting in the late '70s. He turned two-handed tapping into a common guitar technique (thanks to his groundbreaking "Eruption"), while also pushing the limits of whammy-bar and hammer-on expertise. He is also a master at fusing blues-based rock with modern techniques, and his rhythm playing is one of the best examples of the integrated style (combining low-note riffs with chords and double-stops). A guitar hero in every sense of the term. Signature tunes: "Eruption," "Panama."

Chapter 19
10 Guitars You Should Know

• •

In This Chapter

▶ D'Angelico Archtop

▶ Fender Stratocaster

▶ Fender Telecaster

▶ Gibson ES-335

▶ Gibson J-200

▶ Gibson Les Paul

▶ Gretsch 6120

▶ Martin D-28

▶ Ramirez Classical

▶ Rickenbacker 360-12

• •

*N*o musical instrument offers a greater variety of appearance, function, and sound than a guitar. Whether it's the quietly elegant Ramirez, the smoothly debonair D'Angelico, or the raucously funky Telecaster, each guitar presented below has left an indelible mark on the guitar-playing canon and will forever be known as a classic.

D'Angelico Archtop

Manufactured: 1932–1964

Considered by many to be the greatest jazz guitar ever made, D'Angelicos were custom archtop (the tops were arched slightly instead of flat like steel-string folk guitars) hollow-bodies built by the grand master of the genre, John D'Angelico (1905-64). In addition to their warm, lush tone, these guitars were meticulously constructed and graced with some of the most elegant decorations of all time.

Fender Stratocaster

Manufactured: 1954–

The world's most famous electric guitar, the Stratocaster was designed as a space-age instrument in the early '50s, featuring sleek lines, trebly tone, and small body dimensions (at least compared to the huge jazz archtops of the day). In the hands of masters such as Buddy Holly, Jimi Hendrix, Stevie Ray Vaughan, and Eric Clapton, this solid-body ax became ubiquitous, and today, you can't go into any guitar store without seeing at least a few Strats on the wall.

Fender Telecaster

Manufactured: 1951–

Fender's other great contribution to electric guitar lore is the Telecaster, which was also the first commercially made solid-body (1950). The Tele made its mark in the country world, adding a bright, twangy sound to countless recordings. A simple guitar made out of a plank of ash or alder, basic electronics, and a maple neck, it set the standard for electric guitar design and remains a classic today.

Gibson ES-335

Manufactured: 1958–

Introduced in the late 1950s, this ax is a thin "semihollow-body" design, which sought to combine the acoustic qualities of a big archtop with the compactness of a solid-body electric. The result was a superb guitar with a smooth woody tone, good for both clean jazz and heavy rock 'n' roll. This guitar's most famous advocate was '70s jazz-popper Larry Carlton, also known as "Mr. 335."

Gibson J-200

Manufactured: 1937–

For a booming acoustic tone and stylish looks, look no farther than Gibson's venerable J-200. This "jumbo" steel-string was targeted toward country guitarists and quickly became a Nashville classic. Of special note is its highly ornamental rosewood and mother-of pearl inlaid bridge, which is shaped something like a mustache.

Gibson Les Paul

Manufactured: 1952–

Named after Les Paul, the '50s jazz-pop sensation, the Gibson Les Paul model ironically went on to become one of the definitive *rock 'n' roll* instruments. Championed by Jimmy Page and Jeff Beck, this single-cutaway electric exudes the fat, bassy tone that helped define the sound of hard rock and heavy metal. Some original models from the late 1950s — notably the 1959 Standard — can now fetch more than $75,000.

Gretsch 6120

Manufactured: 1954–

Best known as country virtuoso Chet Atkins's main electric guitar, the big, funky tones of this hollow-body were common on many '50s and '60s rock and country records. With its unusual FilterTron pickups and warbly Bigsby vibrato bar, the 6120 also gave early rocker Duane Eddy his signature *twangy* guitar sound.

Martin D-28

Manufactured: 1931–

Martin first mass-produced "dreadnought" (named after a class of battleship) acoustic guitars in 1931 and its D-28 is the quintessential example of that great design. With a fat waist and bass-heavy tone, this big guitar became integral to the sounds of country, bluegrass, and, indeed, just about all steel-string acoustic music.

Ramirez Classical

Manufactured: mid-1800s

Serious classical and flamenco guitarists often consider playing only one kind of guitar — a Ramirez. First built in the mid-19th century, Jose Ramirez's classical guitars helped define the style, with soft gut (later, nylon) strings, superb workmanship, and a luscious tone. Among Ramirez's earliest champions was none other than the master, Andrés Segovia, himself.

Rickenbacker 360-12

Manufactured: 1963–

The ringing guitar tone on early Beatles and Byrds records came from one great guitar: the Rickenbacker 360-12. A semihollow-body electric with 12 strings, this classic has a completely distinctive tone in the guitar universe. The timeless *Rick sound* later resurfaced in the '80s on smash records by Tom Petty and R.E.M., among many others.

Appendix A
How to Read Music

●●

*R*eading music can seem intimidating at first, but it's not difficult at all. Even little children can do it. This appendix explains the concepts of reading music in the context of a familiar song. Armed with this information, you can practice your music reading by practicing the songs throughout this book by using the standard notation instead of the tab. (If you have trouble getting the durations, you can check them against the CD. And if you have trouble with the pitches, you can refer to the tab.)

The important thing to understand about written music is that it tells you three kinds of information all at the same time: *pitch* (the note's name), *duration* (how long to hold the note), and *expression and articulation* (how you play the note). If you think about how it all fits together, you recognize that our written music system is really pretty ingenious — three kinds of information all at the same time and in such a way that any musician can look at it and play just what the composer intended! Take a closer look at these three kinds of information that written music conveys simultaneously:

♪ **Pitch:** This element tells you which notes (or pitches) to play (A, B, C, and so on) by the location of *noteheads* (the oval-shaped symbols) on a five-line *staff*. The notes take their names from the first seven letters of the alphabet (A–G), with the pitches getting higher as the letters proceed from A. After G, the next higher note is A again. (If you call it "H," you're sure to get some funny looks.)

♪ **Duration:** This element of music tells you how long to hold each note *relative to the pulse,* or *beat.* You may, for example, hold a note for one beat or two beats or only half a beat. The symbols that music scores use for duration are whole notes (𝅝), half notes (𝅗𝅥), quarter notes (♩), eighth notes (♪), 16th notes (𝅘𝅥𝅯), and so on.

♪ **Expression and articulation:** These elements tell you *how* to play the notes — loudly or softly, smoothly or detached, with great emotion or with no emotion (that one's rare). These instructions can consist of either little marks written above or below the noteheads or little verbal messages written into the music. Often the words are in Italian (*piano, mezzo-forte, staccato*) because when composers started adding expression and articulation to their scores, the Italians had the most influence in the music scene. Besides, Italian sounds so much more romantic than English or German.

The Elements of Music Notation

Figure A-1 shows the music for the song "Shine On Harvest Moon" with the various notational elements numbered. Read them in order, referring to the explanations that follow for each number. Numbers 1–6 explain the mechanics of reading pitches; 7–19 explain the mechanics of reading durations; and 20–26 explain expression and articulation markings.

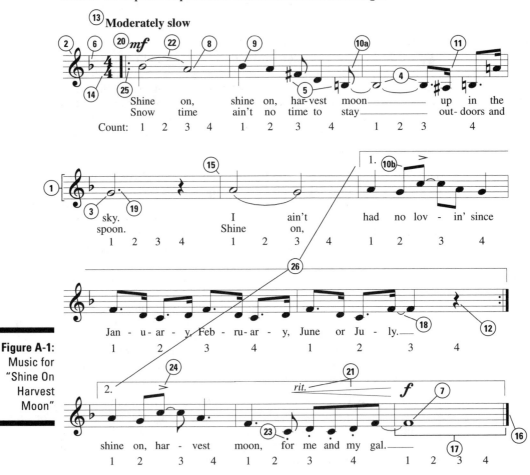

Figure A-1: Music for "Shine On Harvest Moon"

Pitch	Rhythm		Expression/Articulation
1. Staff	7. Whole note	13. Tempo heading	20. Dynamic marking
2. Clef	8. Half note	14. Time signature	21. Crescendo and Ritardando
3. G note	9. Quarter note	15. Bar line	22. Slur
4. Ledger lines	10. Eighth note	16. Double bar	23. Staccato dot
5. Accidentals	a. flagged	17. Measure	24. Accent
6. Key Signature	b. beamed	18. Tie	25. Repeat sign
	11. Sixteenth note	19. Augmentation dot	26. Ending brackets
	12. Rest		

Reading pitch

Table A-1 explains what the various symbols dealing with pitch mean in music notation. Refer to Figure A-1 and this table for the meanings of the symbols.

Table A-1		Pitch Symbols and Their Meanings
Number in Figure A-1	*What It's Called*	*What It Means*
1	Staff	Composers write music on a five-line system called a *staff*. In talking about the individual lines of the staff, refer to the bottom line as the *first line*. Between the five lines are four spaces. Refer to the bottom space as the *first space*. You can place *noteheads* on lines or in spaces. As the noteheads get higher on the staff, they get correspondingly higher in pitch. The distance from one line to the next higher space (or from one space to the next higher line) is one letter of the alphabet (for example, A to B).
2	Clef	The staff alone doesn't tell you the pitches (letter names) of the various lines and spaces. But a symbol called a *clef,* at the left edge of each staff, identifies a particular note on the staff. From that note, you can determine all the other notes by moving alphabetically up and down the staff (line to space to line, and so on). The clef the you use in guitar music is called the *treble clef* (or G clef — see **G note** following).
3	G note	The **clef** that you use in guitar music is the *treble clef* (sometimes called the *G clef*), which vaguely resembles an old-fashioned letter G. It curls around the second line of the **staff** and indicates that this line is G, and any note on that line is a G note. Some people memorize the letter names of all the lines (E, G, B, D, F, bottom to top) by the mnemonic "Every Good Boy Does Fine." For the spaces (F, A, C, E, bottom to top), they think of the word *face*.
4	Ledger lines	If you want to write notes higher or lower than the **staff,** you can "extend" the staff, above or below, by adding very short additional staff lines called *ledger lines*. The notes (letter names) move up and down alphabetically on the ledger lines just as they do on the normal staff lines.

(continued)

Table A-1 *(continued)*

Number in Figure A-1	What It's Called	What It Means
5	Accidentals (sharps, flats, and naturals)	The seven notes that correspond to the first seven letters of the alphabet (sometimes called *natural* notes) aren't the only notes in our musical system. Five other notes occur in between certain of the natural notes. Picture a piano keyboard. The white keys correspond to the seven natural notes, and the black keys are the five extra notes. Because these "black-key" notes don't have names of their own, musicians refer to them by their "white-key" names, along with special suffixes or symbols. To refer to the black key to the *right* of a white key (a half step higher), use the term *sharp*. The musical symbol for a sharp is ♯. So the black key to the right of C, for example, is C-sharp (or C♯). On the guitar, you play a C♯ one fret higher than you play a C. Conversely, to indicate the black key to the *left* of a white key (a half step lower), you use the term *flat*. The musical symbol for a flat is ♭. So the black key to the left of B, for example, is B-flat (or B♭). On the guitar, you play a B♭ one fret lower than B. If you sharp or flat a note, you can undo it (that is, restore it to its natural, "white-key" state) by canceling the sharp or flat with a symbol known as a *natural sign* (♮). The last note of the first staff of Figure A-1, A-natural, shows this kind of cancellation.
6	Key signature	Sometimes you play a particular pitch (or pitches) as a sharp or flat (see the preceding explanation of **accidentals**) consistently throughout a song. Rather than indicate a flat every time a B occurs, for example, you may see a single flat on the B line just after the **clef.** That indicates that you play *every* B in the song as B♭. Sharps or flats appearing that way are known as a *key signature*. A key signature tells you which notes to sharp or flat throughout a song. If you need to restore one of the affected notes to its natural state, a natural sign (♮) in front of the note indicates that you play the natural note (as in the seventh note of figure A-1, where the natural sign restores B-flat to B-natural).

Reading duration

A note's shape helps tell how long you need to hold it. Notes can have a hollow notehead (as in the case of the whole note and half note) or a solid notehead (quarter notes, eighth notes, and sixteenth notes), and the solid noteheads can even have vertical lines (called *stems*) with *flags* (curly lines) dangling off them. If you join together two or more notes, *beams* (horizontal lines between the stems) replace the flags. Table A-2 refers to the symbols numbered from 7–19 in Figure A-1.

Table A-2	Duration Symbols and Their Meanings	
Number in Figure A-1	**What It's Called**	**What It Means**
7	Whole note	The longest note is the *whole note,* which has a hollow oval head with no stem.
8	Half note	The *half note* has a hollow oval head with a stem. It lasts half as long as the **whole note.**
9	Quarter note	The *quarter note* has a solid oval head with a stem. It lasts half as long as the **half note.**
10	Eighth note	The *eighth note* has a solid oval head with a stem and a flag or beam. It lasts half as long as a **quarter note.**
11	Sixteenth note	The *sixteenth note* has a solid oval head with a stem and either two flags or two beams. It lasts half as long as the **eighth note.**
12	Rest	Music consists not only of notes, but of silences, too. What makes music interesting is how the notes and silences interact. Silences in music are indicated by *rests.* The rest in Figure A-1 is a *quarter rest,* equal in duration to a **quarter note.** Other rests, also equal in duration to their corresponding notes, are the *whole rest* (-), *half rest* (-), *eighth rest* (⁷) and *sixteenth rest* (⁹).
13	Tempo heading	The *tempo heading* tells you how fast or slow the song's beat, or pulse, is. As you listen to music, you (usually) hear an immediately recognizable beat. The beat is what you tap your foot to or snap your fingers to.

(continued)

Table A-2 *(continued)*

Number in Figure A-1	What It's Called	What It Means
14	Time signature	Most songs group their beats in twos, threes, or fours. A song's beats may, for example, sound out as "One-two-three-four, one-two-three-four, one-two-three-four" and not as "One-two-three-four-five-six-seven-eight-nine-ten-eleven-twelve." The time signature looks like a fraction (but actually is two numbers sitting one above the other, but with no dividing line), and it tells you two things: First, the top number tells you how many beats make up one grouping. In "Shine On Harvest Moon," for example, the top number, 4, tells you that each grouping contains four beats. Second, the bottom number tells you which type of note (quarter note, half note, and so on) gets one beat. In this case, the bottom number, 4, tells you that the quarter note gets one beat. Assigning the quarter note one beat is very common and so is having four beats per grouping. In fact, 4/4 time is sometimes called simply *common time*, and you sometimes indicate it by using the letter *C* instead of the numbers *4/4*.
15	Bar line	A *bar line* is a vertical line drawn through the staff after each grouping that the **time signature** indicates. In "Shine On Harvest Moon," a bar line appears after each four beats.
16	Double bar	A double-bar line indicates the end of a song.
17	Measure (bar)	The space between two consecutive **bar lines** is known as a *measure,* or *bar.* Each measure consists of the number of beats that the **time signature** indicates (in the case of Figure A-1, four). Those four beats can comprise any combination of note values that add up to four beats. You may have four **quarter notes,** or two **half notes,** or one **whole note,** or one half note and one quarter and two **eighth notes** — or any other combination. You can even use **rests** (silences) as long as everything adds up to four. Check out each measure of "Shine On Harvest Moon" to see various combinations.

Number in Figure A-1	What It's Called	What It Means
18	Tie	A short curved line that connects two notes of the same pitch is known as a *tie*. A tie tells you to not strike the second of the two notes, but to leave the first note sustaining for the combined time value of both notes.
19	Augmentation dot (also called "dot")	A *dot* appearing after a note increases that note's time value by half. If a **half note** is equal to two beats, for example, a dotted half note is equal to three — two plus half of two, or two plus one, or three.

Expression, articulation, and miscellaneous terms and symbols

Expression and *articulation* deal with how you play the music. Table A-3, in conjunction with Figure A-1, tells you about the symbols and terms that deal with these issues. Table A-3 deals with the symbols numbered 20–26 in Figure A-1.

Table A-3	Expression, Articulation, and Miscellaneous Symbols	
Number in Figure A-1	**What It's Called**	**What It Means**
20	Dynamic marking	A *dynamic marking* tells you how loud or soft to play. These markings are usually abbreviations of Italian words. Some of the common markings, from soft to loud, are *pp* (*pianissimo*), very soft; *p* (*piano*), soft; *mp* (*mezzo-piano*), moderately soft; *mf* (*mezzo-forte*), moderately loud; *f* (*forte*), loud; and *ff* (*fortissimo*), very loud.
21	Crescendo and Ritardando	The wedge-shaped symbol is known as a *crescendo* and indicates that the music gets gradually louder. If the wedge-shaped symbol goes from open to closed, it indicates a *decrescendo*, or a gradual softening. Often,

(continued)

Table A-3 *(continued)*

Number in Figure A-1	What It's Called	What It Means
21 (con't)	Crescendo and Ritardando	instead of wedges (or, as some musicians call them, "hairpins"), the abbreviation *cresc.* or *decresc.* appears instead. Another term you can use to indicate a softening of volume is *diminuendo*, abbreviated *dim.* The abbreviation *rit.* (sometimes abbreviated *ritard.*) stands for *ritardando* and indicates a gradual slowing of the tempo. *Rallentando* (abbreviated *rall.*) means the same thing. A gradual increase in tempo you can indicate by using *accel.*, which stands for *accelerando*.
22	Slur	A *slur* is a curved line that connects two notes of different pitch. A slur tells you to connect the notes smoothly, with no break in the sound.
23	Staccato dot	*Staccato dots* above or below notes tell you to play the notes short and detached.
24	Accent	An *accent mark* above or below a note tells you to stress it, or play it louder than normal.
25	Repeat sign	The *repeat sign* tells you to repeat certain measures. The symbol ‖: brackets the repeated section at the beginning (in this case, measure 1), and :‖ brackets it at the end (refer to measure 8 of "Shine On Harvest Moon").
26	Ending brackets	Sometimes a repeated section starts the same both times but ends differently. These different endings you indicate by using numbered *ending brackets*. Play the measures under the first ending bracket the first time, but substitute the measures under the second ending bracket the second time. Taking "Shine On Harvest Moon" as an example, you first play measures 1–8; you then play measures 1–5 again, and then 9–11.

Finding Notes on the Guitar

Figures A-2 through A-7 show you how to find the notes in standard notation on each of the six strings of the guitar. By the way, the actual *sounding* pitch of the guitar is an octave (12 half steps) lower than the written pitch is.

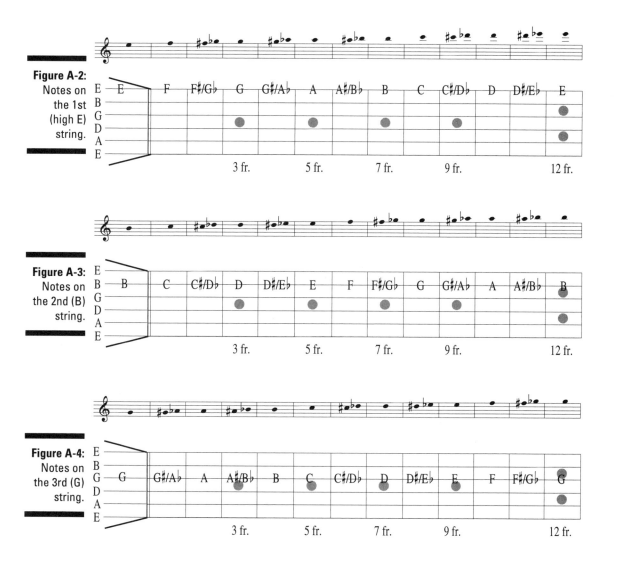

Figure A-2: Notes on the 1st (high E) string.

Figure A-3: Notes on the 2nd (B) string.

Figure A-4: Notes on the 3rd (G) string.

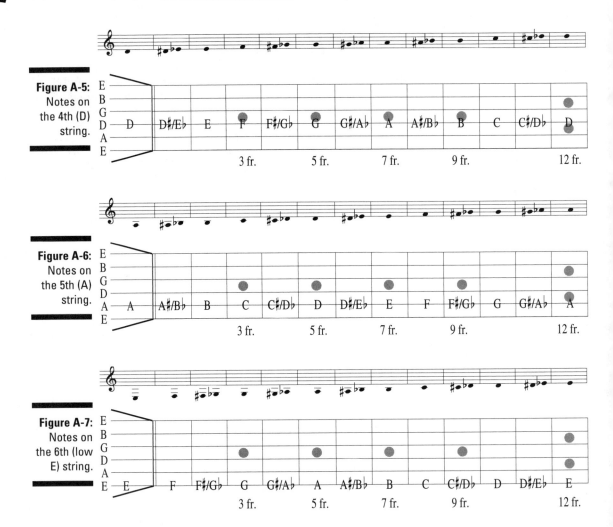

Figure A-5: Notes on the 4th (D) string.

Figure A-6: Notes on the 5th (A) string.

Figure A-7: Notes on the 6th (low E) string.

Appendix B
How to Use the CD

*E*very music example in *Guitar For Dummies* is performed on the CD that comes with this book — over 150 examples! This makes *Guitar For Dummies* a true multimedia experience. You have text explaining the techniques used, visual graphics of the music in two forms — guitar tablature and standard music notation — and audio performances of the music, complete with the appropriate tonal treatment (distortion for rock, sparkly acoustic colors for folk, and so on) and the appropriate accompaniment settings.

One fun way to experience *Guitar For Dummies* is to just scan the text by music examples, looking at the printed music in the book and listening to the corresponding performances on the CD. When you hear something you like, read the text that goes into detail about that particular piece of music. Or go to a particular chapter that interests you (say, Chapter 10 on rock guitar playing), skip to the appropriate tracks on the CD, and see if you can hack it. A little above your head at this point? Better go back to Chapter 5 on barre chords!

Relating the Text to the CD

Whenever you see written music in the text and you want to hear what it sounds like on the CD, refer to the box in the upper-right hand corner, which tells you the track number and start time (in minutes and seconds).

Use the *track skip* control on your CD player's front panel or remote to go to the desired track (indicated in the caption) and then use the cue button of the *cue/review* function (also known as the "fast forward/rewind" control) to go to the specific time within that track (also indicated in the track label in minutes and seconds). When you get on or near the start time, release the cue button and the example plays. In the above example, track skip your way to track #27, and then use the cue (fast forward) control to step your way up to 0:33 (or slightly before).

If you want to play along with the CD, "cue up" to a spot a few seconds *before* the start time. Giving yourself a few seconds head start allows you to put down the remote and place your hands in a ready position on the guitar.

Count-offs

Many of the music examples are preceded by a *count-off,* which is a metro-nome clicking in rhythm before the music begins. This tells you what the tempo is, or the speed at which the music is played. It's like having your own conductor going, "A-one, and a-two . . ." so that you can hit the down-beat (first note of music) in time with the CD. Examples in 4/4 time have four beats "in front" (musician lingo for a four-beat count-off before the music begins), examples in 3/4 have three beats in front.

Stereo separation

We've recorded some of the examples in what's known as a *stereo split.* In certain pieces, the backing, or accompanying, music appears on the left channel of your stereo, while the featured guitar appears on the right. If you leave your stereo's *balance control* in its normal position (straight up, or 12:00), you'll hear both the rhythm tracks and the featured guitar equally — one from each speaker. By selectively adjusting the balance control (turning the knob to the left or right) you can gradually or drastically reduce the volume of one or the other.

Why would you want to do this? If you have practiced the lead part to a certain example and feel you've got it down good enough to where you want to try it "along with the band," take the balance knob and turn it all the way to the left. Now only the sound from the left speaker comes out, which is the backing tracks. The count-off clicks are in *both* channels, so you'll always receive your cue to play in time with the music. You can reverse the process and listen to just the lead part, too, which means you play the chords against the recorded lead part. Good, well-rounded guitarists work on both their rhythm *and* their lead playing.

Always keep the CD with the book, rather than mixed in with your rack of CDs. The plastic envelope helps protect the CD's surface from scuffs and scratches, and whenever you want to refer to *Guitar For Dummies* (the book), the CD will always be right where you expect it. Try to get in the habit of following along with the printed music whenever you listen to the CD, even if your sight-reading skills aren't quite up to snuff. You absorb more than you expect just by moving your eyes across the page in time to the music, associating sound and sight. So store the CD and book together as constant companions and use them together as well for a rich visual and aural experience.

Tracks on the CD

Here is a list of the tracks on the CD along with the figure numbers that they correspond to in the book. Use this as a quick cross-reference to finding more about interesting sounding tracks on the CD. The first number equates to the chapter in which we explain how to play the track. Then just flip through the captions and songs in order until you find the track you're interested in playing. To ease matters a bit, the exercises also contain the track numbers (and times, if appropriate) to help you find just the track you need.

Track	(Time)	Figure Number	Song Title/Description
1		n/a	Tuning Reference
2	(0:00)	4-2	Chord progression using A family chords
	(0:16)	4-4	Chord progression using D family chords
	(0:43)	4-6	Chord progression using G family chords
	(1:10)	4-8	Chord progression using C family chords
3		n/a	"Kumbaya"
4		n/a	"Swing Low, Sweet Chariot"
5		n/a	"Auld Lang Syne"
6		n/a	"Michael, Row the Boat Ashore"
7		5-1	Simple melody
8		n/a	"Little Brown Jug"
9		n/a	"On Top of Old Smoky"
10		n/a	"Swanee River (Old Folks at Home)"
11		n/a	"Home on the Range"
12		n/a	"All Through the Night"
13		n/a	"Over the River and Through the Woods"
14		n/a	"It's Raining, It's Pouring"
15		n/a	"Oh, Susanna"
16		6-6	A 12-bar blues progression in E
17	(0:00)	7-4a	1-2-3-1 permutation exercise
	(0:10)	7-4b	1-3-2-4 permutation exercise
	(0:20)	7-4c	15-14-13 permutation exercise
	(0:00)	7-5	C-major up-the-neck double-stop scale
18	(0:11)	7-6	C-major across-the-neck double-stop scale
19		n/a	"Simple Gifts"

(continued)

Track	(Time)	Figure Number	Song Title/Description
20		n/a	"Turkey in the Straw"
21		n/a	"Aura Lee"
22		n/a	"The Streets of Laredo"
23	(0:00)	8-2	Progression using E-based major barre chords
	(0:13)	8-3	Syncopated progression using E-based major barre chords
	(0:27)	8-4	Progression using major and minor E-based barre chords
	(0:41)	8-5	Progression using major and 7th E-based barre chords
	(0:54)	8-6	Progression using major and minor 7th E-based barre chords
24		8-7	Christmas song progression using E-based barre chords
25	(0:00)	8-11	Progression using A-based major barre chords
	(0:12)	8-13	Progression using major and minor A-based barre chords
	(0:26)	8-14	Progression using major, minor, and dominant 7th A-based barre chords
	(0:42)	8-15	Progression using minor 7th barre A-based barre chords
	(0:55)	8-16	Progression using major and minor 7th A-based barre chords
26		8-17	Christmas song progression using A-based barre chords
27	(0:00)	8-20	Power chord progression in D
	(0:14)	8-21	Heavy metal power chord progression
28		n/a	"We Wish You a Merry Christmas"
29		n/a	"Power Play"
30	(0:00)	9-1a	Open string hammer-on
	(0:07)	9-1b	Hammer-on from a fretted note
	(0:14)	9-1c	Double hammer-on
	(0:20)	9-1d	Double hammer-on using three notes
	(0:27)	9-2a	Double-stop hammer-on from open strings
	(0:34)	9-2b	Double-stop hammer-on from second to fourth fret
	(0:41)	9-2c	Double double-stop hammer-on
	(0:48)	9-3	Hammer-on from nowhere

Track	(Time)	Figure Number	Song Title/Description
31		9-4	Single-note hammer-ons from open strings
32		9-5	Strumming a chord while hammering one of the notes
33		9-6	Single-note hammer-ons from fretted notes
34		9-7	Double-stop hammer-ons & hammer-on from nowhere
35	(0:00)	9-8a	Open string pull-off
	(0:07)	9-8b	Fretted note pull-off
	(0:13)	9-8c	Open string double pull-off
	(0:20)	9-8d	Fretted note double pull-off
	(0:27)	9-9a	Double-stop pull-off to open strings
	(0:34)	9-9b	Double stop pull off from fretted notes
	(0:41)	9-9c	Double double-stop pull-off
36	(0:00)	9-10	Single-note pull-offs to open strings
	(0:19)	9-11	Strumming a chord while pulling off one of the notes
37	(0:00)	9-12a	Slide with second note not picked
	(0:07)	9-12b	Slide with second note picked
	(0:12)	9-13a	Ascending immediate slide
	(0:17)	9-13b	Descending immediate slide
38		9-14	Chuck Berry-like slides
39		9-15	Changing positions with slides
40	(0:00)	9-17a	Immediate bend
	(0:06)	9-17b	Bend and release
	(0:13)	9-17c	Prebend and release
41		9-18	3rd-string bending in a rock 'n' roll progression
42		9-19	2nd-string bending in a lead lick
43		9-20	Bend and release in a lead lick
44		9-21	Bending in different directions
45		9-22	Intricate bending lick
46		9-23	Double-stop bend and release
47	(0:00)	9-24a	Narrow vibrato
	(0:10)	9-24b	Wide vibrato
48	(0:00)	9-25a	Left-hand muting
	(0:08)	9-25b	Right-hand muting

(continued)

Track	(Time)	Figure Number	Song Title/Description
49		9-26	Syncopation through muting
50		9-27	Palm muting in a hard-rock riff
51		9-28	Palm muting in a country riff
52		n/a	"Articulate Blues"
53		10-1	Chuck Berry accompaniment riff
54		10-2	12-bar blues progression in A using double-stops
55		10-4	Box I hammer-ons and pull-offs
56		10-5	Bending in Box I
57		10-6	Double-stop bend in Box I
58		10-7	Box I solo
59		10-9	Typical Box II lick
60		10-11	Typical Box III lick
61		10-12	12-bar solo using Boxes I, II, and III
62	(0:00)	10-13	Suss chord progression
	(0:15)	10-14	Add chord progression
63		10-15	Slash chord progression
64	(0:00)	10-16	Drop-D tuning phrase
	(0:10)	10-17	Power chord riff in drop-D tuning
65		10-18	Typical phase in drop-D tuning
66		10-20	Southern-rock lead-lick in A
67		n/a	"Chuck's Duck"
68		n/a	"Southern Hospitality"
69		11-2	12-bar blues accompaniment
70		11-3	12-bar blues with boogie-woogie riff
71	(0:00)	11-6	Box IV riff with triplet feel
	(0:10)	11-7	Box V lick with slide to Box I
72	(0:00)	11-9	Box I blues lick
	(0:13)	11-10	Box II blues lick
	(0:23)	11-11	Box IV blues lick
73	(0:00)	11-13	Box I blues lick with major third
	(0:10)	11-14	Box I double-stop blues lick with major third
74		11-15	Riff showing typical blues phrasing

Track	*(Time)*	*Figure Number*	*Song Title/Description*
75	(0:00)	11-16a	Typical blues move
	(0:10)	11-16b	Typical blues move
	(0:19)	11-16c	Typical blues move
	(0:29)	11-16d	Typical blues move
76		11-18	Steady bass notes with the E blues scale
77	(0:00)	11-19	Repeated motive at the same pitch
	(0:11)	11-20	Repeated motive at a different pitch
78	(0:00)	11-21	Alternating between a lead lick and a bass groove
	(0:13)	11-22	Alternating between a lead lick and a bass lick
	(0:26)	11-23	Combining fretted notes and open strings
79	(0:00)	11-24a	Blues turnaround 1
	(0:13)	11-24b	Blues turnaround 2
	(0:26)	11-24c	Blues turnaround 3
	(0:39)	11-24d	Blues turnaround 4
80		*n/a*	"Chicago Shuffle"
81		*n/a*	"Mississippi Mud"
82	(0:00)	12-3	Em arpeggio
	(0:07)	12-4	Up-and-down Em arpeggio
83	(0:00)	12-5	Lullaby pattern
	(0:10)	12-6	Thumb-brush pattern
84	(0:00)	12-7	Thumb-brush-up pattern
	(0:09)	12-8	Carter style pattern
85	(0:00)	12-9a	Travis style, Step 1
	(0:08)	12-9b	Travis style, Step 2
	(0:15)	12-9c	Travis style, Step 3
	(0:23)	12-9d	Travis style pinch
	(0:31)	12-9e	Travis style roll
86		12-11	"Oh, Susanna" in Travis style
87		12-12	Travis style with Open G tuning
88		*n/a*	"House of the Rising Sun"
89		*n/a*	"Cruel War"
90		*n/a*	"Gospel Ship"
91		*n/a*	"All My Trials"
92		*n/a*	"Freight Train"

(continued)

Track	(Time)	Figure Number	Song Title/Description
93		13-5	Free stroke classical exercise
94		13-8	Arpeggio classical exercise
95		13-9	Contrapuntal classical exercise
96		n/a	"Romanza"
97		n/a	"Bourée"

Index

Notes

Notes

Notes

Notes

IDG BOOKS WORLDWIDE BOOK REGISTRATION

Register This Book and Win!

We want to hear from you!

Visit **http://my2cents.dummies.com** to register this book and tell us how you liked it!

- Get entered in our monthly prize giveaway.

- Give us feedback about this book — tell us what you like best, what you like least, or maybe what you'd like to ask the author and us to change!

- Let us know any other *...For Dummies*® topics that interest you.

Your feedback helps us determine what books to publish, tells us what coverage to add as we revise our books, and lets us know whether we're meeting your needs as a *...For Dummies* reader. You're our most valuable resource, and what you have to say is important to us!

Not on the Web yet? It's easy to get started with *Dummies 101*®: *The Internet For Windows*® *98* or *The Internet For Dummies*®, 5th Edition, at local retailers everywhere.

Or let us know what you think by sending us a letter at the following address:

...For Dummies Book Registration
Dummies Press
7260 Shadeland Station, Suite 100
Indianapolis, IN 46256-3945
Fax 317-596-5498

...FOR DUMMIES™

BESTSELLING BOOK SERIES FROM IDG